MONSTERS AND SAINTS

Bernadette Marie Calafell, Marina Levina,
and Kendall R. Phillips, General Editors

MONSTERS AND SAINTS

LatIndigenous Landscapes and Spectral Storytelling

Edited by SHANTEL MARTINEZ
and KELLY MEDINA-LÓPEZ

University Press of Mississippi / Jackson

The University Press of Mississippi is the scholarly publishing agency
of the Mississippi Institutions of Higher Learning: Alcorn State University,
Delta State University, Jackson State University, Mississippi State University,
Mississippi University for Women, Mississippi Valley State University,
University of Mississippi, and University of Southern Mississippi.

www.upress.state.ms.us

The University Press of Mississippi is a member
of the Association of University Presses.

Portions of "And He Whispered, 'Yolanda, Yolanda'" were previously
published in *Sagrado* by Spencer Herrera, Levi Romero,
Robert Kaiser, and Luis Valdez (University of New Mexico Press, 2013).
Reprinted with permission from the author.

"cortando las nubes, or, death came on horses" previously appeared
in *flesh to bone* by ire'ne lara silva (Aunt Lute Books, 2013).
Reprinted with permission from Aunt Lute Books.

Library of Congress Control Number: 2023948600
Hardback ISBN 978-1-4968-4873-4
Paperback ISBN 978-1-4968-4874-1
Epub single ISBN 978-1-4968-4875-8
Epub institutional ISBN 978-1-4968-4876-5
PDF single ISBN 978-1-4968-4877-2
PDF institutional ISBN 978-1-4968-4878-9

British Library Cataloging-in-Publication Data available

We pour one out for all of our dead homies.

CONTENTS

PART II. HAZME CASO: MEMOIR, POETRY, AND STORIES

PART III. BRINGING THE BORDERLANDS HOME: PUBLIC DISCOURSES AND THEORIES OF THE FLESH

ACKNOWLEDGMENTS

Together: We would like to thank the University Press of Mississippi for believing in this project. Thank you to Emily, our amazing editor, who has guided us through this process. We would also like to send tremendous gratitude to the authors and contributors of this collection. We originally started this project in February of 2020, not knowing what was waiting for us around the corner. Writing and coordinating a book project during the peak of COVID was no easy task and we sincerely thank everyone who has been part of this journey. COVID taught many people lessons—the importance of community, health, and the power of checking-in on one another. As such, we have led this project through an ethos of community care, empathy, and transparency. Knowledge production and bringing awareness to these topics are critical but not as important as ensuring the health of our communities and friends.

We would also like to thank the desert, borderlands, and the stories for letting us speak their beauty and power into existence.

Shantel: I first want to thank my family for my unconventional childhood and feeding into my interests of family history, ghost stories, tarot cards, astrology, and curanderismo. I want to thank my mom and tías for showing me the importance of being a Martinez woman—even through stories and experiences of intergenerational trauma. Through my family, I learned the importance of love, strength, and engaging one's ghosts. Even though my mom and I have had our ups and downs (never trust a Gemini with a Scorpio moon), I am thankful for how our relationship has developed through time. For teaching me spellwork, the importance of the moons, being connected to nature, and listening/calling in our ancestors. I would also like to thank my dad, Alicia, and my sisters (Rima, Nani, and Chloe) for accepting me for who I am. Specifically, I would like to thank my dad for taking me to the horse races as a kid—where

I learned probability and fractions like a pro at age eight. Also, for teaching me how to play poker when I was six; having a poker face has always served me well. And to both of my parents, who taught me the importance of never putting all my eggs into one basket.

I also want to thank my amazing partner, Vincent. Words honestly fail when it comes to telling you how incredibly grateful I am to have you in my life as my partner in crime. From taking care of me when I am sick, making me laugh in the darkest of days, having a quick eye for details, your lack of proper pronunciation (orrrange), and lack of ass—you are someone who I enjoy walking side by side through this life with. To my little Taurus, Darby, you are such a light in this world. You are my mirror in this world and what gives me hope that intergenerational trauma and hauntings can stop. Your bravery, intelligence, and stubbornness are forces to reckon with. You have no idea how much I am inspired by you and how much I absolutely love you. I cannot wait to see how you grow as you get older. To my dogs: Eli, Margeaux, and Vivie, thank you for your eternal emotional support. From comforting me during panic attacks to cuddling at night, all of your presence creates such joy. You are my babies, always and forever.

To my academic coven: Christine, Tessa, and Long, this project would not be in existence without you all. Thank you for the countless nights of chisme, tarot card readings, and endless support. You are all such great friends and intellectual partners. Thank you for believing in this project. I also want to thank my closest and best friends: Bianca, Allymyr, Michelle, Elspeth, Leandra, Amanda, Sarah, Diana, Bernadita, and Bryce. Y'all motivate me to always do better and be better. Thank you for being my sun and stars. Thank you for all loving me, reminding me to speak truth to power, and centering joy. Also, shout out to Dr. Steve Woodard, Dr. Norm Denzin, and Dr. Juliana Villegas, who have been my mentors and illuminated pathways forward when the heavy mists of disillusionment and depression fogged the way. Thank you for believing in me when I didn't see my own potential.

This project could not exist without years of therapy and healing. So to my amazing therapist, Liana, you have no idea how many times you have saved my life. Thank you for helping me find the importance of living beyond labels. For reminding me of my power and that my stories are worthy of being told.

I want to thank my "sister from another mister" and comadre in arms, Kelly. Girl, you can finish my sentences. You are not a friend—you are my sister, you are my twin. Let us grow old, wear muumuus in the desert together with our gray braids and collection of dogs. I am forever grateful for you and cannot wait till the next time we see each other in New Mexico.

Lastly, I want to thank the smell of Aqua Net, my aunts' obsession with Kate Bush and Depeche Mode, and the sensation of burning my fingers while flipping tortillas on the stovetop for keeping me connected to my roots.

Kelly: My gratitude goes first to the land. Thank you, ancestor, for nurturing me mentally, physically, and spiritually across the ancient and ancestral migratory learning pathway that I've been blessed to walk. To Cruces and to those that have been part of my journey in Paso del Norte, I send my love. To the Phoenix Valley and the Monterey Bay: thank you.

To my ancestors that revolted in 1680 and my kin that revolt today, hoiyu, I see you.

To Ramon: all of my love, forever. I'm glad your mom cursed us. It worked out okay.

La Llorona y Virgencita, gracias por estar siempre conmigo y guiarme en todo lo que hago. To el Santo Juan Diego Cuauhtlatoatzin, Diego the Lieutenant, and Diego: thank you.

Pete stole the chalk, *Fabian No Se Muere*, y los Medina no se rajan, pero nunca nunca.

Shantel, my twin comadre, thank you for grabbing that bizcochito in December 2017 and never letting go.

MONSTERS AND SAINTS

Collecting *Our* Bones

Kelly Medina-López and Shantel Martinez

Little can compare to the beauty of a desert sunset. The pinks, purples, and blues weaving and mixing like braids through the sky while painting rocks with their shadows. Cascading lights shine through cloud bursts illuminating the desert terrain, welcoming a new cast of characters into the delicate ecosystem. Those who claim homespace during the day retreat into the night sky as the nighttime residents come out to play. In this moment, the sunset creates a liminal space and time—where the veil of light and darkness intermixes, and boundaries do not exist. It is in these exact moments, in this exact landscape, where we plant and cultivate the seeds of our stories.

The play of shadow and light, color and contrasts, new and old characters perfectly encapsulate the land—what many perceive to be barren, uninhabitable, and dead are actually the playgrounds and familial homes of countless generations that have come before us, those that are loving in the present, and those who have yet to step foot on this planet. *There is something spiritual about the desert, almost spectral.* It's easy to ignore the signs for those who are unfamiliar with its properties and instead focus on its deficits and "lack" (especially lack of water), but that's what makes this land magical. To live and survive in the desert is to honor the land. Honor its resources. And honor its history. It's about honing your senses to detect when a rainstorm is coming— or a sandstorm. It's about knowing when to leave, when to stay, and when to go back. The land is our greatest teacher and storyteller.

Once you fall in love with the desert, you will always be haunted by its life.

Kelly's abuelita used to tell a story about the desert. In it, the desert wasn't the desert but an old woman: "viejita como yo," she would say, pointing at her faded muumuu and soft, wrinkly-wise skin. Like many desert creatures, desert woman came to life at dusk, the liminal space, the veil, nepantla of the land. Her job was to collect bones, cacti, dead and dry things, the discarded pieces that people thought no longer held life. She would bring them back to her desert home, where she would make a giant fire, flames as high as you could imagine, reaching up, up, up in prayer. Abuelita would lift her arms into the air to imitate the fire, releasing her own prayer out towards the land all around us. Desert woman would assemble the bones she collected into the skeleton of the animal they once carried, lovingly filling in any missing pieces with the dead and dry things she had found, working each bit like clay until it was perfect: a jackrabbit, a roadrunner, whatever the land offered her that day. Then, once the creature was recognizable by its shape, she'd throw it into the flames and say magic words under her breath. Abuelita never said the magic words, even though Kelly begged, but she insisted that when Kelly was ready, she would know them. The fire would consume the creature, cradle it in the hottest part of its heart until all you could see was a bright, bright light, and right when the light was at its brightest and the fire at its hottest, the animal would spring to life, jump from the fire and run into the desert, new.

The desert is not dead and dry things, it is the beginning of abundant life.

Doing the Shadowork

We are here.
　　Breathing.
　　Exhausted.
　　Trying to ground ourselves in a world and land full of trauma. *They always say that shadow work is the hardest work to do in curanderismo and bruje-ria. They, being the ancestors.* It requires the most vulnerability, reflection, and reliving of trauma without shield or protection. You must be willing to open up old wounds that you believed are "healed" as well as unburying memories long forgotten. But, without shadow work, we are stuck within the same vicious cycles and intergenerational traumas that tie us down and commit spirit murder. The same vices and traumas that live freely and are rewarded within academia: ego, control, abandonment, territorialism, unwavering white supremacy, imperialism, racism, internal colonization, cultural genocide,

assimilation, and imposter syndrome. It is easy to be caught up in this world and forget where you come from when academia digs its teeth into your umbilical cord, asking you to split mind-body-spirit-land and instead know only one way. It is easy to forget the power of the land in which your ancestors once walked. It is easy to forget the knowledge that once flowed through your veins like the Turtle River[1]. By silencing trauma for so long, we become haunted, and we pass this haunting down to the next generation and the next. Turning into ghosts and monsters, we are trapped fighting for visibility and survival—but more than anything, to be heard. We scream ourselves into existence, haunting anyone who will listen. But are we actually monsters when all we are trying to do is survive in conditions never meant for our liveability? Like La Llorona, are we to be feared or to be seen as a symbol of resistance?

Displacement, dislocation, and otherness are powerful monsters and ghosts. Rupturing not only roots to the land but also time and space. They cultivate conditions that let us wander aimlessly without hope for any type of return—to ourselves, spirits, communities, or homes. With no purpose, we forget ourselves. In return, we will worship anything that resembles "home." We fight each other for resources. We tear each other apart and recreate cycles of exploitation and oppression. Thinking ourselves Saints when we transcend the borders of our communities only to choke on the holy communion because it is our own blood. We sacrifice ourselves in the name of ourselves.

This is why shadow work is needed. Not just to survive but to name and transcend the trauma that lives within us. To break the scar tissue that blocks the embodied knowledge connecting us to the ghosts, land, spirits, and ancestors. To rethink ghost stories not as stories of fear and harm but rather warnings from our ancestral ghosts who want to protect us from legacies of imperialism, colonialism, racism, misogyny, patriarchy, and so much more. Ghost stories of haunted migrations help us to remember, name into existence suppressed knowledge, and recover our roots. This book's purpose is not only a recovery of long ignored and erased trauma, racial violence, and cultural genocides but flips the script to showcase the power of LatIndiengous stories, knowledge, and land-based knowledge systems that transcend acts of survival, resistance, and healing.

To open the wound, to purge, clean, and begin to heal, we start with a spell that invokes the ancient power of salt. Salt is important to this story because our knowledge begins with it. Salt helps build our bones, and, as a naturally occurring mineral, salt grounds our bones in the earth that we come from: as we consume salt from our land, we fortify our bones with its memory. We invite you to begin with salt and offer this prayer with us.

A protection spell against academia

Take three deep breaths, and clear your mind. Focus on your intentions.

Cast a circle of salt
Call in your ancestors
Call in the directions
Call in the elements
Light three candles:
    white for your own intentions,
    black for protection,
    and pink for selflove
Cast your spell
Repeat three times
Burn the spell

Cutting to the Bone: Removing the Flesh

The US-Mexican border es una herida abierta where the Third World grates against the first and bleeds. And before a scab forms it hemorrhages again, the lifeblood of two worlds merging to form a third country—a border culture.
Borders are set up to define the places that are safe and unsafe, to distinguish us from them. A border is a dividing line, a narrow strip along a steep edge. A borderland is a vague and undetermined place created by the emotional residue of an unnatural boundary. It is in a constant state of transition. The prohibited and forbidden are its inhabitants.
GLORIA ANZALDÚA, *Borderlands/La Frontera*

Settler-colonialism of the US-Mexico borderlands by the Spanish and later US imperial forces worked hard to erase Indigenous presence from the territory that would later become the US-Mexico border. This wasn't just a purposeful imperial tactic; rather, *it is the nexus, or what Santiago Castro-Gómez might call the zero point, of settler-colonialism: in order for the imperial project to work, the land must be devoid of human* life. To turn living, breathing land into an abstract political concept, a place that divides one settler government from the other, it must be framed as an empty, barren space, a division, and nothing more. The project worked, and the border continues to be seen as such: a space that naturally gave way to a divide—mine and yours, but nothing (or no one) in between.

The border is una herida abierta (Anzaldúa), and the life that was disregarded (or marked for/as death/dead) when that incision was made is impacted by its scar tissue. Scar tissue, the haunting of the wound, can cause many complications. It is unyielding trauma, an inability to heal, a constant reminder of the pain. BorderIndigenous people, those who imperial logics, the division of yours and mine and the opening of the wound, marked as dead, live constantly in that scar tissue: the liminal space, the nepantla. And as the wound festers, the tissue grows. It infects, stretches past the land, and is carried into new spaces.

But to understand BorderIndigeneity, it's important to understand the beginning of the incision, the place where scalpel first hit flesh: Paso del Norte, or modern-day El Paso, Texas, USA and Ciudad Juárez, Chihuahua, Mexico. Paso del Norte was an important crossroads—or "pass"—long before any settlers came to the region. Actually, with the discovery of 23,000-year-old human footprints at modern-day White Sands National Monument, only one hundred miles or so north of El Paso, Paso del Norte is the site of the first archaeologically recorded human life in the Americas. What we now know as the US-Mexico border, a politically abstracted lifeless scar, is actually an important beginning. Precontact, the Suma, Humano, and Manso people tended the fertile river valleys of Paso del Norte and traded salt, minerals, the foundation of our bones, in all four directions. But in May of 1598, the scalpel hit flesh and cut deep northwards as Juan de Oñate forwarded Turtle River at Paso del Norte with his team of Spanish colonizers. They brought death, genociding the estimated 248,000 Pueblo inhabitants living across 134 Pueblos to only forty-three by 1640 (not even fifty years later) and just twenty by 1707 (Gutiérrez, 1991, p. xxiii). The thriving Pueblos of Paso del Norte were decimated.

Then, in 1680, Ohkay Owingeh holy man and War Captain Po'pay led a revolt, a revolution that pushed the genociders out of present-day northern New Mexico and its remaining Pueblos and back to Paso del Norte. A crucial but untaught part of US history, The Pueblo Revolt was a successful Indigenous uprising against a colonizing power in what is now North America. As Po'pay fought, so did the colonizing Spanish, enslaving as many Pueblo people as possible as they retreated south to Paso del Norte. These Pueblo enslaved people included Tiwa people from Isleta, near what is now called Albuquerque, Tompiro people from the Manzano Mountains, and Piro people from around what is now Socorro, New Mexico. As enslaved by the Spanish, the Pueblo were forced to build Paso del Norte, pueblos and missions to house the enslaved and imprison anyone who rose up against colonial rule: the beginning of the modern border carceral state.

Let us be very clear: Paso del Norte and its legacy as the scar between two contemporary imperial forces was established as a prison and continues to function as one. Not just a prison, a death camp. When we speak of survival of BorderIndigenous logics, we speak of underground, rebel, renegade prison epistemologies. This is the salt that forms our bones. The minerals, the earth, that teaches us its knowledge. To be BorderIndigenous means housing those bones in your flesh, understanding the renegade logics from inside your bones. Telling stories for survival, speaking those bones back into existence.

The skeleton of this collection is made from those bones. The imperial scar, flesh peeled away from the knowledge we have deep inside. The trauma of colonialism and genocide. The scar tissue that spreads. We refer to this geography of knowledge as LatIndigenous, a term and concept we use to name the land of Turtle Island, formerly colonized by Spain. It is a geography of knowledge linked to people who have survived the wound of colonialism more than once, who have kept their knowledge inside their bones, underneath their flesh. Knowledge which haunts bodies. We frame this through storytelling and explore how ghost stories foreground a LatIndigenous sense of belonging and home that, in return, provide for a nuanced understanding of our intersectional and intergenerational lives, bodies, traumas, and experiences. While we ground our work in a very real scar, the US-Mexico border, an open wound, we acknowledge that space as it historically was: an ancestral crossroads, an important place of confluence and exchange. A trading post for salt. We know through salt, the minerals that form our bones, and as colonized people pass through this important intersection, we acknowledge that we do not stay, but take our knowledge with us, keep it in other ways: house it in our flesh, and share it through our stories. Thus, this research dislocates the concept of "home" away from physical constructions and posits that it is our spectral stories and storytelling practices that actively configure these affective states and spaces of being, becoming, migration, displacement, and belonging.

Arranging the Body: Contextualizing Ideological Interventions

Since the foundational publication of Avery Gordon's (1997, 2008) *Ghostly Matters: Haunting and the Sociological Imagination* to the *Spectralities Reader* by Peeren and Blanco (2013), the subject of hauntology, monstrosity, and "the spectral" has rapidly grown across academic disciplines such as communication, critical rhetoric, sociology, literary studies, photography, media studies, anthropology, diaspora studies, cultural theory, trauma studies, and philosophy. The "spectral turn" is quickly shaping into an instrumental tool for deconstructing experiences and "the horrors of everyday life" (Calafell, 2015, p. 6). The theoretical and academic trajectories of haunting and hauntology (see, for example, Taylor, 1999; Lopez Calvo & Valles, 2018), and the impact these theories have on our ability to understand haunting and hauntology as methodological frameworks, move us to form a LatIndigenous theory of ghosts and hauntings rooted more firmly in the land, connecting tangible, haunted geographies to settler-colonialism and its impact on our lived and embodied realities.

To that end, our choice of the term LatIndigenous is not without careful thought. Although the intersection of Latinx and Indigenous identities has been theorized in previous scholarship (please see: Delgado Shorter, 2021; Gonzalez, 2012; Holling, 2021; Menchaca, 2002; Miner, 2014; Perez, 2018; Saldaña-Portillo, 2016), we wanted a term that recognized not only historic and ongoing processes of settler-colonialism (by Spain, the US, and laterally), but also called explicit attention to geography and geopolitics: the land. Identity terms (Latinx, Chicanx, Hispanic) and other ethnic labels that have histories connected to Spanish colonization are contentious. We want to recognize and honor this tradition and stress that we do not propose LatIndigenous as an ethnic identifier but as a way to name and constellate our thinking across contemporary geographies. It is an effort to bear witness to, and fully name, the layered colonization of the land of Turtle Island, formerly colonized by Spain, and its haunted connections to our embodied realities. As such, and in the context of contemporary US Indigenous studies, southwest studies, and borderlands studies, it recognizes that the colonial history of the desert southwest, US-Mexico borderlands, and parts of the US formerly colonized by Spain is different from the colonial history of non-Spanish colonized geographies and that despite contemporary imperial borders, there continue to be linkages in the Indigenous experience across LatIndigenous geographies. Experiences grounded in the land and expressed through our connection to it. Furthermore, it's important to name that LatIndigenous geographies extend from the territory of former New Spain in the present-day US, Mexico, and through Central and South America. This highlights the political work the term does to make explicit contemporary US border politics and its increasing violence, specifically towards peoples from LatIndigenous geographies, including those from "within" its own borders (like in the case of Texas teen Esequiel Hernandez, Jr.). LatIndigenous, then, is also a political term that

speaks to the contentious relationship of the US-Mexico border in the policing and surveillance of LatIndigenous geographies, both within the US and
broadly, through its immigration policy and rhetoric.

As a land-based concept, LatIndigenous geographies add a tangible layer
to the complex intersectionalities of our hauntings, allowing us to become
real in our experiences. To become real, we tell our stories. Like Gordon
(2008) states, "to write about stories concerning exclusions and invisibilities is
to write ghost stories. To write ghost stories implies that ghosts are real, that
is to say, that they produce material effects" (p. 17). Telling our stories is how
we flesh the wounds of genocide and terror into scar tissue: a reality that does
not ignore how abusive power creates our conditions of modernity: "It is a
case of modernity's violence and wounds and a case of the haunting reminder
of the complex social relations in which we live" (Gordon, 2008, p. 25). Those
complex social relations center on issues of race, gender, ethnicity, class, and
sexuality, all which are frequently included in conversations about haunting
and hauntology (e.g., Holland's (2000) *Raising the Dead*; Cacho's (2012) *Social
Death*; Calafell's (2015) *Monstrosity, Performance, and Race in Contemporary
Culture*), but have yet to be fleshed out in relationship to Latinidades, and
even less so in terms of Indigeneity. And, although Latinx studies is com-
fortable discussing topics of death and haunting (e.g., Dia de los Muertos),
it has yet to be fully analyzed as a widespread theoretical and methodological
framework, except within the fields of folklore and literature (see: Cantú &
Nájera-Ramirez, 2002; Espinosa & García, 2008; Herrera-Sobek, 1990, 2006,
2012; Perez, 2008). These histories allow us to frame our work as a kind of
folklore archive, one that bridges storytelling traditions between Latinx folklore and Indigenous story traditions. Additionally, to make these connections,
we acknowledge the presence of Indigenous histories and storytelling practices as intimately connected to those of the Latinx community while adding nuance through explicit connection to land and land-based knowledges.
This can be exemplified by a ghost that haunts both communities: La Llorona.
Domino Renee Perez (2002) argues that La Llorona "is the physical embodiment of [the] border (racial; sexual, physical, or spiritual). She is a transgressive figure strong enough to penetrate the consciousness of an entire culture"
(p. 109). In the physical landscape of the border, La Llorona, as embodiment
of the border, maps onto the Turtle River that divides the US and Mexico at
Paso del Norte. But the geographic river is itself a shapeshifter, a landscape
haunted by the ghost of the water that should be home there. The water, much
like the Indigenous people who belong to the land, has been regulated, contained, and controlled by the settler-colonial nation-state. For most of the

year, the water that should run through the border Turtle River is turned off at Elephant Butte Dam north of the border in New Mexico, leaving an empty, haunted riverbed behind. In this shapeshifted form, the river does not reflect its true and natural symbiotic relationship with the land but is rather forced into a new monstrosity: it is the "monstrous feminine" of Llorona as Perez recognizes it, but also the monstrosity of settler colonialism and its brutal impact on the land.

Following Levina and Bui (2013), we can recognize the ghostly, haunted Turtle River as a monstrosity that has moved beyond metaphor and become a "necessary condition in the twenty-first century." In the reality of tightly regulated resources and geographies, the Turtle River, and its tangible symbolism as the geographic border, is what Poole (2011) refers to as an "American Monster," that is, a monster "born out of American history. [American Monsters] emerge out of central anxieties and obsessions that have been part of the United States from colonial times to the present and from the structures and processes where these obsessions found historical expression" (4). Thus, Turtle River as a border, a functional, tangible, and contestable reality of the geopolitics of the borderlands, also maps, metaphorically, onto the bodies of bordered Latinx and Indigenous lives through its haunted absence-presence, as narrated through the La Llorona ghost story. In a LatIndigenous context, then, telling La Llorona stories is a way to bear witness not only to the haunting of the "monstrous feminine" as "physical embodiment of [the] border," but also the haunting of a shapeshifting geography, the ghost of water that should be there: the feeling that something is missing and disrupted, the loss of life that should flow free. La Llorona is more than folklore; she is flesh: part of the ecosystem of knowledge that connects body-mind-spirit-land.

Rebuilding the Skeleton: Anticolonial Intersections with Memory-Body-Land-Knowledge

As we have previously discussed, land is central to LatIndinegous histories and storytelling practices as it showcases the ways in which land-based practices map upon bodies and embodied knowledge—when people lose access to space, they also lose access to themselves and their history (haunted migrations). Land also plays a critical role in an expanded understanding of Moraga and Anzaldúa's (1983) concept, theory of the flesh. In this theory, they assert that the body serves as an archive to which we write from. In this sense, the body also acts as an archive of space and memory (e.g., when Anzaldúa talks about walking into a room and immediately recognizing if a fight has just occurred). As such, this directly disrupts Cartesian dichotomies of the mind/body split; thus putting at the forefront embodied knowledge construction. However, LatIndigeneity takes this concept one step further to include land and place. Rather than constructing a "body of knowledge," we are trying to put forth an "ecosystem of knowledge" that demonstrates how mind-body-spirit-land puts into practice a theory of the flesh, where land constitutes as the flesh of Tonantzin, mother earth. *Land is flesh and also acts as an archive to memory and story while also being its own storyteller.* This is especially important to the borderlands as it personifies the landscape—a landscape that can be both a monster and a saint.

If land is both a monster and a saint, then conversations of home become even more complicated. In Pacheco Marcial's chapter, "Becoming Indigenous again: Returning home and making the ghosts visible," he describes being asked the question, "If you could go anywhere in the world, where would you go?" His answer, "home," may appear to be quite simple, but is actually incredibly complicated. Home for him is Oaxaca. But as an undocumented Indigenous immigrant in the United States, the border presents "home" as a place of mourning, death, and pain. A place of memory and longing. The border cultivates scars across his psyche, body, and spirit. By being dislocated from home, how does one resolve trauma? How does one make visible the pain and allow for others to bear witness to the *forever haunting* that is carried within one's body over generations?

Home is *supposed to be* a place of memory and reflection. Through our memories and corporeal narratives, we recreate home—our home—forging our sense of self and belonging. In other words, "we chart our lives by everything we remember from the mundane to the majestic. We know ourselves through the art and act of remembering" (hooks, 2009, p. 5). Our memories travel and are a part of our affective landscapes of home. They craft bridges over ruptured experiences and connect our emplaced emotions with narrations of home. However, for many marginalized and displaced peoples, a sense of belonging is always haunted through historical exclusion from an original homespace. This exclusion further manifests as limited control over our own bodies. By utilizing alternative storytelling practices and critical rhetoric studies to examine a variety of texts and sites, our aim in this book is to expand current notions of spectrality, haunting, and belongingness in LatIndigenous communities. *Simply stated, it is our stories that bring us back. It is our stories that speak to and with our ghosts.* It is our stories that connect us to one another. As Grace Cho (2007) states, "our trauma is tied up in the trauma of another, the way in which trauma may lead, therefore, to the encounter with another, through the very possibility and surprise of listening to another's wound" (p. 165). Making known our shared trauma and displacement helps us return into the real. *Helps us to return home. Helps us return to Tonantzin.*

Returning to the Desert; Returning to Ourselves

There are many ghost stories that exist in the desert. From a land that represents death, it is hard to imagine life. *But all that is living is not undead.* Like a desert sunset, the inhabitants do not always live within a single pane of time—but rather intermix and interweave through time, place, and space. As such, the desert and its surroundings act as an archive of memory and story. The land brings us back to ourselves and helps us remember who we are. By collecting our bones, doing our shadow work, embracing the veil, and retracing our steps, we understand better the ghosts that walk haunted paths within ourselves, families, communities, histories, and spirits. We learn that not all saints are saints, nor monsters are monsters. We are always a little bit of everything.

We conjure together a space for healing. A space for recognition. A space where we can walk hand and hand with death and have no fear. From family curses to La Llorona, dueling border ghosts to haunted migrations, this book bears witness to make real not only to the intergenerational trauma that exists in LatIndigenous geographies but the ways in which we reveal and share suppressed knowledge through ghost stories, from one haunted and wounded tongue to another, to heal body-mind-spirit-land.

In section one, *Ghosts in the Real: Historiography in Our Stories That Becomes Research,* we dive into how our stories become knowledge through mind-body-spirit-flesh. These chapters show an intersectional flow of LatIndigenous thought across borders, searching and researching the knowledge archives of our flesh. For example, in chapter 1, S. de los Santos-Upton and L. Hernández deconstruct La Llorona's plight through a LatIndigenous framework, connecting it to histories of racial violence, police brutality, discriminatory immigration policies, and specters of trauma, arguing that La Llorona holds the potential for transforming grief into resistance. In chapter 2, A. Martinez draws our attention to how "oral traditions have long been the mode of transmission for storytelling about spiritual encounters and the healing practices to restore mind-body-spirit balance across generations of LatIndigenous groups" (p. 42–43). In doing so, she shares transformative testimonios from her own family that remind us that no story is ever singular. In chapter 3, D. Martínez problematizes the Equator's haunted trauma through acts of science and colonialism while also creating potential for spiritual and personal recovery through nepantla. For chapter 4, E. Murillo picks up the theme of dislocation, displacement, and lost family history. Through uncovering research and lost records, Murillo maps together the notion of "triple consciousness" on the borderlands.

Switching gears to Central America in chapter 5 to focus on La Ciguanaba, B. Lara presents her argument on "epistemic haunting:" a form of haunting that reveals suppressed knowledge. Using La Ciguanaba as a metaphor, Lara explores unresolved sexual violence against Central American women while also challenging legacies of colonialism that reach the United States through vessels of broken dreams and unfulfilled promises. For chapter 6, we move to Mexico, where F. Grijalva-Maza exposes the ways in which the triangulation of power between the Mexican government and military, media, along with the Catholic Church have tried to marginalize and bury Santa Muerte, who is the personification of death in the female form. This harsh and calculated response to La Santísima illuminates the ways in which the feminine divine is criminalized—the same feminine divine that Indigenous communities have and continue to worship within Mexico. In chapter 7, M. Gonzales shares a story about culture and resistance through the actions of *la Coyota Perejundia*. Switching from text to art for chapter 8, ceramic artist L. Tecuatl Cuaxiloa shows and tells how Spanish colonization impacted the pottery work of indigenous communities in Cholula, Mexico. Her work challenges what is thought of as "traditional" Mexican pottery and recovers indigenous design and memory through art. Closing this section with chapter 9, S. Ramirez deconstructs the relationship between forgotten agreements, names, and languages and the parallel relationship to decaying space and bodies—who "saves" who when no one is seen as valuable?

In section two, *Hazme Caso: Memoir, Poetry, and Stories*, authors shape connections between body-mind-spirit-land through storytelling, poetry, and art. These chapters celebrate how LatIndigenous ways of knowing are passed through intergenerational oral storytelling practices for survivance, sharing joy, and searching for ways to heal through writing and creative production. To open this section, in chapter 10, B. Zamora, in the act of unmasking a family story of sexual abuse through a poem, presents a space for healing and survival. In chapter 11, S. Herrera argues that decolonization begins with the family and within the confines of family stories. But by excavating his own familial archive, he learns that sometimes ghosts do not want to be bothered, and by unlocking Pandora's Box, familial history can reveal more than one wants to know. Chapter 12, a poem by A. "Velaz" Muñoz digs past colonial understandings of ritual and prayer to reimagine the demons of colonialism as the internal struggle of good and bad, light and dark of Chicanx gang subculture. Using a rosario as a symbol, Velaz illuminates the legacy of the border carceral state and its connection to contemporary police brutality. In chapter 13, S. A. de la Garza's essay illustrates the array of spiritual and cultural influences lost over generations and illuminates the uncanny horror of the metaphysical call to Indigenous practices, which offer a way out of the psychological crises of neoliberal careers. For chapter 14, D. Medina traces the history and intersections of colonization in New Mexico using a metaphorical journey on El Camino Real, or US Interstate I-10. Using modern mile-markers as stopping points, Medina provides an indigenous history of the state juxtaposed against a backdrop of imperial erasure.

In chapter 15, K. Alcalá's essay paints a hauntingly beautiful and contemporary reenvisioning of the La Llorona story. For chapter 16, J. Pacheco Marcial explores being undocumented, indigenous, and displaced. By recalling the pain and trauma the physical border causes on his ability to find "home," he reminds us that the border scar is not just abstract but marked on our flesh. For chapter 17, I. Lara Silva leaves us with a powerful and searing image of how colonialism arrives and continues to arrive, how we might see and name it in historical and contemporary political contexts, and it's complicated and intersectional ties to death. To close this powerful section, R. Sanchez-Avila's stunning photography showcases how visual methodologies can exist within spectral planes, specifically in capturing ghostly desires of LatIndigenous knowledge productions and lineages.

Transitioning into section three, *Bringing the Borderlands Home: Public Discourses and Theories of the Flesh*, we explore the intersections of LatIndigeneity with public and popular texts. These chapters show how LatIndigenous ghosts haunt our public memory and map onto our popular media. In chapter 19, C. Merla-Watson explores the story of La Llorona through the genre of meXicana gothic, employing a "hauntology of the oppressed" framework to do a counter reading of Sandra Cisneros' "Woman Hollering Creek." Finally, in chapter 20, S. Loza grapples with settler colonialism and the haunting of nostalgia in the movie franchise, *Twilight*, where she argues that the series deliberately replicates representations of the Southwest to appease the fragility of white settler colonial memory, at the same time reminding us the imperial wound is far from healed. In our final chapter, Loza also challenges the term LatIndigenous, offering a thoughtful revision which pushes the possibility of body-mind-spirit-land thinking more broadly and offers the potential for future intersections of thought.

Light the Fire and Speak the Magic Words

The desert and its stories are how we knew the colonizer stories we learned in school were wrong. *They didn't respect the desert.* They didn't understand how it was teeming with abundant life. They didn't know that someday all us desert kids would be soft and wrinkly-wise and know the magic words that bring the desert to life. The focus of the colonizer stories is water: it's a drought! It's so dry! Water! Water! Water! NO! We thought, not water! Don't you know the story? We need fire! Fire will bring us life. We did not understand that the conflict we found between the stories was the specter of colonialism, the haunting of the LatIndigenous knowledge of the land we learned in our home stories clashing against imperial logics. *Genocidal logics.*

We decided to write this book to give those hauntings a place: an archive of folklore that connects body-mind-spirit-land, landing us up in a place we can call home. We're both academics from the desert who are sick of academia and its genocidal logics. We returned to fire as the metaphor for new life, purposefully, we're sure, but not intentionally as such. We were comadres from day one. Something clicked. Maybe it was the desert in our bones: desert woman found us both at a tiki bar in Monterey, CA. She collected us, shaped us, and brought us back to the heart of the flames. It started with chisme. Chisme saves lives, and it sure as hell saved ours. Picture us both in worn muumuus of our own, a cup of cafecito, chismeando about just how bad academia really is for two brown and down desert chingonas: "Burn it down!" became our battle cry after every sad story about how the institution screwed us: burn it down! And then we realized, oh shit: BURN IT DOWN. This is our burn-it-down book. Our giant fire, flames as high as you can imagine, reaching up, up, up, in prayer: throw in the bones and whisper the magic words.

We are here to create new life.

Note

1. We use this name for what is known in the US as the Rio Grande and in Mexico as the Río Bravo. Turtle River honors traditional Indigenous names for this ancestor, while also respecting the language sovereignty of those who still speak those sacred words.

References

Blanco, M. D. P., & Peeren, E. (2013). Introduction: Conceptualizing Spectralities. In: Blanco, M.D. P., & Peeren, E. (eds.) *The spectralities reader*. New York: Bloomsbury Academic. 1–28

Cacho, L. (2012). *Social death: Racialized rightlessness and the criminalization of the unprotected*. New York: New York University Press.

Calafell, B. M. (2015). *Monstrosity, performance, and race in contemporary culture*. New York, NY: Peter Lang Publishing.

Cantu, N. E., & Najera-Ramirez, O. (2002). *Chicana traditions: Continuity and change*. Champaign: U Illinois Press.

Cho. G. M. (2007). Voices from the teum: Synesthetic trauma and the ghosts of Korean Diaspora. In P. Ticento Clough & J. Halley (Eds.), *The affective turn: Theorizing the social*. Durham: Duke University Press.

Delgado Shorter, D. (2021). *A Borderland Methodology / Una Metodología Fronteriza*.

Espinosa, G., & Garcia, M. (2008). *Mexican American religions: Spirituality, activism, and culture*. Durham, N.C.: Duke University Press.

Gonzalez, P. (2012). *Red medicine: Traditional indigenous rites of birthing and healing*. Tuscon: U of Arizona Press.

Gordon, A. (2008). *Ghostly matters*. Minneapolis: University of Minnesota Press.

Gutiérrez, R. A. (1991). *When Jesus came, the corn mothers went away: Marriage, sexuality, and power in New Mexico, 1500–1846*. Stanford Univ. Press.

Herrera-Sobek, M. (1990). The Mexican Corrido: A Feminist Analysis. Indiana University Press.

Herrera-Sobek, M. Editor. Chicano folklore: A handbook. (Greenwood Press 2006).

Herrera-Sobek, M. Editor. Celebrating *Latino* folklore: An encyclopedia of cultural traditions (ABCCLIO 2012)

Holland, S. P. (2000). *Raising the dead: Readings of death and (black) subjectivity*. Durham: Duke University Press.

Holling, M. A. (2021). Intersectionalities in the fields of *Chicana* feminism: pursuing decolonization through *Xicanisma's* 'resurrection of the dreamers. In Eguchi, S., Calafell, B.M, Abdi, s., & Delgado Shorter, D. (eds.) *De-whitening intersectionality: race, intercultural communication, and politics*. Lexington Books.

hooks, B. (2009). *Belonging: A culture of place*. New York: Routledge.

Levina, M., & Bui, D. (2013). *Monster culture in the 21st century*. New York: Bloomsbury Publishing.

Lopez Calvo, I., & Valles, V. (2018). *Latinx writing los angeles: Nonfiction dispatches from a decolonial rebellion*. Lincoln: University of Nebraska Press.

Menchaca, M. (2002). *Recovering history, constructing race: The Indian, black, and white roots of Mexican Americans*. Austin: U Texas Press.

Miner, D. (2014). *Creating aztlán Chicano art, indigenous sovereignty, and lowriding across turtle island*. Tucson: U of Arizona Press.

Moraga, C., & Anzaldúa, G. (1983). *This bridge called my back*. New York: Kitchen Table Press.

Poole, W. S. (2011). *Monsters in America: Our historical obsession with the hideous and haunting*. Waco: Baylor University Press.

Perez, D. R. (2008). *There was a woman: La Llorona from folklore to popular culture*. Austin: University of Texas Press.

Perez, D. R. (2018). *New tribalism and Chicana/o indigeneity in the work of Gloria Anzaldúa*. Routledge Press

Saldaña-Portillo, M. J. (2016). *Indian given*. Durham: Duke University Press.

Taylor, D. (1999). Dancing with Diana: A Study in Hauntology. *TDR (1988–)*, 43(1), 59–78.

PART I

Ghosts in the Real: Historiography in Our Stories That Becomes Research

CHAPTER 1

La Llorona

A LatIndigenous Specter of Trauma, Motherhood, and Contemporary Racial Violence

Sarah De Los Santos Upton and Leandra Hinojosa Hernández

According to our abuelas, La Llorona was an indigenous woman who wept because her children were taken from her by a Spaniard. As Joe Hayes, a white man often referred to as the "premier storyteller of New Mexico and the Southwest," tells it, La Llorona was a vain and jealous Mexicana who brutally murdered her children by drowning them in the river. We grew up hearing the legend of the woman who cries out for her lost children in the night and were warned to be careful or she would kidnap us as replacements. As we grew older and witnessed the proliferation of La Llorona-based films—*Mama* (2013), *The Curse of La Llorona* (2019), and *La Llorona* (2020), for example—we also wondered about popular culture's renewed interest in La Llorona's plight and began to make connections between the various histories of La Llorona and our own interests, as Chicana feminist communication scholars, in reproductive justice and critiquing violence against women.

In this essay, we use the story of La Llorona as a LatIndigenous framework to connect cultural and historical conceptualizations of motherhood and trauma to modern-day motherhood traumas associated with caged Latina/o/x[1] and Latin American children and the police brutality that kills brown and Black bodies. LatIndigenous refers to "cultures and peoples that are Indigenous or of Indigenous descent from the American Southwest, Mexico, Central, and South America," and this framework attends to the ways in which Indigenous histories and storytelling practices, especially through ghost stories such as the legend of La Llorona, are woven into Latinx understandings of "being, becoming, migration, displacement, and belonging" (Martinez & Medina-López, 2024, p.8). As mothers continue to publicly mourn and cry out for their lost children, much like La Llorona, they remain shamed and condemned for not raising their children "right" or for making "choices" that put their children in danger. We argue that La Llorona can be used as a specter of trauma that informs how we make sense of the interconnected traumas of colonialism, racism, and violence manifesting upon Black and brown bodies.

While the legend is often used as a cautionary tale to warn young children that they must be on their best behavior to avoid being taken by La Llorona, in the spirit of LatIndigenous storytelling and recounting of histories, Chicana and Mexicana feminists have also used the story to critique patriarchy and colonization (Elenes, 2011). These LatinIndigenous and feminist retellings of La Llorona allow both storytellers and audiences to counter oppression and domination and assert their agency through the construction of new subjectivities and identities (Elenes, 2011; Moreman & Calafell, 2008). Moreman and Calafell (2008) explain that part of the power of these retellings rests in La Llorona's ability to adapt to her given circumstances: "Her lesson is that in our constant self-agentic retellings of her and, therefore, of ourselves can we resignify what is politically most important about ourselves and the time in which we live" (p. 322). We argue that rather than serving as an example of malevolent motherhood, La Llorona is a mother figure who understands pain and loss and is therefore needed more than ever in a moment where BIPOC mothers are mourning the loss of children taken from them unjustly.

Just as Anzaldúa (1995) reimagines La Llorona as a spirit guide who helps a young girl find herbs to cure her mother's illness, we hope to offer this chapter as a guide for supporting BIPOC mothers and healing communities. As we have argued in previous work, true reproductive justice includes the freedom to raise our children in communities free from violence (Hernández & De Los Santos Upton, 2018, 2019). We refuse to perpetuate witnessing the pain of these mothers for the mere sake of witnessing. Instead, we demand that our audience do the work to bear witness (Tait, 2011) by transforming the act of witnessing into tangible action (Hernández & De Los Santos Upton, 2018; Holling, 2014). To this end, we conclude by offering resources for how to begin, continue, and/or sustain the anticolonial, antiracist work of supporting these mothers, their children, and their communities.

La Llorona Origin and Variations

Immediately after the Spanish conquest of México, the legend of La Llorona emerged as a LatIndigenous specter of trauma, a haunting representation of the devastation of conquest and colonialism and the resulting collective anguish for indigenous peoples (Elenes, 2011). The legend has morphed and shifted over time and according to the place of its telling, reflecting multiple subject positions and cultural value systems. As we mentioned in the introduction, the version told to us by our abuelitas was that La Llorona was an indigenous woman who cries out in the night because her children were taken from her by a Spaniard. This telling closely mirrors LatIndigenous versions of the story that link La Llorona to Malintizin, the indigenous translator for Hernán Cortés, who is simultaneously viewed as "the Mexican Eve" and as the mother of mestizas. Martín Cortés, the son she birthed as the result of her relationship with Hernán Cortés (which may or may not have been consensual according to various historical accounts), is widely considered to symbolize the first mestizo (Elenes, 2011). It is not difficult to imagine Malintizin weeping when Martín was taken away from her and sent to live in Spain, and so she becomes La Llorona. Building from this theme, De la Garza (2004) describes hearing that La Llorona wailed because her children were born looking "too Indian," while other tellings say she cries because we, her mestiza children, were born "too Spanish."

Other versions of the story describe La Llorona as a sexualized Mestiza who falls in love with a wealthy Spaniard with whom she has two children. When the Spaniard ultimately leaves her for a woman from his own social class, La Llorona drowns their children in the river and weeps with regret once she realizes what she has done (Pérez, 2002). Pérez (2002) offers a variation of this version, in which a woman married a man with three children and soon became jealous of the love and affection he showed the children. One night, when he was late arriving home, she took the children to the river and drowned them. When she died, she was denied entrance into heaven until she found the lost souls of the children, and so she wanders the earth searching for them. Other versions include a widow in poverty who murders her children to end their starvation and then goes mad as a result, a thief who murders her crying child because he will not be quiet as she attempts to escape the authorities, and a woman burned at the stake after drowning her children to spare them from her husband's vengeful rage (Pérez, 2002). While variations of the legend of La Llorona are endless, most versions tell of a ghostly woman who haunts the site of the original disaster, usually wandering riverbanks or along canals in the dark or sometimes appearing in cemeteries or walking on the side of the road (Pérez, 2002).

As Pedagogy

Elenes (2011) argues that the legend of La Llorona is pedagogical, as it teaches traditional values of obedience and responsibility by demonstrating that a deviation from the norm will result in catastrophe. For children in particular, La Llorona is used as a sort of "boogie man" to keep them from wandering too far away, as children are often reminded that while La Llorona is searching for her own children, she will take any other children she finds (Elenes, 2011, p. 74). Even as a young child, Leandra's mother, abuela, and tías told her stories of La Llorona to discipline her into being a "good young girl" because "La Llorona was always watching." De la Garza explains that the story of La Llorona made sense culturally given the realities she was born into as a "*chicanita*," and this story was, therefore, successful in scaring her into obedience:

> So, La Llorona goes about weeping and wailing and it is a terrifying thing. Since she was such a rotten mother, she would probably do rotten things to us if we were outside and she came around, right? That was the idea. So if it was dark, or we were misbehaving, we'd hear the wind outside our windows and someone would say, "ahí viene La Llorona," here comes La Llorona. And we learned to be scared. (De la Garza, 2004, p. 69)

In addition to using fear to teach children obedience, the multiple variations of La Llorona all attempt to teach appropriate and inappropriate practices of womanhood and motherhood (Elenes, 2011). In other words, this cultural allegory teaches women how they are to live, act, and function within society more broadly and within disciplining Mexican cultural norms more specifically (Pérez, 2002). Because in most tellings, La Llorona fails to live up to these cultural expectations of womanhood and motherhood, she is at best offered as a cautionary tale and at worst portrayed as demonic; "La Llorona is a monstrous feminine or "reproductive demon," mother as traitor, woman as embodiment of negativity or threat, a predatory specter praying upon "innocent" men and children" (Pérez, 2002, p. 103). Although some dominant narratives of La Llorona have served as a pedagogical tool to socialize women and children to behave according to social expectations, La Llorona also serves as a catalyst for resistance and activism through her feminist reimaginings.

As Resistance and Activism

For many Chicana feminists, the specter of La Llorona has created space for critiquing patriarchy and colonization and embodying the culturally specific act of mourning. Anzaldúa, who also learned about La Llorona from her grandmother, explored the multiple and conflicting manifestations of La Llorona, including the varied stories about her described above, but also expanding her analysis to explore Llorona's potential for resistance and activism. As a "tormented soul, wracked with guilt, searching for what has been lost," La Llorona has emerged as a guide, "forever wandering in a physical and psychic borderland" (Pérez, 2002, p. 101). While dominant tellings of La Llorona are embedded with patriarchal implications, Elenes (2011) argues that from its inception, her story inherently critiques both patriarchy and colonization. For Anzaldúa (2007), Llorona's act of wailing specifically embodies the protests of Indian, Mexican, and Chicana women against the various forms of colonization embedded in their lived experiences. In the chapter immediately following this one, Amanda Martinez further explores La Llorona and her children as complex beings with potential and agency. They care for one another and for the dead. La Llorona demonstrates her activist potential as she protects protesters and assists those who are fighting for "their land, their homes, their ties to the earth" (silva, 2024, p. 227).

La Llorona also teaches us how the very act of mourning can be a form of resistance. After generations of betrayal and traumatization, La Llorona haunts us in our unresolved grief as "an ever present specter in the psyches of Chicanos and mexicanos" (Anzaldúa, 2015, p. 88). While haunting us, she holds us in our grief, teaching us how that pain can take us in new directions if we do the work of naming, acknowledging, mourning, and grieving our losses and violations (Anzaldúa, 2015). Through this work, we "learn not just to survive but to imbue that survival with new meaning," engaging in activism to heal not only ourselves but our cultures and communities (Anzaldúa, 2015, p. 88). For Anzaldúa (2009), La Llorona is a manifestation of her personal and collective mourning, grieving over the loss of her health and abilities as she struggled with diabetes and keeping her up at night as she mourned the souls lost on September 11, 2001, counting losses, reflecting on the role the US played in the tragedy, and questioning the role she may have played. La Llorona also embodies cultural mourning; as Chicanxs are confronted with violence, prejudice, and assimilation, she "transcends her legendary status as a wandering specter punished for her feminized transgression and becomes emblematic of an entire generation of people who are becoming lost" (Pérez, 2002, p. 109).

La Llorona also maintains her status as a mother in mourning, and she guides other mothers through their grief. De la Garza (2004) describes being pressured into an abortion that she did not want and waking herself up screaming for her baby. When she cries out about this and other experiences, it scares people, and they turn their backs on her and her story, leaving De la Garza to conclude that society at large is more fearful of La Llorona's ability to tell her story than they are of her potential to harm children. Instead, they pretend she has no story of her own to tell and turn her into a story they can use for their own purposes (De la Garza, 2004). For De la Garza (2004), La Llorona embodies the very act of mourning:

> Ves, yo soy una Llorona tambien. I am a woman who weeps, too. I think I am a lot like you. Well, I don't know really—because like I said earlier, I don't even know your name or where you're really from. But I know what it feels like to have a pain so big in my heart that I want to cry for-ever. That if I cry out, I am afraid I will never stop crying—like you. (De la Garza, 2004, p. 71)

La Llorona has become a symbol of personal, collective, and cultural loss; however, she also holds the potential for transforming grief into resistance (Pérez, 2002). If we allow her, La Llorona can teach us how to acknowledge and hold our own grief, and this has implications for us individually and for our cultures and communities collectively. As Anzaldúa (2009) explains, "En estos tiempos de La Llorona we must use creativity to jolt us into awareness of our spiritual/political problems and other major global tragedies so we can repair el daño" (Anzaldúa reader, p. 312). La Llorona ultimately teaches us how to grieve and gives us the space to do so.

In her extensive writing and theorizing on La Llorona, Anzaldúa relies on feminist and LatIndigenous retellings to illuminate her potential as a guide. In her children's book, *Prietita and the Ghost Woman / Prietita y la Llorona*, she reimagines La Llorona as a spirit guide who helps a young girl named Prietita find an herb that the curandera needs to heal her mother. Through this reliance on LatIndigenous retelling, Anzaldúa transforms La Llorona from a terrifying ghost to a guardian angel. Throughout her other writings, Anzaldúa often describes the ways in which La Llorona calls out to her, guiding her through her grief and toward her potential. When she is stranded on a bridge, La Llorona calls to Anzaldúa: "'Adelante,' la Llorona whispers. 'You have a task, a calling. Only you can bring forth your poten-tial.' You yearn to know what that ever present inner watcher is asking of you" (Anzaldúa, 2015, p. 136). La Llorona is here for all of us to serve as a guide if we will accept her as such.

Whether you think she is to blame or she is an innocent victim, La Llorona is a mother who has lost her children. She is also a figure who helps us make sense of the grief that accompanies colonization culturally, spiritually, and within our own family units (Pérez, 2002). It is no coincidence that her legend centers on the loss of children, as losing a child represents a loss of both the past and the future, and colonialism has threatened to take cultural ways of knowing and self-determination away from the colonized (Elenes, 2011). At the heart of this chapter, we are concerned with the ways in which the loss of children and the legacy of colonialism are deeply intertwined for mothers of color. BIPOC mothers are forced to parent under legacies of colonialism that threaten the physical, emotional, and spiritual safety of their children, and when violence occurs in the home or on the streets, mothers are often the first to be blamed. We argue, then, that La Llorona is a specter of trauma that informs BIPOC motherhood. As De la Garza (2004) demonstrates, this is a truth that is not documented, but embodied:

> La Llorona cries at night, crying for her children, as a sort of eternal pun-
> ishment for her crime or loss, depending on how you look at it. If it is a
> crime, well, then she is damned to suffer because of her evil actions. If it
> was a loss, then she is damned to suffer, I guess, because she is a woman
> and that is what women do when they have children: Suffer. This is not a
> book-truth, not historically documented narrative truth. This is the kind
> of truth you make from hearing stories. (De la Garza, 2004, p. 69)

The legacy of conquest and colonization that informs contemporary motherhood for BIPOC mothers in the United States means that we are all La Llorona. Existing as La Llorona is a spectrum of experiences that, on one side, has us struggling to parent our children (and reparent ourselves) within violent colonial paradigms (Latinx Parenting, 2018), and on the other, has our children ripped from us violently through state-sanctioned violence such as police brutality and family separation.

Motherhood and Trauma

In our earlier research, we have traced the contours of the relationship among reproductive justice, gendered control, and violence against women

(Hernández, 2019; Hernández & De Los Santos Upton, 2018, 2019, 2020). At a broader level, violence against women is a global public health concern (Krantz, 2002; Ellsberg, 2006; WHO, 2017). In the United States, violence against women occurs in various spaces—the doctor's office, the birthing room, the home, and also in public spaces and spheres, as we have seen with violence against transgender women of color, Latin American migrants at the Mexico-US border, and police brutality against women of color. Such violence necessitates the use of an intersectional framework to consider how such structures—the government, the police, and more—facilitate spaces for violence and harm. Here, we utilize theoretical grounding points of violence against women and reproductive justice to consider an alternative reading of La Llorona that posits her as a mother figure who understands pain and loss. As we noted in the introduction, we contend that such a reading of La Llorona is needed more than ever in a moment where BIPOC mothers are faced with violence and are mourning the loss of their children taken from them unjustly at the hands of the US government. By extension, we hope to put our alternative reading of La Llorona in conversation with earlier readings of La Llorona written by white men (such as the reading by Joe Hayes, who refers to La Llorona as a jealous, vain, and violent woman). All too often is the history of Mexicanas patriarchally and misogynistically written by white men (Heidenreich, 2020)—here, we seek to re/envision La Llorona's historical and contemporary significance through the lens of Chicana feminist and reproductive justice lenses.

According to Ross and Solinger, reproductive justice is a conceptual framework and activist praxis that splices reproductive rights with social justice. Moving beyond notions of "choice," which center on the reproductive right to legally choose to have an abortion, reproductive justice crosses linguistic borders and expands the scope of activist interventions in reproductive health. As de Onís (2015) explains, the word "pro-choice" has no direct translation in Spanish, and so the use of this terminology around reproductive health creates a boundary between English and Spanish speakers. Reproductive justice, on the other hand,

> easily translates to justicia reproductiva, which features the concept of <justicia>, a familiar ideograph in the Spanish language and in Spanish-speaking cultures. Because Latin America and the Caribbean have endured dictatorships and colonialism—often facilitated by corrupt, U.S.-backed regimes—pursuing social <justice> is a well-accepted imperative and motivation. (de Onís, 2015, p. 9)

In other words, reproductive justice not only has a direct translation, but this translation also holds cultural relevance for many Spanish speakers, making it a more accessible term for multiple, overlapping reasons.

Reproductive justice surpasses pro-life/pro-choice binaristic approaches to reproductive health, advocates on behalf of sexual autonomy and gender freedom, and has three primary tenets: "1) the right to *not* have a child, 2) the right to *have* a child, and 3) the right to *parent* children in safe and healthy environments" (Ross & Solinger, 2017, p. 9, emphasis original). Moreover, reproductive justice demands that all fertile/parenting individuals require a "safe and dignified context for these most fundamental human experiences" (Ross & Solinger, 2017, p. 9). A safe and dignified reproductive context includes access to healthcare, a living wage, a healthy environment, housing and education, and additional resources in both prenatal and postnatal contexts across the lifespan (Hernández & De Los Santos Upton, 2018; Ross & Solinger, 2017).

Within the context of reproductive justice, we have analyzed the sociopolitical and sociocultural structures that have facilitated reproductive feminicidios, a concept defined as a "signification of the murdering of women as a result of their reproductive capacities and/or a structural limitation of their reproductive options during times of violence, poverty, and barriers to healthcare" (Hernández & De Los Santos Upton, 2018, p. 72). While a comprehensive overview of reproductive feminicidios in the US and Latin America is outside the scope of the chapter, we stress that such feminicidios include the following: the murdering of Black and brown communities at the hands of the police state, the reproductive violences faced by women of color throughout the United States both historically and contemporarily, and the separation of Latin American migrant families at the Mexico-US border (Hernández & De Los Santos Upton, 2018/2019b). White supremacist violence—family separation, police brutality, and reproductive violence and control—fundamentally disrupts families, inflicts generational trauma upon families, and thus violates the tenets of reproductive justice while at the same time communicating the perceived inhumanity of communities of color. As we have discussed in past research (Hernández & De Los Santos Upton, 2018/2019b; Hernández, 2019), recent lines of violence are congruent with the United States' history of reproductive racism and reproductive nonviolence. In our current day, however, we are able to see the violence occur in real-time on a national and international scale with the advent of smartphone technology. For example, in 2019, George Floyd's brutal murder shocked the United States. When George Floyd was murdered, and the story was streaming on social media and news outlets across the country, we watched in horror for several reasons: 1) we watched as the eight minutes felt like hours, felt like a lifetime; 2) we watched as the police officers inflicted violence upon him as he cried for help; and 3) we watched in horror as he called out for his mother. We immediately felt his cries—Sarah as a mother herself—and saw the connection between George calling out for his mother and the ways in which La Llorona called out for her children. On screens across the country and beyond, the much-needed relationship and bond between mother and child was called to the fore, the bonds severed and a Black man murdered at the hands of the police state.

As we noted above, La Llorona helps us make sense of reproductive injustices both in the US and at the Mexico-US border. As a being in a constant state of mourning, we recall how La Llorona's cries, outbursts, and pain can serve us as a mode of power to resist dominant structures that seek to rip apart families of color and dismantle family structures that serve to keep families and traditions together and ultimately keep children safe. Over the past several years, we have witnessed the severing of family bonds through the separation of families at the Mexico-US border (Hernández, 2019; De Los Santos Upton, 2019). Both cases—George Floyd's murder and family separation—are tools of white supremacism. In this chapter and in past research, we contend that both actions are acts of trauma against communities of color in line with the US's historical violence against black, brown, and Native/Indigenous communities (Hernández, 2019; Hernández & De Los Santos Upton, 2019). The Trump administration's illegal family separation processes "that have prolonged the length of time such children are held in government custody have exacerbated the significant trauma that many of these children already have suffered" (Center for American Progress, 2019, para. 2). Children who were forcibly separated from their families at the Mexico-US border have suffered from physical and mental traumas including anxiety, pain, frustration, self-harm, and suicidal ideation (Center for American Progress, 2019). Moreover, the organization Physicians for Human Rights published a report detailing family separation trauma and violence and found the following:

> Medical experts documented psychological trauma, including post-traumatic stress disorder, depression and anxiety. In nearly every case, the group's medical evaluators 'noted that the trauma suffered by the parents and the children warranted further intervention and ongoing therapeutic support.' The report concluded that the forced separation in those cases constituted torture and enforced disappearance, in that there was a period where parents did not know where their children were and were not able to contact them. (Mejia, 2020, para. 3–4)

Taken together, within a reproductive justice framework, both cases are physical manifestations of violent colonial paradigms with histories and actions written by and implemented by the hands of white individuals onto Black, Latinx, and Native American/indigenous communities. Whether exploring the ways in which earlier histories of La Llorona were written by white men or when exploring white supremacist violence perpetrated against communities of color, La Llorona serves as a liberatory Chicana feminist figure who assists us in reclaiming our fears, anger, and rage. She also serves as a space within which we can further critique white colonialist systems of domination and violence and find modes of solidarity and action with others. La Llorona is but one feminist figure in Chicana histories—alongside La Malinche—who has served as a cultural scapegoat for Mexican conquest, failed femininity, and failed motherhood as part of the historical revisionist goals of white supremacy. However, as we have discussed, a Chicana feminist reproductive justice reading of La Llorona's cultural history and impacts can serve to assist us in developing new modes of activism and solidarity in powerful ways.

Reproductive Justice, Witnessing, and Resources

La Llorona wailing, beckoning, encouraging the artist to rail against injustices. She calls me to act.
ANZALDÚA READER, p. 295

La Llorona creates space for the grief of BIPOC mothers, teaching us to lean into it and holding us as we wail. As Anzaldúa argues, she also serves as a guide, demanding that we act out against injustice and showing us the way. Too often, scholars and journalists write about unspeakable violence without offering the potential to work against such violence. This approach to journalism and scholarship allows readers to experience mundane witnessing (Ellis, 2009) of such violence; however, it does little to transform the act of witnessing into tangible action (Hernández & De Los Santos Upton, 2018; Holling, 2014). La Llorona begs us to do better. Pérez (2002) describes being startled awake at night, imagining La Llorona has come for her, not to take her, but to "ask something of me, proof that I have been working, doing something with my life" (Pérez, 2002, p. 110). In this essay, La Llorona calls out to us, asking what we are doing to support BIPOC women and children. We must continually revisit this question, but in this essay, we answer her call by offering a list of resources and strategies for readers looking to begin and/or sustain such work. We recognize that many of the stories of reproductive injustice are not ours to tell; however, we hope that by following the lead of Black women and other women of color and compiling a sample of the strategies they have employed in the fight for justice, we can encourage readers of this chapter to take action in some form. These five strategies are in no way exhaustive; rather, they are starting points on this journey.

1. Support BIPOC Mothers in Prenatal, Birth, and Postpartum

As we described above, BIPOC mothers experience reproductive feminicidio on a spectrum, ranging from mistreatment, neglect, and violence in prenatal, birthing, and postpartum contexts to losing their children to police brutality. As SisterSong (2021) has argued, it is important to approach reproductive justice by supporting mothers, children, and communities holistically, and there are multiple ways of offering such support through the donation of time, money, and other resources. For example, several organizations have created funds and scholarships for BIPOC birthing people to assist with expenses during prenatal care, birth, and the postpartum period. The SisterSong Birth Justice Care Fund covers the cost of prenatal, labor, and postpartum support and essential items such as breast pumps, diapers, wipes, car seats, and strollers. The San Antonio Nurse Midwife Birth and Wellness Center is a "loving, compassionate, listening safe space available for Black birthing people" and offers birth scholarships to "lift Black families up" through free or reduced care (McIver-Brown, 2020, para. 1). In addition to monetary donations, there are multiple ways to support reproductive justice for BIPOC families. Black Mamas Matter offers literature to become better informed and a toolkit for advocates to "lay the groundwork for policy change while highlighting Black mamas' human right to safe and respectful care" (p. 5). Forward Together is an organization working towards rights, recognition, and resources for all families, and their website offers free access to multiple tools, including *We Keep Each Other Safe: A Guide By and For Black, Indigenous, Latinx, POC and LGBTQ Communities Navigating the COVID-19 Pandemic* and *The Road to Reproductive Justice: Native Americans in New Mexico.*

2. Donate Time and Resources to End Police Brutality

On the other end of the spectrum of reproductive feminicidio, police brutality against BIPOC bodies is such a prevalent issue that it can be difficult to know where to begin addressing it. It is important to follow the lead of Alicia Garza,

Patrisse Cullors, and Opal Tometi, the radical Black organizers who created the #BlackLivesMatter movement in response to the acquittal of Trayvon Martin's murderer. As described by the organization itself, Black Lives Matter is "an ideological and political intervention in a world where Black lives are systematically and intentionally targeted for demise. It is an affirmation of Black folks' humanity, our contributions to this society, and our resilience in the face of deadly oppression" (Black Lives Matter, 2021, para. 3). The Black Lives Matter website contains various resources for getting involved with the movement, including toolkits for *Healing Action* and *Healing Justice*, and toolkits centered on Trayvon Martin's story and the beginning of the movement, including *#TrayvonTaughtMe* for Black and Non-Black POC organizers, *#TalkAboutTrayvon*, a toolkit for white people, and *#TrayvonMeEnseñó*, a toolkit in Spanish. Several other organizations and individuals have created resource lists detailing various ways to get involved and education guides for learning more about the ways in which racism and white supremacy function in US society. The American Civil Liberties Union (ACLU) has created a community action manual on fighting police abuse, which includes identifying the problem, meeting community goals, and developing strategies for organizing to meet these goals.

The Movement for Black Lives also offers several ways to get involved, including specific actions like the *Week of Action in Defense of Black Lives* and resources, including a safety guide for staying safe and assessing risk when participating in actions such as protests. Another important way to support efforts to end police brutality is to post bail for protestors.

Finally, education is a powerful way to not only begin but sustain antiracist work. The Michigan League for Public Policy has created the 21-Day Racial Equity Challenge, which can be completed individually with a log to track participation or in conversation with a cohort of other participants. The Chicana M(other)work Collective has created a *Social Justice Summer Curriculum for Children of Color*. The six-week curriculum was created for children ages four to ten and includes discussion topics, activities, and recommended videos and books to engage topics including race, colorism, and white supremacy, and the movements to end these systems of violence in accessible terms.

Activists have also compiled Google Documents and Google Drive folders with educational materials and action guides. Carlisa Johnson's document, *Resources for Accountability and Actions for Black Lives*, includes a list of victims of police brutality, links to information and updates about each case, numbers to text to stay informed, email addresses and sample emails scripts, donations, petitions, resources for protestors, and various other ways to take action. Charles Preston's *Black History Month Library* on Google Drive includes electronic copies of complete works by Black authors, artists, and academics. To facilitate antiracist work in white communities and encourage "white folks to become allies, and eventually accomplices," Anna Stamborski, Nikki Zimmermann, and Bailie Gregory created the Google Document *Scaffolded Anti-Racist Resources* based on stages of white identity development. More resources to deepen antiracist work in white communities and households can be found on Sarah Sophie Flicker and Alyssa Klein's Google Document, *Antiracism Resources.*

3. Donate Time and Resources to End Family Separation

Although the Trump administration is no longer in office, and we no longer see family separation at the forefront of news coverage, it remains a pressing reproductive justice issue. It can be overwhelming to know where to begin, especially if you live in a community far removed from the Mexico-US border or migrant detention centers. There are, however, multiple ways to get involved, and organizations like the Refugee and Immigrant Center for Education and Legal Services (Raices) and the ACLU have streamlined ways to take action according to the amount of time one has to offer. The "take action" sections of Raices' websites ask visitors if they have "a few minutes," "some time," or if they are "up for anything," and offer several strategies for getting involved to end family separation, among other causes. For those with limited time, there are options to donate money, sign petitions, send emails and texts, Tweet, call representatives, and even start a conversation about immigration with family members, all with support and sample messaging provided by the organization. For those with more time, there are opportunities to organize and host community events, volunteer, and intern. Raices, for example, has multiple volunteer opportunities, including *The Karnes Pro Bono Project*, which provides free legal services to people in ICE custody at Karnes. Raices also presents several remote volunteer opportunities, perfect for offering flexibility and opportunities to those who live far away from the border and detention centers and continuing this important and necessary volunteer work during the COVID-19 pandemic.

4. Decolonize Parenting and End Chancla Culture in Your Home and Community

In addition to addressing state-sanctioned violence against BIPOC mothers and children, we argue that reproductive justice also involves a shift away from violent, colonized views of children and approaches to parenting. Adult supremacy is a worldview that asserts "children are inferior, adults are superior, and that children must comply to adult expectations and environments" (Tootoosis, 2020, para. 3). This normalized oppression of children is rooted in colonization and ultimately leads to the socially accepted dehumanization of children (Tootoosis, 2020). An example of this normalized oppression is Chancla Culture. La Chancla is a reference to the use of a sandal or flip-flop to threaten or actively cause physical harm to children, and it has become a pop culture icon and the subject of jokes for many Latinxs. Leslie Priscilla Arreola-Hillenbrand of Latinx Parenting argues that Chancla Culture is "the use of oppressive strategies—including corporal punishment, shame, and fear—to manipulate children into behaving which cause significant harm to a child's development and emotional development especially when employed long-term" (2020, p. 4). Latinx Parenting is dedicated to decolonizing parenting and ending Chancla Culture through nonviolence, supporting families with education and advocacy, and there are multiple ways to get involved and support this important work (Latinx Parenting, 2018). Latinx Parenting offers decolonized nonviolent parenting workshops, like the *Ending Chancla Culture Workshop*, and intensive series, such as the *Decolonized Nonviolent Parenting 6-Week Series* and the *Criándome, Cuidándome: Reparenting Ourselves While Raising Our Children 8-Week Series*. Workshops are offered on a sliding pay scale according to privilege, and scholarships and payment plans are available to ensure accessibility. Latinx Parenting also hosts panel discussions like the *Brown Fatherhood Panel* and offers more individualized support through parenting circles and parent coaching. In addition to participating in these offerings, there are opportunities to get involved with Latinx Parenting by following the organization on social media and joining their mailing list, where they share insights and resources, donating to their scholarship fund, and becoming a patron on Patreon, which helps sustain the growth of the movement to end Chancla Culture and grants access to additional resources to support nonviolent parenting journeys.

5. Be a Comadre

To us, La Llorona is a comadre on the journey of motherhood and quest for reproductive justice. The concept of comadrisma is rooted in female friendship; however, this bond moves beyond surface-level friendship to encompass relationships that are rooted in support of mothers, whole families, and allies in workplaces and activist circles (de Hoyos Comstock, 2012; Scholz, 2016).

As a guide, La Llorona shows up for us as a comadre by teaching us to be comadres to one another, both through formal comadre organizations and informal community-based networks. For example, as described above, organizations like SisterSong and Latinx Parenting have structures and programs in place to support reproductive justice on a nationwide scale, as well as in community settings and individual homes. At this historic moment, both organizations have facilitated connections for COVID-19 relief, drawing on their vast networks to create and strengthen mutual aid efforts and ensure struggling families do not go without food and shelter during the pandemic. We argue that this is what reproductive justice looks like in practice. In addition to supporting their efforts, we can find ways to follow La Llorona's lead and show up as comadres in our communities every day. Something as simple as being welcoming to children in multiple spaces can allow parents to show up and participate without struggling to find childcare. Holding a friend's baby at an academic conference (thanks, Leandra), allowing students to bring children with them to class, or welcoming families with children to participate in meetings where organizing for activist events is taking place are all small examples of embodied reproductive justice that can have a big impact on both parents and children.

Concluding Thoughts and Future Directions

Inspired by LatIndigenous tellings and retellings of the story of La Llorona, we are drawn to her mothering potential as a spirit guide leading us towards enactments of reproductive justice. Engaging in the strategies outlined above by taking a stand against reproductive violence is a way to work towards reproductive justice and create a world where parents are empowered to raise their children in safe and healthy communities. We have provided these strategies as a starting point to assist academics, practitioners, activists, and community members in participating in the continued fight for reproductive justice. Future directions for research, engagement, and activism include combatting colorism and anti-Blackness in Latinx spaces and communities, continued efforts to support prison reform and defunding the police in hopes of fostering safer and more resourced BIPOC communities and exploring the intersections of reproductive justice with other movements, such as coalition-building with environmental justice organizations (de Onís, 2019), Black Lives Matter, and more.[2]

Ultimately, through La Llorona's guidance, influence, and calling, we are able to join each other in spaces to mourn and also collectively act to create change and more equitable health spaces for BIPOC families.

Notes

1. Latina/o/x individuals are often racialized/ethnicized as brown, erasing the experiences of AfroLatinos and perpetuating colorism and anti-Blackness. We acknowledge that race and ethnicity intersect in powerful ways, particularly in reproductive justice contexts, and we use the term Latina/o/x with the understanding that our communities are made of up individuals who identify, or are marked as, Black, brown, Indigenous, white, Asian, and mixed-race.

2. We wish to thank the anonymous reviewer from NCA 2021 who not only offered encouragement and thoughtful advice for strengthening this manuscript, but also inspired us to think through how we can build off these strategies in future research and activist efforts.

References

Anzaldúa, G. (1995). *Prietita and the ghost woman*. San Francisco: Children's Book Press.

Anzaldúa, G. (2007). *Borderlands/La frontera: The new mestiza* (3rd ed.). Aunt Lute Books.

Anzaldúa, G. (2009). *The Gloria Anzaldúa Reader*. Duke University Press.

Anzaldúa, G. (2015). *Light in the dark/Luz en lo oscuro: Rewriting identity, spirituality, reality* (A. Keating, Ed.). Duke University Press.

Arreola-Hillenbrand, L. P. (2020). *Ending Chancla Culture: Decolonizing our familias & raising future ancestors Mini e-book*. Latinx Parenting.

Black Lives Matter. (2021, March 4). *Herstory*. https://blacklivesmatter.com/herstory/.

Center for American Progress. (2019). New Report Details the Traumatic Effects of Family Separation on Children. Retrieved from https://www.americanprogress.org/drumbeats /new-report-details-traumatic-effects-family-separation-children/.

De Hoyos Comstock, Nora. 2012. "Introduction." In *Count on Me: Tales of Sisterhoods and Fierce Friendships*, ix–xiii. New York: Atria.

De la Garza, S. A. (2004). *María speaks: Journeys into the mysteries of the mother in my life as a Chicana*. Peter Lang.

de Onís, C. M. (2019) Reproductive Justice as Environmental Justice: Contexts, Coalitions, and Cautions. In L. O'Brien Hallstein, A. O'Reilly, & M. Vandenbeld Guiles (Eds.), *The Routledge Motherhood Companion*. Routledge.

de Onís, K. M. (2015). Lost in Translation: Challenging (White, Monolingual Feminism's) with Justicia Reproductiva. *Women's Studies in Communication*, 38(1), 1–19. https://doi.org/10.108 0/07491409.2014.989462.

Elenes, C. A. (2011). *Transforming Borders: Chicana/o Popular Culture and Pedagogy*. Lanham, MD: Lexington Books.

Ellis, J. (2009). Mundane witness. In P. Frosh, & A. Pinchevski (Eds.), *Media witnessing: Testimony in the age of mass communication*. Palgrave Macmillan.

Ellsberg, M. C. (2006). Violence against women: a global public health crisis. *Scandinavian Journal of Public Health*, 34, 1–4.

Heidenreich, L. (2020). *Nepantla2: Transgender mestiz@ histories in times of global shift.* University of Nebraska Press.

Hernández, L. H. (2019). Feminist approaches to border studies and gender violence: Family separation as reproductive injustice. *Women's Studies in Communication, 42*(2), 130–34.

Hernández, L. H., & De Los Santos Upton, S. (2018). *Challenging reproductive control and gendered violence in the Américas: Intersectionality, power, and struggles for rights.* Lanham, MD: Lexington Books.

Hernández, L. H., & De Los Santos Upton, S. (2019a). "Insider/Outsiders, Reproductive (In) justice, and the U.S.-Mexico Border." *Health Communication,* 1–5.

Hernández, L. H., & De Los Santos Upton, S. (2019b). Critical health communication methods at the US-Mexico border: Violence against migrant women and the role of health activism. *Frontiers in Communication, 4,* 34.

Holling, M. A. (2014). "So my name is Alma, and I am the sister of . . . : A feminicidio testimonio of violence and violent identifications." *Women's Studies in Communication, 37*(3), 313–38.

Krantz, G. (2002). Violence against women: a global public health issue! *Journal of Epidemiology and Community Health, 56,* 242–43.

Latinx Parenting. (2018). *Latinx Parenting: Crianza con Corazón y Cultura.* https://www.latinxparenting.org/.

McIver-Brown, N. (2020, June 10). *SANM Birth Fund: Lifting Black Families Up.* GoFundMe. https://www.gofundme.com/f/birth-scholarships-for-black-birthing-people.

Mejia, B. (2020, February 25). Physicians group releases report on psychological effects of family separation. *Los Angeles Times.* https://www.latimes.com/california/story/2020-02-25/family-separation-trauma.

Moreman, S. T., & Calafell, B. M. (2008) "*Buscando para nuestra latinidad*: Utilizing *La Llorona* for Cultural Critique." *Journal of International and Intercultural Communication, 1*(4), 309–26.

Pérez, D. R. (2002). Caminando con La Llorona: Traditional and contemporary narratives. In *Chicana traditions: Continuity and change* (pp. 100–113). University of Illinois Press.

Santos Upton, S. (2019). Nepantla activism and coalition building: Locating identity and resistance in the cracks between worlds. *Women's Studies in Communication, 42*(2), 135–39.

Scholz, Teresa Maria Linda. "Beyond "Roaring Like Lions": Comadrismo, counternarratives, and the construction of a Latin American Transnational subjectivity of feminism. *Communication Theory* 26, no. 1 (2016): 82–101.

SisterSong. (2021, March 4). *Reproductive justice.* https://www.sistersong.net/reproductive-justice.

Tait, S. (2011). "Bearing witness, journalism and moral responsibility." *Media, Culture & Society, 33*(8), 1220–35.

Tootoosis, C. (2020). The cunning of the adult supremacist [Freedom Rising]. *Writings.* http://www.colbytootoosis.com/writings/adult-supremacy.

World Health Organization. (2017). Violence against women. Retrieved from https://www.who.int/newsroom/factsheets/detail/violence-against-women.

CHAPTER 2

Legacies of Land, Cultural Clashes, and Spiritual Stirrings

A Testimonio of New Mexican Ghost Stories

Amanda R. Martinez

Traveling north of Albuquerque, the southwestern desert transforms gradually from buildings and cityscapes to neighborhoods and apartment complexes to sprawling rural lands. Passing Rio Rancho, the Sandia Mountains shade the picturesque scenery east of the major highway that traverses the north/south state route. Tumbleweeds bounce across the lowlands and thin streams of water flow from the arroyos. New Mexico boasts a slogan on souvenirs: "the Land of Enchantment," a well-deserved claim to fame.

Land Legacies and Identity Politics

Signs mark "reservations" to indicate where one sovereign community's land ends and another begins. Leaving Rio Arriba County, now entering the Reservations of San Felipe, Tesuque, Pojoaque . . . The signs are more than space designations. They speak volumes about Southwest history, documenting legacies of colonization, mestizaje, land grants, and sovereignty (Dunbar-Ortiz, 2014; Gonzales, 2019). At an academic conference in Albuquerque years ago, I had the following conversation with a Chicano historian:

Our people had few choices, all with different costs. Are you Native? Okay, then you belong on reservation land. Are you Mexican? Okay, then back you go to the other side of this border. Are you Spanish? Okay, then here is some land and you can stay.

Each summer, the Spanish Market and the Indian Market inhabit the Santa Fe Plaza in successive weeks. Locals and tourists browse the art, pottery, and jewelry and enjoy the cultural dance and music performances. We eat fry bread, Navajo tacos, roasted corn on the cob, and stuffed sopaipillas topped with Christmas-style red and green chile. New Mexico is my familial homeplace. I am a descendant, local, and tourist when I navigate these multigenerational spaces.

Beyond Santa Fe, the Land of Enchantment exudes a notable LatIndigenous aura. Española connects the other nearby rural cities through two-lane roads. My matrilineal family is from Medanales, just before Abiquiu, and my patrilineal side is from Alcalde, just past the San Juan Ohkay Owingeh Pueblo.

I grew up hearing relatives self-identify as "Spanish" or "Hispanic." I did not question this tendency much as a kid, but as a young adult, I realized that "Spanish" identification privileges the conquistadores, eclipsing the complex ethnic mixes of New Mexico, laden with sociopolitical, class-based historical reasons such as distancing New Mexico culturally from Mexico after the Treaty of Guadalupe Hidalgo in 1848 (Lamadrid & Gonzales, 2019). Identity complexities persist for centuries, given the historical presence of Genízaros and indigenous groups alongside the Spanish (Gonzales, 2019), rendering claims to a fully simply Spanish identity incomplete (Trujillo, 2019). Pride, shame, cultural confusion, and hope shape our shifting avowed identities powerfully, such as claiming a pure European ancestry or embracing mestizaje and rediscovering and embracing ancestral indigeneity (Romero, 2019; Trujillo, 2019).

My ears perked up as a kid when my great/grandparents would tell stories about indigenous members in our family lineage alongside los conquistadores from provinces of Spain, corroborating the state's colonization amidst shifting borderlands. Grampa Ben told me that our Garcia family descends from the Spanish province of Extremadura. His wife, my Gramma Ramona's family, has a multiethnic history, though she lost both her parents as a child and knows fragmented bits about her ancestral lineage. Gramma Ramona's family, according to my mom Susan, "has Black, Indian, Spanish, and Arabic lineage." Once Gramma Ramona met one of her aunts, a Black woman, and perpetually thereafter described her as "Black-Black" in all familial conversations, characterizing her tía's skin color as an anomaly. On my dad Eugene's side, my Gramma Grace talked about "la India" Grandma Kika, noteworthy for her indigenous features. Comments abound for those who look "muy India" with high cheekbones or dark skin complexion or "muy güero" for having light features like los Españoles, such as the green eyes some of my tías and tíos have, or the light hair and white skin of my Gramma Grace and Uncle Joe. Personal accounts of ambivalence, hazy memory, lost knowledge, shame, and pride towards our indigenous history are not uncommon patterns among some New Mexican families (Romero, 2019). The importance of raced and classed historical, social order lends insight into attitudes about the intersections of racial/ethnic and regional cultural allegiance (Brown, 2013), and arguments flourish about how we should identify (Medina, 2014).

New Mexico exists among many regional, national, and global histories that include massive dislocation and privilege/disadvantage shifts (Moraga, 2011). The regional cultural legacies intertwine with experiences of trauma, exploitation, and oppression that animate hauntings and make home feel sometimes disorienting due to unresolved social violence (Gordon, 2008), such as slavery, genocide, and colonization (Ortiz, 2018). Identity invokes complicated emotions, politicized tensions, and personal struggles. Still, alongside histories of colonization exist histories of resistance. Ultimately, "we are not a conquered people" (Cuevas, 2019).

New Mexico is a majority-minority politically blue state that only recently elected Native women to federal government positions, though Chicano/as/Hispanics have long held political roles. My relatives agree: Everything here is political. It's about who you know. When I studied abroad in college, I experienced an awakening that prompted a deep self-identity exploration. The message that Spain/Spanish means white people stunned me, especially because my New Mexican family identifies as Spanish, and few of us would pass for Spanish in Spain. As one of few in my large extended family to ever set foot on the motherland, I was confused. Even my Spanish peers thought me having my last name was odd because I am a brown US-American woman with ancestry in the southwest. I thought, *you don't know your own colonizer history?* They imagined only white people were US-Americans, and they assumed I was from practically any and every country in South America instead. Higher education and young adult experiences have helped me embrace my mestizaje (Galván, 2014) rather than the longstanding historical race/class, societal status, and power-driven reasons to privilege Spanish identity (Brown, 2013).

Anzaldúa (2009) emphasizes the strength and power derived from mestizaje and Chicanx consciousness and the borderlands as a holistic both/and way of thinking and acting that includes a transformational tolerance for contradiction. Blackwell (2018) quotes Anzaldúa in an interview: "I felt very strongly that the Native American movement was the closest that I felt to the Chicano movement just because we shared the same history of colonization, attempted genocide, and basically the same blood because Chicanos are primarily Indian, but they've just forgotten it" (p. 118). New mestiza consciousness as a concept of personhood synergistically embraces the historically contradictory Euro-American and indigenous anchoring of the US-Mexico borderlands (Anzaldúa, 1999; 2015). Gonzales (2019) draws our attention to the prevalence of Genízaro communities across the region, urging us to "embody our mixed indigenous heritage as a defiant act in honor of our ancestors and challenge the colonial power of the nation-state to dominate our identity" (p. 246). Racism and colonial terror histories result in intergenerational trauma that manifests in myriad ways. In the stubborn binary-centric racial histories of the world, Chicanx/Latinx mestizaje complicates the intertwining of race, ethnicity, class, and cultural, regional claims. It is "through knowledge [that] we liberate ourselves" (Anzaldúa, 2015, p. 91).

In my testimonio (Reyes & Curry Rodriguez, 2012), I bear witness to the stories that follow to engage LatIndigenous places, spaces, spiritual mestizaje that intertwines elements of both Catholicism and indigenous practices (Elenes, 2014), and proximity to ancestral knowledge. Delgadillo (2011) defines spiritual mestizaje as "the transformative renewal of one's relationship to the sacred through a radical and sustained multimodal and self-reflexive critique of oppression in all its manifestations and a creative and engaged participation in shaping life that honors the sacred." (p. 1) Reckoning with settler-colonial power structures, I weave the intergenerational "ghost stories" passed down through my family—and others I have experienced personally—with the grand narratives that commemorate inextricably linked historical events and common knowledge infused with Spanish Catholic religiosity and Native indigenous spirituality. I invoke the monstrosity of we and our multiply colonized histories of the Southwest (Calafell, 2016) alongside mestizaje realities to shed light on the decolonial possibilities within intergenerational ghost storytelling. I focus on the tensions inherent in representational monstrosity (Levina & Bui, 2013) as the "ghost stories" I share keep these tensions and subsequent repression from fading while retold through a particular frame that shares cultural power with Chicanx/Hispanic and indigenous people. Cultural stories help us to talk about ourselves; they are a way we teach the youth about survival and the salient power of homeplaces, and for those places to act as a release for the subconscious thoughts we cannot control (Alcalá, 2001). Oral traditions have long been the mode of transmission for storytelling about spiritual encounters and the healing practices to restore mindbodyspirit balance across generations of LatIndigenous groups for "complex reasons, including survival and protection from the Inquisitions" (Buenaflor, 2018, p. 35). Calling our souls back in when they wander is a healing strategy, and storytelling acts as a form of medicine for us (Garcia Lopez, 2019; Torres, 2005).

The Coco Man

Entering Pojoaque before arriving in Española, the Koko Man Fine Wine and Liquors sky-high sign holds meaning beyond its catchiness, spelled with k's in playful, clever reference to the disciplinary boogeyman. The Coco Man conjures childhood memories with my cousins recounting curiously detailed yet vague stories about him, a beast whose presence is intimately tied to the land. My dad, uncles, or grandpa would slyly creep around the corner, back hunched over, face squinted into a monstrous distortion, a big toothy grin . . . and he would jump out with a roar to scare us or limp forward slowly, as classic horror movie villains do, and somehow still catch up and capture his prey scrambling desperately to escape! "Oooooh. . . . WoooooOooooooWooooooOooooooh . . . The Coco Man is coming!" Dad, personifying the Coco Man exclaimed, raising his voice and lowering it rhythmically for an ominous effect that only the most intimidating boogeymen can achieve.

"Aaaaaah!!!!!! Eeey, don't get us!!! Nooooo!" we kids would shriek, provoking each other to scream louder or jerk our bodies away vigorously in response to the intensity of each other's escape attempts. Dad would cackle in deviance and dominance, satisfied by our terrified reactions, knowing he had fulfilled his goal: to keep the children on edge and in line, well-behaved and reminded of our vulnerability to the Coco Man if we acted up. Though the origins of the Coco Man stories likely evolved over time, the "Coco" word usage is a result of a misinterpretation of translated meaning. Avila and Parker (2000) explain:

> . . . Indian women sang lullabyes to the Spanish children they cared for, singing, "Coco, coco," [and] the Spaniards completely misunderstood. "Coco" means "the boogie man" in Spanish, while in Nahuatl it simply means "go to sleep." So, while the Indian women were singing, "Sleep so that you can rest and not get sick," the Spaniards thought they were saying, "The boogie man is going to get you if you don't sleep."

Figure 2.1. *Koko Man*, original
drawing by Moises Gonzales.

The disciplining, patriarchal power of the Coco Man conveys an unmistak-
able fear appeal to frighten children to keep them out of harm's way, like
the Chupacabra, el Cucuí, or La Llorona, monsters lurking in the dark for
centuries (Anaya, 2006). A common warning from parents to frighten kids
away from trouble rings familiar, as the late Chicano author and New Mexico
native Anaya (2006) describes: "Don't be a malcriado, my parents said. Get
home on time" (p. 27).

Into young adulthood, we took a somewhat agentic role in the Coco Man
story's evolution when we told the stories amongst ourselves, spiraling them
into spookier versions. I remember my cousin Little Daniel, serious in tone,
saying that "Pa'de [Padre] Juan," an old local man often spotted walking slowly
along the side of the road with a limp in his step, was coming to get you, so
you better watch out. Pa'de Juan is always around, readily on call to regulate
all manner of disrespectful or displeasing behavior, even in our adult ages,
now far beyond childhood! We joked that, obviously, Little Daniel just wanted

to scare us, so we should brush off his stories. But then we would see Pa'de Juan trudging along the side of the road—the highway even, with speeding cars whizzing by him!—and the scene would send a chill down our spines. Our postures tightened, and we drew our skepticism back with a shallow inhale. Not only did the Coco Man maintain relevance beyond our childhood spooky stories, but he now morphed into a human form by way of Pa'de Juan's image as embodied host. Coco Man is here to stay, and he is still terrifying, whether as an imagined beastlike ominous predator or a lone old man walking as his primary means of transportation around town. The shifting nature of the Coco Man as monstrous signals he is undoubtedly everywhere at once.

One summer, the Martinez family went camping in the mountains. As we set up camp, all the cousins changed into swimsuits to dip our feet, and eventually our waist-up bodies, in the clear, chilly stream water that poured into a large lake in the distance. I remember using my toes to stroke the dark green, velvety moss that covered the pebbles and large boulders lining the bottom of the shallow river. We were warned by the adults to be careful not to slip and fall on the soft moss. As we shivered but braved the water's chill, my eldest cousin, Maria, began to tell the tale of La Llorona, the legendary story of the wandering woman who drowned her children and now weeps in the waters, perpetually searching and longing for their return. As my cousin described La Llorona, she detailed her flowing straight hair and how the water current's hum created a deafening sadness and sorrowful drowning out of her cries— but you could still hear those cries if you listened closely. I looked down at the green moss and imagined how sad it must be for a mother to lose her children, and I was unable to empathize with what could have possibly driven her to make this reality her own. The inability to shore up empathy for even the most heinous actions has historically meant moral superiority and distance between oneself and another. This is how I experienced the tale of La Llorona as a child. The story easily made La Llorona into a monstrous albeit feminine figure, conforming to familiar gender roles as a weeping mother, and yet her actions made her a dark figure akin to the Coco Man, a cautionary tale of discipline, power, and control over our youthful fates.

Maria laughed maniacally as she saw the unease register in our expressions. "Ooooeeeey! You're scared, hahahahaha! She's gonna come and get you later tonight so you better watch out!" Our small bodies tightened as we struggled to contain our new fear, managed to be cold but also brave enough to stay in the water with the cousins. As the sky grew darker and our campfire's brightness faded, we cousins begged to sleep in the camper. Finally, upon permission from Grampa Floyd and Gramma Grace, we climbed onto the large *bed side*, eventually squeezing our grandpa out of the bed. We wanted him to stay in the camper with us for protection should we need him to defend us against a Coco Man; Grandpa was a skilled hunter, a sharpshooter, and an outdoorsy masculine man who was staunchly aware of and thoroughly immersed in his religious, spiritual practices and the mountains. His booming, deep voice alone could scare the wits out of anyone, and it often *did* scare us as young kids. Grampa Floyd moved to the smaller bed and left Grandma to comfort her grandchildren crowding her bed.

Despite my Gramma Grace's insistence that we go to sleep, we kept giggling at any little sound, screaming when poked by a cousin attempting to provoke a scare. After we wore our poor grandma out and she fell asleep, we crammed into the small camper bathroom and threw water on the mirror in total darkness. Then, at cousins Maria and Loriann's instruction, we chanted "Bloody Mary" together three times, then screamed frantically because we swore that we saw a face appear in the mirror, another manifestation of the faceless boogey person manifesting after our conjuring, eerily attending to our search for spiritual spookiness that carries power to discipline us as children. Our minds wandered to imagine the possibilities that lie in the unknown.

Los Matachines de Alcalde at St. Anne's Church

In the cold winter air, the smell of firewood burning inside homes fills the mountainous desert outdoors as families gather for the Christmas holidays. The women scurry around the kitchen, tending to the crock pot of beans, enchiladas in the oven, posole and chile simmering on the stove, a fresh batch of homemade tortillas keeping warm on the counter and available for snacking. The men tend to the firewood, chopping it with an axe before lugging it inside and carefully positioning it in the fireplace. The children run in and outside of the house together, playing games, teasing each other, and making up stories. We cram into several cars and parade ourselves a short distance to St. Anne's Catholic Church. We fill the pews for mass, linger afterward to greet others in attendance, light a candle to send loving intentions to our deceased family members, make the sign of the cross with blessed water, and say a prayer for them and for ourselves (Buenaflor, 2018).

Though we vary in our devout religiosity, everyone practices cultural Catholicism because the Catholic spirituality binds our cultural practices and beliefs together (Téllez, 2014). We all know the prayers, songs, and responses expected from the priest. We know when to stand, sit, and kneel, and it is a reflex to simply remain quiet, attentive, and respectful as a member of the congregation. As Mom says, "It's good to take the holy water and make the sign of the cross to ward off evil." Religious and spiritual beliefs maintain utmost importance because they operate as a safeguard against unknown forces to which we and others might be susceptible, even if we are mostly do-gooders, though flawed, sinning humans by nature.

Everyone files outside to watch los Matachines dance in front of the church, the perfect symbolic and sacred scenic backdrop for the reenactment of the first encounter and ongoing tensions and battles between the Natives and the Spanish conquistadores. The Matachines dance-drama "is an important annual obligation for the people of Alcalde, who express warm pride in it and for whom it embodies a self-conscious sense of cultural heritage and continuity." (Rodriguez, 2009, p. 106). Importantly, the reenactment "reconciles the spiritual conflicts of conquest and colonization" (Gandert, 2019, p. 19). The tradition began hundreds of years ago, and the dancers who participate in keeping the Matachines tradition alive come from many generations of families from Alcalde (Campos, 2018). At least three generations of men on my patrilineal side have participated in los Matachines de Alcalde; as Rodriguez (2009) notes, "Today almost all men in the community have participated in the dance at one time or another" (p. 106). The village of Alcalde was once a "colonial administrative center with a substantial population of Genízaros," and today, the locals still remember this complex history by celebrating "both Matachines and the spectacular Comanches equestrian play that dramatizes the 1779 defeat of the powerful Comanche leader Cuerno Verde (Green Horn)" (Gandert, 2019, p. 23). The region is distinctly Catholic-dominant, existing alongside many Native spiritualities outside of organized religious structures; there are twenty-three federally recognized tribes in the state (New Mexico Secretary of State).

As the controversies over slavery-era confederate monuments have aggravated the public's imagination anew recently and prompted a critical reevaluation of how and why we pay tribute to certain historical figures as a nation, New Mexico, too, has grappled with its own colonial past, igniting tensions among Latinxs/Hispanics and Native Americans. For example, the annual 1692 reconquest of New Mexico depicts a celebration, known as the Entrada, of the Native Americans' succumbing to the Spanish Empire after intense resistance and revolts (Romero, 2018). The reenactment ceremony intends to keep Hispanic history alive but has been the subject of harsh criticism for its celebration of the Spanish colonizers' atrocities committed against Native communities. The ceremony came to an end in 2018, and instead, a

Figures 2.2. and 2.3. Los Matachines: The Indigenous encounter the Spanish conquistadores, Alcalde, NM, 2009, photos by Amanda R. Martinez.

multidenominational prayer gathering marks the start of the annual Fiesta de Santa Fe (Romero, 2018). The reenactment ceremonies center on conquest and powerfully illustrate the struggle to assimilate indigenous groups away from their spiritual practices and beliefs and into Christianity, namely Catholicism, in northern New Mexico (Guzmán, 2017). Local journalist Guzmán (2017) describes the Matachines: "The dance bares forth all the contradictions and complexities of identity that have become essential to northern New Mexico. It is an embodiment of mestizaje, a racial and cultural mixing of Europeans and Natives." The Alcalde tradition holds unique ties to the Penitentes, an organized religious brotherhood present in New Mexico at least since 1610 (Gutiérrez, 2019), who play a pronounced role in both the Rosario and procession (Rodriguez, 2009). My Grampa Floyd was a Penitente, and my dad and Tío Danny participated for years as Matachine performers on horseback, donning ornate costumes full of symbolic colors, threads, war bonnets, and palmas handcrafted by locals.

The Indians dance synchronously in lines as they surround the young Indian princess, La Malinche (aka Malintzin), dressed in a white dress and veil. The Alcalde version of the Matachines "is devoid of the overtly Indian elements" (Rodriguez, 2009, p. 104) apparent in other regional renditions, which signals a prioritization of the Spanish conquistadores' perspective, as it is rooted in the Moro-Cristiano format of the Iberian reconquest dances. Guzmán (2017) reminds us that "in Mexico it is widely known that with Cortez, La Malinche bore the first mixed-race children of the Americas. It is through her that the dance telescopes from the continental to the local and

ure 2.4. Los Matachines: St. Anne's Catholic Church, Alcalde, NM, 2009, photo by Amanda R. Martinez.

back again" (para. 2). Among the longstanding points of "internal opposition seems to be religious-ethnic: Christianity is always symbolically juxtaposed to Indian religion, and Pueblo people seem drawn to this particular dance according to the intensity of their Catholicism" (Rodriguez, 2009, p. 95).

The indigenous dancers wear brightly colored capes with a vibrant stream of ribbons that flow down their headdresses, swaying with rhythmic movement. The important figures include El Monarca, who holds the most symbolic power and occupies front and center space, and then El Torito enters the scene, a bull figure characterized unmistakably as a troublemaker. The toro, or bull dancer, is only found in northern New Mexico and "symbolizes evil and imperial Spain" (Gonzales, 2019, p. 241). The authoritarian figure, El Abuelo, dances around the others and cracks his whip often as a reminder to all to behave well and respect their places.

Guzmán (2017) captures the essence of the scene: "The music, the people, the Spanglish conversations on the sidelines, and the viejitos perched in the seats at the very front—it's all very Norteño." As Rodriguez describes, "Los Comanches involves approximately ten men on horseback, divided into two opposing groups, who ride toward each other, face off, and engage in a mock battle narrated by their spoken -or shouted- lines" (Rodriguez, 2009, p. 105).

Figure 2.5. *El Abuelo y El Toro*, original drawing by Moises Gonzales.

My Tío Danny trots into the scene on his horse, confidently masquerading in his cape, knight-like war bonnet head gear, and leather cowboy boots, a sarape adorning the saddle on his horse, yelling out his lines in Spanish to amplify the escalating tension as the Natives and the Spanish clash over the land upon which they battle. Religious compartmentalization is readily apparent, and the fusion of Catholic and indigenous elements symbolically communicates volumes in these rituals (Rodriguez, 2009).

Sacred Lands and Spiritual Stirrings

One time, my dad and his brother-in-law, my Tío Gerald, decided to take a day trip up to the mountains near Abiquiu. They were enjoying the mountain environment for a brief time before their visit took an unexpected turn. They noticed in the distance a white, bonelike structure, so they carefully drew nearer only to discover that it was a fully intact human skull! My dad recalls, "The gophers native to that area dug up the skull from its shallow grave, or the grave probably became shallow over the course of time and made it easy for them to do." Not far off from the skull that lay bare in the dirt, they noticed more bones protruding from the dirt and rocks.

Avila and Parker (2000) assert, "We should not be afraid of ghosts. They have an important message for the living. If we do not want ghosts to visit us,

Figure 2.6. Despite some differences in performance and costume, the San Juan and Alcalde Matachines versions are very similar (Rodriguez, 2009). Los Matachines: Daniel Sr. Martinez, Spanish conquistador on horseback, San Juan, NM, 2009, photo by Amanda R. Martinez.

we should pay the dead their proper respect" (p. 68). The two, without many words exchanged, immediately knew what they must do: try and carefully bury the skull back into the ground where it lay and gently throw some dirt over the other bones they could see above ground. My dad speculated, "It was probably a sacred burial ground, like an old Indian cemetery from years ago, and we just so happened to stumble upon it and see those gophers nearby to realize what likely happened here." Not wanting to disrespect the sacred land or disturb the spirits that surely linger long past the dead have been laid to rest, my dad and Tío Gerald bolted back down the mountain, spooked by the possibility of being perceived as treading disrespectfully atop the sacred land and spiritual presence resonant up there.

Another time, my Tío Roland went into the mountains for a day of hunting and fishing with his brother, Russell. As locals very familiar with this area, they knew when to start making their way down the mountain to avoid navigating back in the pitch-black darkness of night. In his truck, driving down the dirt path, suddenly, Tío Roland felt swept up into an unfamiliar vortex of disorientation, a feeling of unease and confusion overcoming him. He stopped his truck, got out, and walked slowly around to the back because he heard a whirlwind of many voices at once competing for his attention, some whispering, others yelling. "Roland! Hey! Over here!" A flurry of indecipherable voices stirred in his ears, and a fog appeared to where he could not tell which direction that his truck was in, even though it was just moments ago that he stepped down from it because he thought he heard his brother calling out to him. He could hear some voices get very close, then very far away, and he tensed up, on guard, standing steadfast in case he felt an attack creeping on due to the unsettling out-of-body experience he was enduring. Tío Roland recalls, "It was just creepy because I could hear my brother yelling for me and after a little while, I thought, *what are you doing?* And I started to get mad, thinking he was playing a joke on me." But then the stirred-up spiritual forces came to a halt, and finally, he could see clearly.

The dizziness he experienced dissipated, and he could regain his footing, both literally and mentally, to move in a direction he felt confident was the right one to get back to his brother and truck. When he got to the truck, his brother was inside asleep! Tío Roland, at this point, was very confused because, just moments ago, his brother was yelling out for him, which is what prompted him to abruptly stop and get out to see where his brother's voice was coming from in the distance. He shook his brother awake. They began to argue because Tío Roland, still unsure of what exactly had just taken place, angrily accused his brother of playing a joke, making sure that he understood that this practical joke was way out of line. His brother was not faking being asleep inside the truck, and he swore that he was asleep and unsure of what had just happened, similarly perplexed based on Roland's account.

Tío Roland tells this story to our family regularly because it was such a bizarre out-of-body experience that confronted them abruptly and powerfully. The family in the region, knowing these lands, believes that he and his brother accidentally stumbled upon ancient burial grounds of the indigenous native to the land spanning centuries. The other-worldly dimensional experience he felt pummeled him into an uneasy realm of disorientation and spatial confusion when, just moments before, he was mere feet from his vehicle. In a way, this powerful multisensory experience and mental disorientation my tío felt serves as a cautionary tale for nonbelievers. Some eagerly attempt to convince him to take them there so they can witness the vortex for themselves, but Tío Roland refuses. A big burly softspoken countryman, my tío recounts the experience with such emotionally infused, intricate detail we believe him sincerely each time he retells it. He vows to stay away from that area to avoid disturbing the spiritual ancestral occupancy of these soils. We respect the unknown and tread carefully to not disturb the spiritual peace and unrest.

LatIndigenous Culture Clashes

Stories about witches who shapeshift into animal forms, such as coyotes, burros, or owls, proliferate in New Mexican history, a sign of the spiritual/ religious coexistence rooted in history and occupation of the lands (Anaya, 2006). My mom recalls when her dad and grandpa would detail scenes when a witch abruptly turned back to human form, unveiling their identity to onlookers. Once, some family members were traveling to Santa Fe in a covered wagon, and they spotted a figure lying motionless on the roadside, and owls were circling her body. The family slowed their wagon to a stop, formed a circle around her, made the sign of the cross, and she suddenly disappeared after they splashed holy water over the area.

Mom remembers, "There was this one time when I was a kid and my dad got sick and there was no medical reason that could explain it but the illness stubbornly lingered." So finally, frustrated, especially with the new owl who had recently taken up residence in the big tree outside their house, he told his wife he was off to the neighbor's house to borrow a rifle because he was going to shoot the big owl. When he marched back, determined with the rifle in tow, he did not get the chance to shoot because the owl disappeared and never returned!

When my mom was twelve years old, her strict Catholic parents allowed her to have a rare sleepover with a friend. The two girls stayed up late and were peering across the window towards the cemetery across the street when they noticed a giant red fireball bouncing from post to post on the fence. Chills ran down their spines, and they went to bed immediately because they knew what they had seen but would rather not continue to think it into their current reality. The common occurrence of witches traveling "as balls of fire across the countryside" (Anaya, 2006, p. 39), jumping from side to side of the arroyo or from post to post on a fence (Herrera-Sobek, 2006), and owls as symbols of evil prevail among the locals who believe in the existence of brujeria in its many manifestations.

Witches coexist alongside the Catholic religious dominance in New Mexican society; the fireballs are witches under the framing of Catholic definitions of deception and evil thought to roam the land listlessly and indefinitely with purpose to their conjures. Different forms of witchcraft were introduced to indigenous cultural life by the Spaniards, and these belief systems often clashed with the indigenous systems (Brown, 2013). The Spanish lumped sorcery (inflicting illness) and healing (curing illness) together under the term "witchcraft," but Pueblo communities drew important distinctions between the two. This overly generalized category helped criminalize even indigenous healing spirituality, which made it easier to punish under Spanish rule and law (Brown, 2013).

Sometimes the play-it-safe innocent children make for easy believers and reflexively look away out of sheer fear and a healthy respect for the spiritual potential powers of the unknown, like with my mom and her childhood friend at age twelve. However, teens and young adults may be more inclined to embrace that intoxicating invincibility and confidence that comes with the cusp of adulthood. The two youngest siblings of the ten in the Garcia family, just a couple of years apart in age, grew up very close as sisters. When my Tía Joy began experiencing the onset of a strange illness without a medical explanation but with severe symptoms that put her near death, my grandparents intervened and insisted on pursuing the healing powers of a curandera to undo the bad energy by hopefully finding its root cause. Curandera/os are deeply spiritual religious healers who treat problems both within and outside the bounds of Western medicine using holistic wisdom engaging the body, mind, and soul (Avila & Parker, 2000; Torres, 2005) and earth elements such as plants, fire, and water in their limpia rituals (Buenaflor, 2018). These entanglements signal an ethic of "embodied relationships with the earth's minerals, elements, animals, and landscapes" (Garcia Lopez, 2019, p. 5), and curanderas may typically use multiple treatment regimens at once for treating a given ailment (Herrera-Sobek, 2006).

"The curandera was running late," Tía Bea recalls, "and we were waiting around for a while when she finally arrived. She told us she had just come from another meeting that required an exorcism," she said, laughing incredulously. "Joy and I looked at each other like, what? Okay . . ." My tía admits that she was skeptical, and her bad attitude, including exaggerated eye rolling and loud sighs to express annoyance, communicated this clearly to the curandera. The curandera confronted Tía Bea nonchalantly: "I know you don't believe in me. You'll believe soon."

As writer and curandera Avila and Parker (2000) state, "By coming to a curandera, they are acknowledging that medical science can take them only so far, and that some diseases will only heal when the wounds of the heart and soul have been healed as well" (p. 42), and wellness assumes a cocreation process that carefully considers the entire being of the person, including the mind, body, emotions, soul, and spirit. At the permission of my grandparents, whose idea this trip was in the first place, the two young girls followed the curandera into a separate room. Tía Bea, serious in tone now and aghast just recalling the secrets the curandera knew, said, "She knew things that no one else knew, things that only Joy and I did together when no one else was around at all. So, I freaked out!" The likely explanation for Tía Joy's ill state was jealousy, or *envidia*, which concerns a two-way interaction of manifested envy as an emotional disease, and, sadly and surprisingly, this incident involved someone she thought was her good friend. Avila and Parker (2000) describe *envidia*: "The first way concerns the envious individual, the person who is sick in her soul. The second concerns the *envied* individual, the person who is receiving energy that is not hers. When someone is the object of envy, she gets sick in her *tonal* (spirit)" (p. 51). The curandera described the friend who had cast the negative energy of *envidia* in such detail that the two went from skeptics to true believers, now hinging on her every word.

The curandera instructed them with a course of action after she completed her rituals to spiritually cleanse my Tía Joy in an effort to rid her of the mindbodyspirit susto she had endured for a persistent time now. Tía Bea said, "After that, and I witnessed the curandera tell us all these details about things there is no way she would know, I followed her exact instructions. The next day, I insisted to go with my sister to move her out of the apartment she shared with this so-called friend, and I told Joy that she was to never speak to this girl again. End the friendship. That's it. There's no other way."

Young (Forbidden) Intertribal Love

My mom moved into her dorm room to attend a nearby university after she graduated from high school. One of her first new friends was her roommate in the dorm room, Sherrie, a member of the Isleta Pueblo. Sherrie began dating a young man from the Navajo Nation. The relationship was new and exciting, as young love tends to be, especially in those initial butterflies-in-the-stomach stages. Soon after the courtship began, Sherrie's health noticeably declined, and she experienced a wide range of symptoms that could not be attributed to one specific health explanation. She got very ill and required hospitalization on a few occasions, and yet the doctors could not find anything medically wrong to explain her escalating symptoms. They were stumped. Sherrie was surprised. My mom was worried. The family was notified.

A turning point arose because Sherrie's family could not stand idly by as she suffered so much and without medical treatment to effectively help her health improve. So, the family turned to the Native spiritual leaders in search of answers, hoping for adequate treatment regimens to heal Sherrie. After careful timeline considerations of Sherrie's sickness onset and the noted persistence of her symptoms, even after multiple medical intervention efforts, the family realized that her sickness had begun shortly after she started dating the young man from the Navajo Nation. When this timeline information came to light, her family suspected the intertribal romantic relationship as possibly part of the root cause of the medically inexplicable symptoms.

The Native spiritual leaders had to come together and cooperate on a healing pathway that would rid Sherrie of the mysterious sickness she endured, a common belief surrounding collaborative healing practice if the cure were to be effective for such interpersonal problems (Brown, 2013). The suspicion was that a young woman member of the Navajo Nation, perhaps a fellow college student at the university, had noticed the intertribal relationship and the fact that Sherrie was an outsider as a member of the Isleta Pueblo. Sherrie's status as an indigenous woman proved trivial because she was not a member of the Navajo Nation specifically. This upset the onlooker and fueled her jealousy, resulting in a spiritual transference of ill will cast upon the innocent young woman of the Isleta Pueblo. This energy was not Sherrie's, but it afflicted her as the target for her role in the intertribal dating partnership. Simply dating a man from another indigenous tribal affiliation thrust the bad energy upon her. Avila and Parker (2000) explain, "Envy is an energy that is contrary to love, and when someone feels that emotion, she can transmit it by her presence without saying anything . . . Envy is the twist in the heart that we feel in the presence of someone else's good fortune" (p. 52).

In New Mexico, where there exists a large, thriving, visible cultural presence of indigenous groups—each a distinctive cultural community, as opposed to the monolithic and "people of the past" stereotypes often attributed to them in mass media and popular culture—the priority to maintain the various cultural distinctions remains highly important. Therefore, the intertribal young love provides an example of the strong teaching about the importance of ingroup cultural sustenance, which sometimes includes explicit advocacy of only having romantic relationships with fellow members of your same Native group. This within-group pattern or preference is likely a residual outcome from centuries of attempted total genocide at the hands of colonizers. Some Chicano families in New Mexico and much of the US Southwest hold similar views about romantic partnerships that result in children and grow the familial lineage.

Mom was relieved to witness her roommate begin to show signs of improved health after the spiritual leaders worked together to try to heal her; it was a multistep and long-term process of calling the soul back after the spiritual trauma (Garcia Lopez, 2019). Upon returning to the dorm room after one of her visits to see the healers, Sherrie brought my mom a set of sticks that she insisted she always carry. Sherrie instructed her to put one of the blessed sticks at the bottom of the dorm doorway, especially when they were settling in for the night. Another stick was placed on the windowsill. Then, there were the blessed sticks that both must carry in their purses or bookbags when they left the dorm for various outings, like attending classes. Mom remembers, "I kept my sticks for many years after we parted ways and even when I had moved away after getting married, I still carried my sticks that she gave me, just to be safe. You just never know." The spiritual clashing among Native tribes rooted in intertribal young love that only Native healers and blessed sticks can deflect powerfully demonstrates that protections for Chicanx/Spanish/Hispanic bystanders assume importance for fear that these bystanders, by being in mere proximity to the afflicted, may potentially become collateral victims.

Respect the Land and Embrace a Spiritual Mestizaje

The stories I share in this testimonio illustrate the transformative power of the lands that bear the remnants of their rich, complicated historical legacies alongside evolving interpretations infused with modern-day religious and spiritual belief systems: a spiritual mestizaje (Delgadillo, 2011). The Spanish, Native, and LatIndigenous cultural and religious-spiritual encounters woven thematically throughout show that "spirituality, in the end, is how we relate to each other as human beings, independent of theology" (Téllez, 2014, p. 156). Medina (2014) encourages us to embrace a Nepantla spirituality as a fluid third space that changes and shifts with the integration of new thinking, wisdom from old religious practices, and the rediscovering of indigenous ancestral knowledge that leads us to a holistic "spirituality [that] is fundamentally about being in relationship; being aware of one's interdependence or connectedness to all that can be seen and all that is unseen" (p. 167). Garcia Lopez (2019) refers to this sentiment as a totality of "embodied spirituality that intersects with social contexts and natural environments. The emphasis on balance, integration, and relationality gestures toward a necessary decolonization of binary worldviews that split the self from the environment and the body from the soul, and which guide our everyday experiences in a capitalist society steeped in the residues of colonialism" (p. 9). Romero (2019) reminds us that "the Indio-Hispano may not have been raised in the Indian way, but his heart beats with the rhythms of his ancestral past" (p. 300). We must listen to these rhythms, these beating hearts inside us, and hear the ancestral wisdom we embody by virtue of not just our existence but also the embracement of our modern-day spiritual mestizaje. Let us exist in this in-between space as a whole in and of ourselves, as we already are. Defining moments, like the stories I have just shared in this chapter, lead us to recognize our LatIndigeneity: we are both/and, not either/or.

This both/and decolonial approach allows us to exist in all our complexity and grow into an identity of spiritual mestizaje that we can "call the new tribalism by propagating other worldviews, spiritual traditions, and cultures to your árbol de la vida" (Anzaldúa, 2015, p. 141). Anzaldúa (2015) further describes this both/and position that, at first, "resembles Frankenstein's monster -mismatched parts pieced together artificially- but soon the new rendition fuels your drive to seek alternative and emerging knowledges. It inspires you to engage both inner and outer resources to make changes on multiple fronts: inner/spiritual/personal, social/collective/material" (p. 141). Surrounding ourselves with the LatIndigenous potential that we already hold within us and within our reach based on mestizaje inherent to our ancestral homeplaces serves as a coping mechanism, a resistance to pressures of assimilation or acculturation, to choose or be one or the other, to give up one part of ourselves to conform to another's ways. As New Mexican natives, we have always occupied a space of both/and, from these LatIndigenous spiritually vibrant lands that hold the cautionary tales, life teachings, and the cures for mindbodyspirit peace and restoration. We just need to keep our minds and hearts open to listening to the land and hearing the whispers of our ancestral past to inform, protect, and heal our collective past, present, and future.

Note

I dedicate this testimonio to my Martinez family of Alcalde, my Garcia family of Medanales, and all our beloved kin who have transitioned to the ancestral realm. I am grateful for my big extended family for sharing in community with me over the years, especially as we recounted the experiences depicted in these stories. For confidentiality, pseudonyms are used in place of real names in some of the stories.

References

Alcalá, K. (2001). "Introduction." In R. Johnson (Ed.). *Fantasmas: Supernatural stories by Mexican American writers*. Bilingual Press.

Anaya, R. (2006). *Curse of the Chupacabra*. University of New Mexico Press.

Anzaldúa, G. (1999). *Borderlands/La frontera: The new mestiza*. Second Edition.

Anzaldúa, G. (2009). *The Gloria Anzaldúa reader*. Duke University Press.

Anzaldúa, G. (2015). *Light in the dark/Luz en lo oscuro: Rewriting identity, spirituality, reality.* Duke University Press.

Avila, E., & Parker, J. (2000). *Woman who glows in the dark: A curandera reveals traditional Aztec secrets of physical and spiritual health.* Penguin Group Inc.

Blackwell, M. (2018). "Many roads, one path: A testimonio of Gloria E. Anzaldúa." In D. Espinoza, M. E. Cotera, & M. Blackwell (Eds.). *Chicana Movidas: New Narratives of Activism and Feminism in the Movement Era.* University of Texas Press.

Brown, T. L. (2013). *Pueblo Indians and Spanish colonial authority in eighteenth-century New Mexico.* The University of Arizona Press.

Buenaflor, E. (2018). *Cleansing rites of curanderismo: Limpias espirituales of ancient Mesoamerican shamans.* Bear and Company Books.

Calafell, B. M. (2016). *Monstrosity, performance, and race in contemporary culture.* Peter Lang Incorporated, International Academic Publishers.

Campos, G. (2018, December 27). Los Matachines keep Alcalde tradition alive. Santa Fe New Mexican. https://www.santafenewmexican.com/news/local_news/los-matachines-keep -alcalde-tradition-alive/article_42981f64-e0c1-5f8f-8583-70136ab3659d.html.

Cuevas, J. (2019). "We are not a conquered people." In L. Medina, & M. R. Gonzales (Eds.). *Voices from the Ancestors: Xicanx and Latinx Spiritual Expressions and Healing Practices.* The University of Arizona Press.

Delgadillo, T. (2011). *Spiritual mestizaje: Religion, gender, race, and nation in contemporary Chicana narrative.* Duke University Press.

Dunbar-Ortiz, R. (2014). *An indigenous peoples' history of the United States* (Vol. 3). Beacon Press.

Elenes, C. A. (2014). "Spiritual roots of Chicana feminist borderlands pedagogies: A spiritual journey with Tonantzin/Guadalupe." In E. Facio & I. Lara (Eds.). *Fleshing the Spirit: Spirituality and Activism in Chicana, Latina, and Indigenous Women's Lives.* The University of Arizona Press.

Galván, R. (2014). Chicana/Latin American feminist epistemologies of the global South (within and outside the North): Decolonizing el conocimiento and creating global alliances. *Journal of Latino/Latin American Studies, 6*(2), 135–40. https://doi.org/10.18085/llas.6.2.1160715 w62582591.

Gandert, M. A. (2019). *Visualizing Genízaro cultural memory and ritual celebration.* In M. Gonzales & E. R. Lamadrid (Eds.). *Nación Genízara: Ethnogenesis, place, and identity in New Mexico.* University of New Mexico Press.

Garcia Lopez, C. (2019). *Calling the soul back: Embodied spirituality in Chicanx narrative.* The University of Arizona Press.

Gonzales, M. (2019). "Genízaro settlements of the Sierra Sandía: Resilience and identity in the land grants of San Miguel del Cañón de Carnué and San Antonio de las Huertas." In M. Gonzales & E. R. Lamadrid (Eds.). *Nación Genízara: Ethnogenesis, place, and identity in New Mexico.* University of New Mexico Press.

Gordon, A. F. (2008). *Ghostly matters: Haunting and the sociological imagination.* U of Minnesota Press.

Gutiérrez, R. A. (2019). "The Genízaro origins of the hermanos Penitentes." In M. Gonzales & E. R. Lamadrid (Eds.). *Nación Genízara: Ethnogenesis, place, and identity in New Mexico.* University of New Mexico Press.

Guzmán, A. I. (2017, December 29). Que viva los Matachines: A conversion drama becomes a local staple. Santa Fe Reporter. https://www.sfreporter.com/arts/2017/12/29/que-viva -los-matachines/.

Herrera-Sobek, M. (2006). *Chicano folklore: A handbook.* Greenwood Press.

Lamadrid, E. R., & Gonzales, M. (2019). "Introduction." In M. Gonzales & E. R. Lamadrid (Eds.). *Nación Genízara: Ethnogenesis, place, and identity in New Mexico*. University of New Mexico Press.

Levina, M., & Bui, D.M. T. (Eds.). (2013). *Monster culture in the 21st century: A reader*. Bloomsbury Publishing USA.

Medina, L. (2014). "Nepantla spirituality: My path to the source(s) of healing." In E. Facio & I. Lara (Eds.). *Fleshing the Spirit: Spirituality and Activism in Chicana, Latina, and Indigenous Women's Lives*. The University of Arizona Press.

Moraga, C. (2011). *A Xicana codex of changing consciousness: Writings, 2000–2010*. Duke University Press.

New Mexico Secretary of State (2021, February 27). *23 NM Federally Recognized Tribes in NM Counties*. https://www.sos.state.nm.us/voting-and-elections/native-american-election-information-program/23-nm-federally-recognized-tribes-in-nm-counties/.

Ortiz, P. (2018). *An African American and Latinx History of the United States* (Vol. 4). Beacon Press.

Reyes, K. B., & Curry Rodríguez, J. E. (2012). Testimonio: Origins, terms, and resources. *Equity & Excellence in Education, 45*(3), 525–38. https://doi.org/10.1080/10665684.2012.698571.

Rodriguez, S. (2009). *The Matachines dance: A ritual dance of the Indian Pueblos and Mexicano/Hispano communities*. Sunstone Press.

Romero, L. (2019). "Sangre de Indio que corre en mis venas: Nativo poetics and Nuevomexicano identity." In M. Gonzales & E. R. Lamadrid (Eds.). *Nación Genízara: Ethnogenesis, place, and identity in New Mexico*. University of New Mexico Press.

Romero, S. (2018, September 8). New Mexico grapples with its version of confederate tributes: A celebration of Spanish conquest. *The New York Times*. https://www.nytimes.com/2018/09/08/us/new-mexico-la-entrada.html

Téllez, M. (2014). "Pero tu no crees en dios": Negotiating spirituality, family, and community." In E. Facio & I. Lara (Eds.). *Fleshing the Spirit: Spirituality and Activism in Chicana, Latina, and Indigenous Women's Lives*. The University of Arizona Press.

Torres, E. C. (2005). *Curandero: A life in Mexican folk healing*. University of New Mexico Press.

Trujillo, M. L. (2019). "Genízaro salvation: The poetics of G. Benito Córdova's Genízaro Nation." In M. Gonzales & E. R. Lamadrid (Eds.). *Nación Genízara: Ethnogenesis, place, and identity in New Mexico*. University of New Mexico Press.

CHAPTER 3

Dueling Border-Ghosts
Exploring the Equator as a Space of Spirituality and Resistance

Diana Isabel Martínez

I left Guayaquil, Ecuador, when I was six in the 1980s, so my memories of the country are especially vague, fleeting, and incomplete. Learning to navigate being in the United States meant not knowing about my home country. For example, I learned about the US Constitution instead of the constitutions in Ecuador. I had difficulties pronouncing the name of the US president and forgot who it was from the country I left. I knew some words in Spanish only and was learning others in English. These hauntings stemmed from feeling like an empty vessel—too young to remember what made me Ecuadorian but too old to understand what it meant to be *estadounidense*. I now realize that I have, as cultural critic Diana Taylor (2003) explains of her identity, always been American in the hemispheric sense. I do not claim my American identity by living in the US; instead, I make this identification by being born in South America and residing in North America. And yet, the opposing rotational forces pulling the northern and southern hemispheres were a lot for a six-year-old to bear. It was exhausting. I consider the plethora of feelings that I was too young to recognize as trauma, such as living somewhere that did not always see me as human or deserving of the same treatment as my peers and did not have the language or recourse to make itself known. I now have pictures, the privilege afforded to me based on my education, and elapsed time to help me retrace those old unnamable experiences. Among the photographs I have of myself as a child, one that

Figure 3.1. My mother and me at the
Museo Mitad del Mundo (childhood).
Courtesy Diana Isabel Martínez.

anchors me in my country dates back to when I visited the equator. In the
picture, I am sitting with my mother and a childhood friend (Figure 3.1) in
front of a structure that materializes the competing forces that would haunt
me throughout my life and those ghosts from the northern and southern
parts of the hemisphere pulling me in different directions. Therefore, I write
this chapter to consider the meaning of the equator—which I define as an
interplay between people and land in the middle—to give language to that
little girl's experiences and validate the bodily knowledge produced in that
in-between and contested nepantla space.

As I made sense of my experiences in (re)learning Ecuador and the role
of the equator for the international community, I came across contested
information. The equatorial space has been challenged by writers, scientists,
tourists, governments, and Indigenous populations, to name a few. Where an
author stands geographically and ideologically determines the representations
of this space. This chapter calls into question popular conversations regarding
the equator, explores how this nepantla space provides knowledge for making
sense of my experiences, and highlights the generative possibilities for others
with similar geographical, figurative, or spiritual experiences. These dueling
border ghosts need not rip the person apart; they can be opposing forces *and*
serve as a line drawn across the globe with connective potential.

I argue that Gloria Evangelina Anzaldúa provides examples of dueling border ghosts through one definition of nepantla, physically situated on the equator and discursively located at the cross-section of effects of colonization and LanIndigenous knowledge. In *Nepantla-The Theory and Manifesto*, an essay situated at the Gloria Evangelina Anzaldúa archive at The University of Texas at Austin, she describes the Nahuatl term through the disparate forces of nature, grounded in the laws of gravity, opposed to one another by definition, concentrated more in some spaces, and observable most clearly from the equator. Anzaldúa (1995) describes this nepantla space as a bodily location:

> Living in in-between liminal spaces is like living on the equator. North of the equator water flows clockwise, south of the equator it flows counterclockwise—two radically different perspectives, two different conocimientos, two different world views. We on the equator are pulled in different directions. But el nepantla is a postmodernist topos: a space capable of accommodating mutually exclusive, discontinuous and inconsistent worlds. (Gloria Evangelina Anzaldúa Papers, 1995, Box 61.21)

This LatIndigenous dueling force that pulls and simultaneously accommodates multiple worlds is a heuristic space discussed by scholars, cultural critics, and writers. As colleagues and I have written elsewhere (Martínez, 2022; De Los Santos Upton, Bowen, & Hernández, 2019; Hernández, De Los Santos Upton, Bowen, & Martinez, 2019; Bowen, 2018; Bowen, 2017) and Anzaldúa herself has noted, nepantla comes as a continuation of the theory of borderlands. Anzaldúa explains that the term comes from

> people using metaphors such as 'Borderlands' in a more limited sense than [she] had meant it, so to expand on the psychic and emotional borderlands [she's] now using 'nepantla.' Nepantla emphasizes the connection to the spirit world is more pronounced and the connection to the world after death, to psychic spaces. It has a more spiritual, psychic, supernatural, and indigenous resonance. (Anzaldúa, 2000, p. 176)

In her introduction to *Interviews/ Entrevistas*, Keating (2000) explains that for Anzaldúa, "nepantla has multiple meanings that overlap and enrich each other. *Nepantla* represents liminal spaces, transitional periods in identity formation . . ." (p. 5). Gutierrez-Perez (2012) also notes the bodily pain associated with this space, how it pulls the subject in multiple directions, and how those pieces are placed back together in new and sometimes incompatible ways.

As an Ecuadorian, my identity connects to this spectral location on the globe, and I understand those contradicting forces—opposing forces that I have termed LatIndigenous dueling border-ghosts—from a physical and discursive level. I have pictures along the monument celebrating the country's place in the world, and the separate museum run by locals more accurately reads 00°00′00″ latitude. As a researcher of Anzaldúa's work and having grown up in Southern California, I have studied the physical and psychological borderlands from which she writes and felt the intensity of the border, the "open wound" from which she speaks. I have moved in and out of terms such as migrant, generation and a half, foreigner, citizen, second language learner, diversity award recipient, child of divorce, illegitimate, bastard child, and survivor, to name a few. I found language to fall short of describing experiences with the dueling forces in nature; the LatIndigenous ghosts that show up for me in nature most accurately describe my identity. This experience through dueling ghosts that pull me in different directions points to different physical borders but nonetheless converge at specific sites and on specific bodies to create a unifying force.

I argue that these LatIndigenous forces in nature manifest themselves materially on the body through impulses that appear to be elemental or out of control but are natural, meaningful, and generative. Anzaldúa's theory of nepantla encompasses a LatIndigenous space where dueling ghosts haunt the equatorial region. The official monument, situated at the Ciudad Mitad del Mundo (Middle of the World City) in San Antonio parish of the canton of Quito, and the Museo Solar Inti-Ñan, located a few hundred feet out at the zero latitude location run by locals, highlight these dueling energies. The essay considers those movements between each equatorial place as an extension of the physical forces of nature pulling the land in opposing directions, dueling border LatIndigenous ghosts, and interrogating belonging as haunted. Since the official monument celebrates acts of European colonialism and references to "accuracy" place blame on the Ecuadorian republic for misrepresenting the "true" equator, the continued historical exclusion of locals persists far beyond the bounds of the equatorial space. These exclusions manifest themselves in how I navigate my identity and belonging from afar.

Defining the Equator: Ghosts of Colonialism in "Scientific Precision" versus Ghosts of LatIndigeneity of Place

The criticism of the equator is characteristic of a more prominent global ghost of colonialism, one that blames the Ecuadorian government and republic for an error that lies deep in European roots. A quick lesson in the history of the disputed equatorial space reveals that the Ciudad Mitad del Mundo monument commemorates a French Geodesic Mission in 1736 to measure how long a degree of latitude was at the equator. This space forms part of a broader fascination with Ecuador for scientific discoveries and experiments. For example, Darwin's well-known visit to the Galápagos Islands and the inclusion of his findings in his theory of evolution. In other words, Ecuador has long served the needs of the global, western scientific community. It has been observed, prodded, and conquered by European scientists, explorers, and, as this essay will show, tourists.

Scholars have discussed the intersection between Indigeneity, colonialism, and haunting. In their definition of settler colonialism, Awvin, Tuck, and Morrill (2013) explain that this is "persistent social and political formation in which newcomers/colonizers/settlers come to a place, claim it as their own, and do whatever it takes to disappear the Indigenous peoples that are there" (p. 12). Additionally, as a prerequisite for colonizers to attain power, they needed to take the sovereignty of Indigenous populations: "In order for settlers to usurp the land and extract its value, Indigenous peoples must be destroyed, removed, and made into ghosts" (Awvin, Tuck, & Morrill, 2013, p. 12). While the quotation focuses on how colonialism turns the colonized into ghosts, this essay considers the LatIndigenous dueling ghosts created by colonialism by accounting for multiple hauntings. Namely, this essay considers how the process of colonization described above also produces LatIndigenous spirits. This section focuses on how the ghosts of colonialism haunt the present moment and then explores how Indigenous populations were also pushed to the margins, silenced, and made into LatIndigenous ghosts.

This chapter explores how colonialism is reenacted long after the initial attack on sovereign people on their land and how it sets up a system of western domination to understand how defining the equator results in dueling LatIndigenous ghosts. Ecuadorian history books explain the "conquistadores," or colonists who profoundly shaped the republic's history. And even the term emblematic of Latin, a romance language that spills over into descriptions of colonialism. I remember learning about the conquistadores as a child. Based on the term's connotation, which can also be a synonym for making someone fall in love with you or seducing them, I had difficulty understanding that the term used in these moments was a violent takeover of people and land. The ghost is evident in the linguistic connotation of the term, which would impact how the story of colonialism is told in history books and passed down from generation to generation. It was not a violent attack; the language subtly explains that the Indigenous populations were "seduced" into colonialism. The rhetorical blame shifts from the colonizer to the colonized, which comprises the linguistic lure of defining colonialism through "conquista." It gives the aggressors the means to blame the people they have oppressed. It also created a discursive contract that praises the colonizers for any successes they achieved and faults the colonized for all the shortcomings of the aggressors.

This issue over praise and culpability becomes relevant in the colonizing ghosts' quest to define the precise location of the equator, which blames the shortcomings of the scientific community and its effects on the people of Ecuador. The French Geodesic Mission participants determined the site of the 00°00'00" latitude on the equator by building a monument and a museum dedicated to the cultural history of Ecuador. This original monument would reside in Calacalí, Ecuador, as it would get replaced by a much larger Ciudad Mitad del Mundo monument in the 1980s. It would become one of many official and unofficial equatorial monuments worldwide in Indonesia, Kenya, Uganda, the Dominican Republic of Congo, Gabon, Sao Tome and Principe Islands, and Brazil. What seems unique about the Ciudad Mitad del Mundo monument is that it has been the object of blame for not residing on the exact 00°00'00" latitude when technological advances revealed that the line was inaccurate. Several questions surfaced. Who is to blame for the errors made during the scientific experiments on the land? How do the wider circumference of the country and its corresponding islands benefit from the immense contributions to scientific thought that they have made? Why does the republic, or any colonized people, receive the brunt of the blame for colonial errors? Interestingly, the zero-longitude line does not have the same scrutiny attached, even though Europeans drew a line on the metaphorical sand. Additionally, the designation of this space in England occurred due to the country's global dominance and colonizing force.

While Ecuador has served the scientific imaginary for the west, the republic as a whole has been blamed for scientific inaccuracies regarding the exact place of the equator by colonizing ghosts who set the wrong location. Upon searching for information regarding the Ciudad Mitad del Mundo monument, many magazine articles and blog posts followed an archetypal journey that goes something like this: Man goes to Ecuador. Man visits the Ciudad Mitad del Mundo monument. Man "discovers" it is in the wrong place and goes to the "right" place. Man takes out his phone. Man recognizes that the spot is also a tad wrong. Man came. Man conquered. This journey serves as the performance and reenactment of colonialism via tourism. It is impossible to search on the monument without running into articles published by institutions such as the Smithsonian or individual blogs dedicated to these attacks.

While it is not my prerogative to prove or disprove scientific observations conducted in Ecuador, and I am not an apologist for these enactments, I find it essential to point out some apparent details. Much like scientific theories evolve, a new understanding emerged with time, namely that the calculation for the location of the equator was incorrect when using Global Positioning System (GPS) measurements. The evolution in scientific thought and instruments reflected that this space is contested, fluctuating, and imprecise. In doing this research, it is clear that this space is much more disputed than was initially thought. Whether the equator exists perfectly is not as relevant as the need to pinpoint the exact location and point fingers when that need goes unmet. It is also not just the scientists who make these expeditions. Now, tourists engage in a similar search for discovery, tracking their experiences on blogs, reviews, and smartphones.

The description of the space above shows that it is contested and has seen colonialism's violent tactics and the glossy eyes of the tourist gaze. Both of these forces serve as colonizing ghosts. As such, it fits the description of a nepantla space. Sarah De Los Santos Upton (2019) explains that this

> . . . is a liminal, in-between stage characterized by chaos and disorientation, where individuals experience disassociations, breakdowns, and buildups of their identities. In this transformational space, individuals begin to question ideas, tenets, and even identities inherited through family, education, and culture as different perspectives collide . . . Anzaldúa explains that nepantla becomes a sort of home . . . (pp. 124–25)

In other words, this is not a space that one wills oneself into for creativity or self-expression, but the subject lunges into this space of chaos. Notably, I argue that trauma haunts this space and can produce change—this location includes haunted, hallowed, and LatIndigenous forces. Once here, the nepantlera creates out of necessity and generates knowledge from the body's experiences. This location is a transgressive space that defies categorization imposed by external agencies. Anzaldúa uses multiple descriptions to theorize the revolutionary potential inherent in this space, including a painful birthing process that brings life into the world through its revolutionary transformation. She also describes this location as an equatorial space with opposing forces pulling the subject and how this allows for an ability to live in uncertainty of the new identity formed in that process. Much like

Figure 3.2. My mother and me at the Museo Mitad del Mundo in 2013. Courtesy Diana Isabel Martínez.

finding the official equator, it is impossible to pin down a single definition of nepantla as that would defy its very nature.

After all of this, I wonder if I imagine things regarding the official monument. Popular sources state that the 1982 structure was replaced by the giant splendor of a memorial today. I was born in 1982, and I visited the site before I was six and moved to the United States. Did I miss the giant structure? Why do I remember a much smaller one? I remember my mom holding me up to place my hand on the top of the monument. While studies on public memory would say that how I remember things is just as important as the accuracy of what happened, I wonder where the narrative I have learned about the equator eclipsed my experience in this space. This memory haunts me because it doesn't seem to make sense. I don't have enough tools at my disposal to know what the monument looked like when I was there. I felt like I had my hand on the globe next to my mother, which felt so powerful when I was there. She had placed my hand on top of the world. As an adult, I stood in front of the enormous structure. Our reenactment of the image had a different appearance as we both tried to make sense of the space and discussed that it looked unlike what we remembered (Figure 3.2). She and I are different at this point too. We moved to the United States, and our relationship took many twists and turns. Our lives changed. But we eventually made it back together, and that relationship between my mother and me and our trip to this place made it the equator. I placed the photograph of my mother and me in a collage picture frame and pictures of my children.

With this understanding that the equator is a ghostly set of forces, neither the monument nor the energies it represents lack precision. I do not blame the republic for adopting a monument that would draw people from around the globe to celebrate the forces that make our planet what it is. Instead, I find it necessary to consider the larger nepantla space of the equator. This essay now discusses the Museo Solar Inti-Ñan and its contributions to equatorial history, heritage, and experiencing this beautiful space.

Expanding the Equator Geographically and Spiritually via LatIndigenous Hauntings

The reality that the equator rests on locally owned land and not in Ciudad Mitad del Mundo not only disproves the ghostly settler presence that claimed the land but also provides evidence that LatIndigenous ghosts continue to haunt today's colonizing forces on the space. As Arvin, Tuck, and Morrill (2013) state, "The experiences and intellectual contributions of Indigenous women are not on the margins; we have been an invisible presence in the center, hidden by the gendered logics of settler colonialism . . ." (p. 14). While Arvin, Tuck, and Morrill focus on Native feminist theory as it applies in the US context, the logic translates well in this case. The equator and the people on whose land it rests have always been there, bringing another set of hauntings, dueling ghosts that challenge the ghosts of colonialism.

These hauntings duel between banal suggestions by knowledgeable outsiders and intellectually through the planned educational experiences created by the LatIndigenous hosts. First, the power of a planned coincidence may spring up from a mere suggestion or feeling that emerges in the colonizer, settler, or tourist. When a tourist questions the colossal monument's location, rebels in the thought of having "conquered" this bucket list destination, or desires to learn more about their identity, the LatIndigenous ghosts enter and explain that there is another place that is also associated with the term "equator." The colonizer's mind—tickled with curiosity and hunger for discovery—sets forth to find the authentic equator. The LatIndigenous ghosts of memory, nostalgia, and trauma provide context and history where colonizing forces aim for erasure and death. I locate my point of entry into this space and offer my experience.

The dueling LatIndigenous ghosts of memory move between recovery (remembering) and erasure (unmembering) of the trauma of colonialism. In other words, the effects of the French expedition from the perspective of Indigenous people in that space are unavailable to the intellectual tradition from which I currently write. Nor can I, as someone still working on understanding the nature of my identity as mixed with colonizing and colonized blood, marked by working in the academy, understand the materiality of colonization and genocide faced by my ancestors. With this understanding of the incommensurability of experience and position, as explained by Byrd and Rothberg (2011), and the haunting silence reminiscent of violence that occurred in these spaces, the space becomes one of possibility. In other words, these hauntings open up space for LatIndigenous ghosts.

The LatIndigenous ghost took her time to let me into the story. Growing up, I never knew of this second "unofficial" equator, but I did have an opportunity to visit it during my last trip to Ecuador in 2013. Recognizing that there was another equator was both exhilarating and saddening. On the one hand, I was happy to have an opportunity to learn more about my home. On the other hand, learning about my home country as a tourist made me feel less Ecuadorian.

It reminded me of all the times that, upon hearing that I am from Ecuador, white people have jumped at the opportunity to brag about their travels there. Sometimes, they have been to places I am from, and other times, they want to talk about their visits to the Galápagos Islands, a place I know is part of my home country but to which I have never been. Even in academic circles, I often find myself reading journal articles or books written by people who have had the privilege to study there or carry out a Fulbright grant. (This is a great honor, by the way, just not one I have experienced.) These privileges were not available to me as an immigrant whose mother gave everything she had for the opportunity to start a new life in the United States. I think of people who talk to me about being mugged while there, of the food, asking me if I have tried cuy, a traditional entrée in Andean South American culture, with a particular disgust on their face. I tend to walk away from those conversations. I miss my country and don't need more people to make me feel ashamed about my background. Writing about Ecuador and learning more about the culture—my culture—is a privilege I didn't think I would ever have. I realize the privilege of visiting and beginning the process of learning about who I am and the land from which I came. I take a deep breath and get ready for the tour.

When the mistake regarding the official monument came to fruition, the discovery of the "true" 00°00′00″ latitude would place it in privately owned land approximately two hundred meters away. The owners created a museum that includes Indigenous relics and a shrunken head. People have called the unofficial museum a tourist trap, fake, and a sham due to the demonstrations that have people balance an egg on a nail or watch leaves go down a sink in different directions of the red line marking the equator. Some have commented that the exhibitions that discuss Indigenous cultures and cuy take away from the whole point of visiting the equator. Many have attempted to answer the question of whether or not visiting this site is worth the trouble. And yet, others claim that the tour guides at the official monument are trying to hide the fact that it is not truly the equator.

This distinction between privately owned land and that which the government owns provides a fascinating story of two parallel hauntings. The first official story celebrates the history of scientific discovery, and the LatIndigenous museum that explores the history of the people of Ecuador seems to be secondary. I honestly did not even know about it when I visited the site. Now, I understand that it includes views of the country using special glasses. The privately owned museum places LatIndigenous heritage at the forefront of the exhibition, something that some visitors criticize as a "detraction" from the purpose of educating the public about the equator. This educational and cultural portion of the tour is not there by accident; it is an exercise in resistance, a haunting, by the landowners. It is impossible to begin the presentation on the equator without first learning about aspects of Ecuadorian heritage. The owners understand entirely what the visitors are there to see. They have created a tour that eventually gets them to that attraction after a history lesson on Indigenous cultures. In this museum, the nepantla space felt even more powerful than the official monument. I got the sense that multiple audiences gathered there, and as an Ecuadorian, I would see a history that I might not have learned even if I had never migrated to the US. The stories felt historical and personal. The space did not seem "dressed up" for the world's stage. It felt sacred. I walked the line. I took pictures of the archaeological markers and the location, proudly stating that GPS captured the measurement. I unsuccessfully attempted to balance an egg on a nail. I marveled at the demonstrations with the water going down the drain in different directions and wondered whether it mattered if this effect was factual or not. I also considered what it would be like when the sun was directly above you, and you cast no shadow. Where would the ghost, my shadow, be at that moment? Is it in me? I appreciated the tour and the guide, and I wondered why it was such an inexpensive tour. I thought about how expensive it is to go to museums across the globe, especially in Europe. I think about the lines of people waiting to get into the gates of museums and the souvenirs available for purchase. I did experience opportunities to buy leather, Panama hats (rumored to come from Ecuador by locals), and the little miniature monument from the other official site. I might have missed it, but I did not see such options at this unofficial location, although my memory might be failing me. I appreciated learning what I learned and tried hard to remember the tour guide's face and imprint as much of what she said in my memory. We took pictures of hummingbirds. They were everywhere, and I was home.

Conclusions

One of the biggest lessons I learned by being a tourist in my home country, a land I love and live so far away from, is that the equator is the interplay between the culture and the land. Regardless of the exact location of the equator, the truth is that Ecuador is a country that occupies and is defined by its relationship to both the northern and southern hemispheres. It experiences the physical and psychic gravitational forces pulling the earth in opposing directions. It also shares the opposing forces of culture, heritage, history, Indigeneity, colonization, violence, erasure, and more as a colonized land. As a LatIndigenous space, it experiences the hauntings that stitch together portions of its past and affect how we remember our historical place. Through dueling ghosts of colonization and LatIndigenous identities, memory via re/dismembering, trauma, and nostalgia, the contested nature of the space, impulses, and regroundings may occur.

Of course, these (im)possibilities become possible in nepantla. This chapter elaborated on Anzaldúa's conception of nepantla as a dual set of opposing forces seen at the equator. Significantly, this space goes beyond a mere liminal identity and considers a contested terrain with several, often contradictory, dueling forces. The violence inherent in colonization is ubiquitous; it is seen even in the meaning of "conquistar." Continuing to romanticize these painful experiences only furthers a colonizing agenda. Instead, scholars should reflect on where we stand and acknowledge the incommensurability of Indigenous experiences represented by the gaps in what has been brought up in the essay and the possibilities that open up when considering the various hauntings discussed herein.

When I think back to the little girl in the picture with her mother at the site of the equator, I speak to that inner child. Migrating to the US would change my life forever, but I would always hold on to those moments that brought me back home. I would support my mother as she navigated starting over in the US, a foreign country, being a single mother. I wish I could let that little girl know that, together, we would learn the language to try to explain our experiences and be open to creating new terms to describe things that felt impossible to say with words. Those dueling ghosts would be a part of who we are, and we didn't need to be afraid of them—if anything, we need to continue to find them and bring them back in our moments of need.

References

Anzaldúa G. (2000). *Gloria E. Anzaldúa: Interviews/entrevistas* (A. L. Keating, Ed.). New York, NY: Routledge.

Arvin, M., Tuck, E., & Morrill, A. (2013). Decolonizing feminism: Challenging connections between settler colonialism and heteropatriarchy. *Feminist Formations* 25(1), 8–34.

Bowen, D. I. (2018). Gloria Anzaldúa: From borderland to *nepantla*. In *Oxford Research Encyclopedia of Communication*, edited by Dana Cloud. Oxford University Press, 2018. doi: 10.1093/acrefore/9780190228613.013.606.

Bowen, D. I. (2017). Voices from the archive: Family names, official documents, and unofficial ideologies in the Gloria Anzaldúa papers. *The Journal of Multimodal Rhetorics* 1(1), 26–41.

Byrd, J. A., & Rothberg, M. (2011). Between subalternity and indigeneity: Critical categories for postcolonial studies. *Interventions* 13(1), 1–12.

De Los Santos Upton, S. (2019). Communicating *nepantla*: An Anzaldúan theory of identity. In *This bridge we call communication: Anzaldúan approaches to theory, method, and praxis*, edited by Leandra Hinojosa Hernández and Robert Gutierrez-Perez, 123–42. Lanham, MD: Lexington Books.

De Los Santos Upton, S., Bowen, D. I., & Hernández, L. H. (2019). Nepantla activism in *Braiding Borders + Trenzando Fronteras*. In *Latina/o/x communication studies: Theories, methods, and practice*, edited by L. H. Hernández, D. I. Bowen, S. De Los Santos Upton, & A. R. Martinez, 229–50. Lanham, MD: Lexington Books.

Gloria Evangelina Anzaldúa Papers, Benson Latin American Collection, University of Texas Libraries, the University of Texas at Austin.

Gloria Evangelina Anzaldúa Papers, Nettie Lee Benson Latin American Collection, University of Texas Libraries, The University of Texas at Austin, Box 61.21 Nepantla-The Theory and Manifesto, 1995.

Gutierrez-Perez, R. M. (2012). Warren-ting a "dinner party": *Nepantla* as a space in/between, *Liminalities: A Journal of Performance Studies* 8(5), 195–206.

Hernández, L. H., De Los Santos Upton, S., Bowen, D. I., & Martinez, A. R. (2019). Introduction: Latina/o/x communication studies: Current considerations and future directions. In *Latina/o/x communication studies: Theory, method, and practice*, edited by L. H. Hernández, D. I. Bowen, S. De Los Santos Upton, & A. R. Martinez, 1–44. Lanham, MD: Lexington Books.

Keating, A. L. (2000). Risking the personal: An introduction. *Interviews/entrevistas: Gloria E. Anzaldúa* (pp. 1–15). New York, NY: Routledge.

Martínez, D. I. (2022). *Rhetorics of nepantla, memory, and the Gloria Evangelina Anzaldúa archives: Archival impulses*. Lanham, MD: Lexington Books.

Taylor, D. (2003). *The archive and the repertoire: Performing cultural memory in the Americas.* Durham, NC: Duke University Press.

CHAPTER 4

Closing the Circle

Eric Murillo

A few years ago, during graduate school at the University of Texas El Paso, I was blessed with the opportunity to work with the Piro/Manso/Tiwa Indian Tribe of the Pueblo of San Juan de Guadalupe (PMT) and assisted them with genealogical and historical research, mainly focusing on the archives from the Paso del Norte Missions in the El Paso-Cd. Juarez metroplex. During that time, I was also researching my own family's links to the missions and tried to understand why those doors had suddenly opened and why my prayers had been answered.

I grew up in Dell City, Texas, in the 1980s and '90s and had never really known where I came from. Most people assumed we were Mexican Americans, and I never really questioned or even understood what that meant. Among the things that made us different than most of the Mexican and Mexican American families was that we never went to Mexico to visit family. We would travel to New Mexico, primarily to Chamberino and Las Cruces. My family also never celebrated Mexican traditions like Día de los Muertos, Mexican Independence, or other staple traditions.

I also remember my grandmother Celia Dominguez Murillo referring to people from our town as "los Mexicanos" and often feeling confused when she would other them. If they were "los Mexicanos," then "who were we?," I wondered. In some strange way, I thought my grandmother was being hateful towards other Mexicans but did not understand that it was her way of preserving her and our identity that wasn't "Mexican."

During my research, I was able to establish my ancestral links to several of the Paso del Norte Mission Indigenous communities, including Senecu,

Socorro, Guadalupe, and Ysleta. I was also able to meet relatives that are tribal members with the PMT, and they have accepted me and continue to teach me about the tribe's complicated history and its many challenges today, including the struggle for federal recognition that has been hampered by historical errors in classification. I am forever grateful for the Moreno family, particularly my cousin and mentor Gilbert Moreno, First War Captain of the PMT and who was always willing to teach despite enduring so much pain during the time that I knew him. He has since passed, and although an ancestor to us, his presence is still felt among us who remain to walk on this earth.

Piro Manso Tiwa

The Piro-Manso-Tiwa Indian Tribe of San Juan de Guadalupe (PMT) is a Native American tribe currently seeking federal recognition and official status as a Native American tribe through the Bureau of Indian Affairs (BIA). Their members have strong genealogical and historical ties to the Piro, Manso, and Tiwa Indigenous communities that lived in the Paso del Norte region (today's El Paso-Juárez borderplex) during the Spanish colonial period (1600s–1820), and most of their ancestors are clearly identified as "Indio" or Indian. Others are not, and their relatives are classified as "vecinos" or citizens of their respective pueblos. While some Spanish colonial research equates vecino with Spaniard, Diana Velasco Murillo (2016), whose research examines Zacatecas, México from 1546–1810, challenges that logic. She states:

> This inclusiveness diverges from the scholarship that tends to equate "vecino" status exclusively with Spaniards or that defines it as the antithesis of "indigenous." In many areas of New Spain vecindad was neither formal nor official and hence not legally restricted to Spaniards. (p. 145)

Therefore, the vecino status did not necessarily mean that a person was of Spanish ancestry in Spanish colonial Zacatecas, México. This supports the findings of Richard Gutiérrez (1991), who studied Spanish colonial New Mexico from 1500–1846, or roughly the same period covered in Murillo's study. He found that racial classification in New Mexico during that period was subjective and that "there was no direct correspondence, except perhaps at the extreme ends of the classification scale, between race and actual physical color" (p. 198). That race is a social construct is plainly evident in the various ways in which people were classified according to perceived race or social status. The implications are that some of the Paso del Norte vecinos may have been of Native American and mixed-Native American ancestry, particularly the ancestors of PMT tribal members. While Spanish officials assigned racial classifications to individuals and families, we do not know how those individuals saw themselves. Nor do we know, from records, if they participated in native ceremonies or had other ties to the Piro, Manso, and Tiwa communities of Paso del Norte. While some of their ancestors may have served as Presidial soldiers, members of vecino and Spanish militias, or in other capacities for the Spanish, they may have maintained their ancestral ties to their native communities or had other immediate family members who did.

Double Consciousness, Triple Consciousness

This essay will explore the question of Indigenous identity and tribal recognition through the lens of W. E. B. Du Bois's Double Consciousness theory, where Native Americans, particularly those near the US-Mexico borderlands, must navigate being Native, "Mexican/Hispanic," and citizens of the United States. According to Dubois' (1903) theory of Double Consciousness, African Americans experience an internal conflict in navigating a divided identity. Like the experiences of Black people in the US, Native Americans on the US-Mexico borderlands must navigate through several imposed identities; they can be identified as Native American, Hispanic, American, or Mexican (formerly Spanish). Unlike Native Americans in places outside of the US-Mexico borderlands, who are usually identified as Native American, European-American, or a mixture of both; Native Americans in the US-Mexico borderlands are often identified as "Mexican," which can be understood by the veil in Dr. Du Bois's writings where Native Americans struggle to be seen or acknowledged as Native Americans. For many Native American communities in the US-Mexico borderlands, maintaining an Indigenous identity is even more challenging because often their tribes, pueblos, nations, or bands were supposed to have disappeared and become "Mexicanized" as many researchers, historians, and others who have studied the region have suggested. Therefore, unless they are wearing identifiable Native American regalia for ceremonies or other occasions or fit the stereotypical expectations of outsiders, they often appear to be part of the larger Mexican and Mexican American population to outsiders. As former Tigua Governor Joe Sierra once stated, "We have three cultures that we are trying to fit into: our own, the Spanish, and the American" (as qtd. in Comar, 2010, p. 6).

The Spanish culture that Tigua Governor Sierra identifies is now mostly seen as Mexican culture, which features the Catholic Church, the Spanish language, and other cultural markers that are remnants from Spanish colonization in the borderlands. There are holidays, foods, music, and other cultural phenomena that include the participation of the region's Indigenous people, causing many non-informed people to assume that they are part of the greater "Hispanic" or Mexican-origin population.

Like the Tiguas, the PMT have navigated the various imposed cultures and ethnic labels while maintaining a strong Indigenous identity that survived despite incredible socioeconomic pressures from the Spanish, Mexican, and US governments to assimilate into the dominant cultures. Each of these powers sought to eradicate or limit their existence as tribal people. However, the PMT's shared historical struggles, ceremonies, and strong kinship network, along with their strong sense of identity, ensured that they would maintain a tribal identity.

This triple consciousness did not necessarily mean that native people lost their core identity as native people, rather that they would and did exhibit agency when forced to navigate the multiple imposed identities along with their own self-identity. In some situations, they may have felt common bonds with their Mexican and Chicano neighbors and identified *with* them against discrimination and other injustices committed against them, such as occurred during the El Paso Salt Wars (1877–78), and at other times they were targets of ridicule and discrimination from those same communities because they were Indigenous. As citizens of the United States, they assimilated into the greater US society to various degrees, including intermarriage with non-Indians, living and working outside of their core communities, adopting US customs, and serving in the US Armed Forces as some examples. However, they have not lost their core identity as Indigenous people, and their continued participation in ceremonies and traditions serve as a way for them to reaffirm their commitment to the ways of their ancestors and to each other.

Additionally, they have overcome erasure by records where time, warfare, natural disasters, and human misdeeds have led to the destruction of valuable documents that recorded their existence as native people. The US occupation of Paso del Norte in 1846–1847, for instance, resulted in the "destruction of a portion of the municipal archives by soldiers quartered in government buildings, who used the manuscripts to light their candles" (Timmons, 1990, p. 96). In this example, it is difficult to estimate the extent of the destruction of the archives, but it helps account for the limited amounts of records from Paso del Norte that are available today. The PMT members of today have the unenviable task of providing official records to the BIA that clearly document their ancestor's tribal affiliations, and they are faced with piecing together surviving documents that are extremely limited and often in poor condition.

Aside from the lack of official records, some of the PMT's ancestors, including some of my own, "lived outside the state" and maintained many of their cultural practices and ties to their native communities, even if not always documented like the Native peoples in Ned Blackhawk's *Violence over the Land* (2006, p.13). They also had to travel for "food, work, worship, and recreation" (Blackhawk, 2006, p. 13), sometimes leaving the core native communities for extended periods of time, making them "invisible" in official records and adding to the difficulties in tracking them today.

These periphery native communities maintained ties to the core native communities, and members of the periphery native communities could become part of the core native communities and vice versa. These groups were fluid and featured families whose members could be part of both groups. The periphery groups featured relatives of the core group who primarily left the core group due to work, but assimilation, internal disputes, or other factors were also causes. Blackhawk's own ancestors, who he describes as "non reservation Shoshone families," resemble some of the PMT's ancestors, who also do not appear in official records as members of the core tribal communities but lived in the periphery and outside of "state surveillance" (2006, p. 13).

Today's PMT tribal community also features core and periphery tribal members and the same fluidity that their ancestor's tribal communities featured. Core tribal members can be said to live in and around the areas where other core members live or travel and participate in most tribal meetings and ceremonies. They often are knowledge holders within their families, responsible for passing down stories and traditions, educating tribal members, and helping maintain tribal traditions. Core members include the Tribal Council members, Tribal leaders and elders who are responsible for organizing ceremonies and meetings to include gathering materials and preparing ceremonial grounds. In addition, core tribal members are responsible for maintaining tribal chants and prayers, dances, and ceremonial regalia, in addition to ensuring that traditional protocols are respected and followed.

In general, periphery tribal members may be siblings or relatives of core tribal members who live outside of the core communities and who are not actively participating in tribal ceremonies and functions. Periphery members may still have some connections to the core tribal community, either through limited participation or through kinship networks, and may become active core members. However, because of geographical distance or limited knowledge or participation, periphery tribal members may not always be seen as tribal members or see themselves as such. Their knowledge of tribal traditions and practices is likely to be limited, especially when compared to that or core tribal members.

1787 and 1814 Paso del Norte Census Records

The University of Texas El Paso is home to various archives from the Spanish Colonial Period, and while most of the records are difficult to read, mostly due to neglect, or quality of record, the 1787 census that was particularly well preserved and easy to read. It was also rich in demographic information and featured the Spanish Casta system of classification. After the Mexican Independence war, the Spanish Casta system was phased out, and for many descendants of the Paso del Norte Indigenous people finding roots was even harder.

I decided to compare the 1787 census records, which featured the Heads of Household, and an 1814 census record, that featured a total census count. While it would have been ideal to compare the 1787 census, which featured heads of household, with 1814's heads of household, I was unable to find it among existing records. However, it is still possible to track the demographic changes, and it is clear that there was, in fact, a dramatic shift during this period.

In the 1787 Heads of household census, Indigenous people could fall into various categories: Indios del Pueblo, Indios "vecinos, and Genizaros. The Indios del Pueblo had specific tribal affiliations for each pueblo—Piro for Senecu and Socorro, Tiguas at Ysleta, Sumas at San Lorenzo, and Mansos and Piros at Guadalupe. A separate Indio category could be found among the vecinos for each pueblo, which most likely meant that they were Natives with biological links to the Indios del Pueblo for their respective communities who held vecino status. The Genizaros were primarily Apache and Comanche in the Paso del Norte region, although other non-pueblo Indians were among them. Mestizos, Lobos, and Coyotes all had Indian ancestry to varying degrees but included African and Spanish as well. Africans were also among the 1787 population and were listed as Negros. The Españoles, as previously mentioned, were themselves a mixture of European and other ethnicities, and they were a minority, composing only 35 percent of the total heads of household that year. This supports the research findings of Murillo (2016), who argues that during the Spanish colonial period, "Native peoples, Africans, and castas regularly outnumbered their colonizers" (p. 7), which is clearly the case in the Paso del Norte community in 1787.

1787 Paso del Norte Heads of Household and 1814 Paso del Norte Census

	Senecu	Socorro	Ysleta	San Lorenzo	Guadalupe	Total
Indios	75	29	74	33	59	270
Mestizos	3	66	11	28	122	230
Coyotes	20	12	0	6	28	66
Lobos	0	2	0	11	5	18
Genizaros	0	0	0	1	0	1
Negros	0	1	0	0	0	1
Españoles	12	11	19	5	274	321

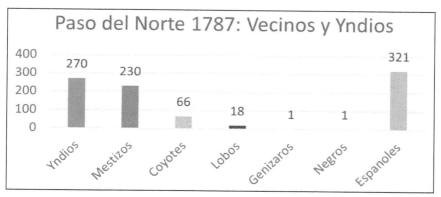

Figure 4.1. Paso Del Norte Heads of Household 1787.

By 1814, all of the previous ethnic/racial categories were combined into just two: vecino and Indio. There was also a dramatic shift in the demographics of all the Paso del Norte communities, which saw a dramatic drop in the Indio population while a corresponding increase occurred among the vecino population for each of the communities. While constant warfare and occasional diseases would have affected the populations of Paso del Norte, it is unlikely that Indigenous families in the region would have simply disappeared or died off in large numbers, as the census records suggest. It is most likely that many of the Paso del Norte Indians were simply absorbed into the vecino population for various reasons, which I will explore further in the conclusion.

The dramatic shift in the population from Indios to vecinos from the periods studied can be attributed, in part, to the increased assimilation and "Hispanicization" of the Mission Indians, Genizaros, and other non-Spaniards who "acquired new ethnic classifications" (Blackhawk, 2006, p. 80) as did the Genizaros in Blackhawk's study. He documents a major growth in the

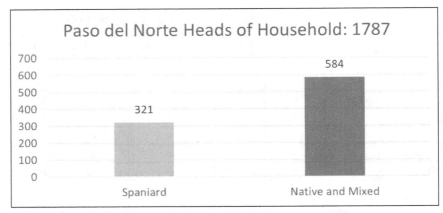

Figure 4.2. (Spanish: 321 = 35 percent, Native and mixed: 584 = 65 percent of population heads of household)

Figure 4.3. Paso del Norte 1812 Census (Vecinos 87 percent, Indios del Pueblo 13 percent).

proportion of vecinos of the New Mexican village of Abiquiu, while the proportion of genizaros in that village decreases from 1760 to 1821.

The El Paso del Norte Indigenous people, in a similar fashion, also became absorbed into the Vecino population, at least in official records. While the Pueblos of Senecu and Ysleta still maintained relatively large Indigenous populations, the rest of the communities in the Paso del Norte region saw a major decline in official "Indios del Pueblo" and corresponding growths in their vecino populations.

The best explanation for this shift, as this research indicates, is due to a change in classification and not racial/ethnic composition of the Paso del Norte community. What led to this shift is not easily answered in this research because of the gaps in census records, the other issues related to record keeping, and the fluidity of classification, but what is evident is that Indigenous people were absorbed into the greater vecino population and erased as Indigenous people at least on the records.

Conclusion

Indigenous people from the Paso del Norte region, like their counterparts in other regions in North America, have had to navigate several layers of colonization, each with its own methods of classification. Whether they were erroneously classified as vecinos, Mexicans, or other, they undoubtedly found ways to maintain their own identity, similar to African Americans in the double consciousness theory of W. E. B. Du Bois. They navigated several identities while maintaining a Native identity, even when their "Indianness" was challenged by others.

The PMT tribal members had to negotiate a Spanish (later Mexican), Native American, and American identity, unlike the African Americans in Du Bois's theory, who had two identities to navigate. This unique situation where Native Americans in the US-Mexico borderlands had a third identity to navigate is why I thought that triple consciousness is perhaps a more accurate way to view the Indigenous people from the US-Mexico borderlands. This third space may seem redundant, but it is necessary to carve out a place for Indigenous people in the US-Mexico borderlands where history often treats us as ghosts.

Like in Du Bois's theory, there exists a unique or internal perspective of identity for Native Americans on the border along with the outside perspective, which could label them as Indians or Hispanic Mexicans. Because of these two imposed identities, American and Mexican, and their own identities as Indian people, the PMT tribal members, like African Americans, struggle with a fragmented identity.

As Indigenous people, the PMT tribal members have mostly lived among other tribal members in reconstituted Indian communities, which featured mostly Indigenous and Mestizo people. In that environment, they also lived as tribal people who maintained many of the customs and traditions of their ancestors, including using and understanding the local flora and fauna, drumming and singing traditional chants, participating in tribal ceremonies and communal activities such as the traditional rabbit hunt, and having an understanding and awareness of the tribal leaders and other tribal members.

However, PMT tribal members also lived around Spanish and later Mexican American majority communities, and because of the Indigenous

heritage of some Mexican Americans, they often shared some similar phe-
notypes, which can be confusing for outsiders who are unfamiliar with those
distinctions. When PMT members navigate the Mexican American world,
they are not likely to face as many internal conflicts because of their familiar-
ity with the culture. Many borderlands Native Americans speak Spanish, listen to Mexican music, and participate in some Mexican American traditions
and holidays, for instance.

In other settings, such as the workplace, school, or in some cases, the
neighborhood could be a white majority, which creates a separate awareness
for Indigenous people who may have to act and think in a totally different
way than they do in their home community. PMT members, in these settings,
may be identified as Native or Mexican American by White Americans and,
thereby, must work to fit into the white world while still maintaining their
own internal identity. This means that PMT members might have to speak
and act differently in this setting, sometimes fitting into stereotypical roles
and at other times fighting against those roles. In this environment, PMT
members are likely to behave and act differently than they would in their own
home communities.

Diana Velasco Murillo's "urban Indian" concept helps us understand how
native people were able to maintain that Indian identity, despite living in close
proximity to the colonizer. She argues that the "adaptation of Spanish-style
civic identities did not lead to the erosion of indigenous societies, but actually facilitated their persistence" (p. 5). Native peoples in Zacatecas, as well
as in the Paso del Norte region, established their own communities, maintained traditional ways of existing, and adopted Spanish customs, all while
creating a distinct Indian identity within those communities. In the Paso del
Norte community, each Native pueblo had its own Indigenous leaders who
were recognized as such by the Spaniards. They also had their own distinct
ceremonial feast days, celebrating particular saints or other Catholic symbols:
Ysleta del Sur and Senecu del Sur celebrated San Antonio, or Saint Anthony,
on their feast day on June 13th, and the Guadalupe Mission Indians celebrated the Virgin of Guadalupe in December. The ceremonies and events that
occurred during these celebrations featured Indian dances, traditional races,
and other ancient practices in conjunction with adopted Catholic traditional
practices. This negotiation between two seemingly conflicting spiritual traditions allowed for the Paso del Norte Indigenous communities to continue to
practice their ancient traditions, even if modified, allowing for the survival of
those traditions that might have otherwise disappeared.

The Enlightenment inspired eighteenth-century Bourbon Reforms, which sought to "centralize authority and increase economic activity" (Murillo, 2017, p. 161) would have a tremendous impact on Indigenous communities across the Spanish empire, interrupting all aspects of their lives. The Bourbon Reforms weakened Indigenous leadership, religious organizations, land rights, and even identity. In Zacatecas, for example, the Indigenous population at the end of the eighteenth century was no longer exempt from tribute, or free labor, and other rights and privileges were no longer recognized. In addition, long-standing Indigenous communities and communal lands were increasingly under threat from the expanding Spanish pueblos.

While these changes occurred in Zacatecas, it is very likely that similar changes resulting from the Bourbon Reforms affected the Paso del Norte Indigenous communities. This would help explain why such a dramatic demographic shift occurred from 1787 to 1814 in the Paso del Norte region. This shift from Indio to vecino was, in part, imposed upon the Indigenous people of the region and, in part, an example of the agency of the Paso del Norte Natives. Vecinos were allowed to purchase and own private land, something not generally afforded to the Indios del Pueblo. Evidence of this tactic can be found in Houser's 2002 analysis of Ysleta del Sur land transactions. In his analysis, Houser identifies several Ysleta del Sur Tiguas who are listed as both Indian and vecino among the land records. In the index, for example, he documents a Pedro Gonzales (pg. 2), who is listed as an Indian and vecino who sold land to Jacinto Telles, Pablo Marquez, who is classified as a Ysleta Indian and a vecino (pg. 6), and Masedonio Trujillo who is listed as Yndigena or Indian and as a vecino of Ysleta as some examples.

The arrival of the Anglo population to the Paso del Norte region in the mid-nineteenth century further added to the challenges of maintaining an Indian identity, at least to outsiders who found it difficult to distinguish between Indians and Mexicans. "Tiguas and Mexicans often dressed alike, and their houses were similar," according to Houser (2002, p. 4), and it was easier to classify them as a homogenous people rather than to learn about the nuances that distinguished them as separate people.

PMT Tribal members were mostly disappeared from official records to varying degrees by Spanish colonial authorities, Mexican and US officials, and by numerous academics in the past. It is not uncommon to read narratives about the El Paso-Juarez borderlands where the Indigenous people seemingly disappear by the late 1800s and are no longer visible or active and part of the vanishing Indian narrative where we are swallowed up by Western progress.

Despite these challenges, PMT tribal members remain committed to each other and their way of life that connects them to tens of thousands of years of history in the lands known as the US-Mexico borderlands. Their resilience is a testament to the strength of their leaders and the tribal members who continue to fight for recognition.

References

Blackhawk, N. (2006). *Violence over the Land: Indians and Empires in the Early American West*. Cambridge, Massachusetts: Harvard University Press.

Comar, S. C. (2010). *Indigenous Resistance in the El Paso Borderlands: The Tigua Indian Land Dispossession and The Salt War of 1877*. University of Texas El Paso.

Du Bois, W. E. B. (1970). *W. E. B. Du Bois: A Reader*. (M. Weinberg, Ed.) New York, Evanston, and London: Harper and Row.

Du Bois, W. E. B. (1903). *The Souls of Black Folk*. Chicago: A. C. McClurg & Co.

Gutierrez, R. A. (1991). *When Jesus Came, the Corn Mothers Went Away: Marriage, Sexuality, and Power in New Mexico, 1500–1846*. Stanford, California: Stanford University Press.

Houser, N. (2002). *From the Place of Beginning: An Analysis of Land Transactions and Their Effect on Ysleta del Sur Pueblo*. El Paso: University of Texas El Paso Press.

Márquez, P., Ramos Navarro Wold, L. (1998). *Compilation of Colonial Spanish Terms and Document Related Phrases*. Second Edition. SHHAR Press, 1998, (Society of Hispanic Historical and Ancestral Research). P. O. Box 490 Midway City, CA.

Murillo, D. V. (2016). *Urban Indians in a Silver City: Zacatecas, Mexico, 1546–1810*. Stanford California: Stanford University Press.

Nuestra Señora de Guadalupe del Paso del Rio del Norte. (1707–1890). Local Census. Microfilm Collection. Catholic Archives of Texas.

Staff, Special Collections (1999). Guide to MF489 Archives of the Cathedral of Cuidad Juarez, 1671–1945). Guides to Microfilm Collections. 3. https://digitalcommons.utep.edu/guides/3.

Timmons, W. H., (1990). *El Paso: A Borderlands History*. University of Texas at El Paso.

Ysleta del Sur Pueblo (2018). Ysleta del Sur Pueblo: About Us. http://www.ysletadelsurpueblo.org/about-us.

CHAPTER 5

Ciguanabas, Refugees, and Other Hauntings

Three Salvadoran Women's Epistemic Hauntings as Resistance Against Heteropatriarchy

Brenda Selena Lara

Las Ciguanabas

I first learned about La Ciguanaba as a first-year graduate student in Karina Alma's 2018 "Central Americans Making Memory" course. As Alma recalls, La Ciguanaba was an Indigenous woman enslaved by a plantation owner who attempted to sexually assault her. She escaped his clutches but not for long; scorned by her refusal, the plantation owner sent his goons to murder her by the local riverbank. His murder cursed her to exist alongside the riverbank for the rest of her afterlife. For misogynist men like the plantation owner who dare confront her, they are initially met with her beauty, and then quickly, her physical body shifts as she transforms into an old hag to terrify them. As a Mexican American Chicana, I heard *historias de espanto* (scary stories) throughout my home, including *El Cucuy, brujas, duendes,* and the infamous *Llorona.* As a child, I was told La Llorona was a woman who scornfully drowned her children in a river and then drowned herself as a punishment for her children's murders. It was not until years later that Chicana feminist scholars exposed me to a complex Llorona, who was not a bad mother but a representation of Chicana subjectivity and resistance. Like this feminist

Llorona, as a queer Latinx woman, I felt connected to La Ciguanaba's transformation, rebellion, resistance, and haunting.

La Ciguanaba's folklore is not a lone haunting. Nor is it only her haunting to bear. Drawing from sociologist Avery Gordon's (1997, p. xvii) haunting
as a "repressed or unsolved social violence that is [repetitively] making itself
known," I argue that La Ciguanaba's haunting transcends linear temporality
to highlight the unresolved sexual violence against Indigenous and Mestiza
Central American women and nonbinary femmes. I trace this haunting, first in
the twentieth century with cisgender Salvadoran refugee Reyna Marroquin and
continue into the twenty-first century to highlight two trans women refugees.
In the 1970s, Reyna Marroquin fled El Salvador to escape domestic abuse and
financial scarcity. Although, the sexual violence she experienced did not stay in
El Salvador; instead, she was introduced to another misogynist evil that led to
her death in New York. Four decades later, in 2017, LGBTQ+ refugees began the
trek from Central America to Mexico. By 2018, the caravan had made its way to
the Tijuana US-Mexico border. Among the individuals in the Central American
Caravan were Francia Camila and Jade Quintanilla (Ottoway & Daliwal, 2017).
As trans-identifying women, Francia and Jade fled El Salvador to escape sexual
abuse and transphobia. But like Reyna's narrative, El Salvador's political borders
did not halt their hauntings. The social violence Francia and Jade fled continues
to go unresolved; in their journey through Mexico, they were met with transphobia, anti-Central American sentiment, and sexual violence.

Reyna, Francia, and Jade's hauntings are reminiscent of the Central
American folkloric icon La Ciguabana. Building on Gordon's (1997) interpre-
tation of haunting and Karina Alma's (2017, pp. 110–11) "cigua resistance" as a
gendered Indigenous and Latina resistance that draws from La Ciguanaba, I
argue that the social violence Reyna, Francia, and Jade experienced embodies a larger phenomenon I name *epistemic haunting*. Epistemic haunting is
a framework that unveils marginalized living and deceased individuals' suppressed histories and delegitimized knowledge to expose an ongoing injustice. I contend that Reyna, Francia, and Jade are modern-day Ciguanabas. La
Ciguanaba's folklore embroiders colonialism and heteropatriarchy's power
dynamics. Expanding on "cigua resistance," I establish that La Ciguanaba's
mythology is an epistemological framework for comprehending LGBTQ+
and gender-nonconforming Central Americans, including trans and sexually
deviant women. Though Francia and Jade's experiences occur decades after
Reyna's story, they are also reminiscent of La Ciguanaba's haunting.

I center these women's narratives because it allows for a humanized
understanding of how heteropatriarchal violence continues to haunt not

only Central American women and LGBTQ+ refugees' experiences but also the United States and Mexico's memories. These are nation-states that have continuously ignored and marginalized Indigenous and Central American women's experiences throughout history. My intention here is not to speak for Indigenous, Central American, or Salvadoran subjectivity and identity creation. As a Mexican-American Chicana (who has been severed from her Indigenous ancestry), it would be unethical to do so; what I do intend to do is analyze La Ciguanaba's legend to understand these women's resistance. La Ciguanaba's narrative is still relevant in the twenty-first century as it gives insight into women's sexual and gendered violence. These epistemic hauntings are dialectical, meaning that (1) these power structures haunt Central American women and LGBTQ+ refugees' experiences as they continuously ignore and marginalize Central Americans' experiences, and (2) these same ignored and marginalized communities also haunt the United States and Mexico with their testimonies and archives.

La Ciguanaba Folklore

La Ciguanaba's legend transcends several geographies and times. Variations of La Ciguanaba-like stories (including her other names, La Siguanaba, La Cigua, and La Ciguamonta) span Southern Mexico, Central America, and South America (Clara de Guevara, 2010, p. 106). Notably, La Ciguanaba is most associated with El Salvador and Guatemala. While storytellers depict La Ciguanaba as an Indigenous woman, scholars like Ceslo Lara-Figueroa (1984, p. 28) argue that her tale is a product of a ladino (mestizo) mixture of Spanish sirens and Indigenous myths. As a mixture between Spanish and Indigenous mythology, La Ciguanaba is a Ladino figure that acts as a LatIndigenous icon for Central American individuals. LatIndigeneity is a term coined by Shantel Martinez and Kelly Medina-López (2024) to highlight Latin American Indigenous descent individual's borderlands spectrality. Recino emphasizes the significance that La Ciguanaba has to Salvadorean modernity. Though Lara-Figueroa establishes a distinct racial and cultural Ladino component to La Ciguanaba, Guatemalan scholar Adrian Recino (1918, p. 560) contends that La Ciguanaba and La Llorona are different names for the same myth. While Recino's claims broaden La Ciguanaba's identification, it is also a reminder that La Ciguanaba's narrative transcends nation-state borderlands. As such, La Ciguanaba's narrative does not just impact individuals in Central America but also diasporic refugees. Salvadoran folklore scholar Rafael Rodriguez

(2000, p. 431) disputes that La Ciguanaba and La Llorona are the same entity and establishes that La Ciguanaba is symbolic of El Salvador's modern society. Whether La Ciguanaba's narrative is transnational, nevertheless, Recino emphasizes La Ciguanaba's significance to Salvadorean modernity; by doing so, he reminds us that when scholars utilize La Ciguanaba's to analyze Salvadorean individuals—as it is in this article—her folklore should be read within El Salvador's historical and contemporary cultural context.

Despite disagreement on La Ciguanaba's ethno-racial significance, her legacy's gendered implications cement her status as a "bad woman." Chicana scholar Alicia Gaspar de Alba (2014, p. 19) coins the "bad woman" term to describe women who deviate from heteropatriarchal norms, and consequently, society punishes them. La Ciguanaba's "bad woman" status is apparent in her LatIndigenous status, as her name contributes to her gendered haunting. Clara de Guevara (2010, p. 106) traces La Ciguanaba's etymology to two Nahuatl phrases. The first translation, "*cihuat nahauli*," means "witch woman." The second "*cihuat huethuet*" translates to "old woman." "*Cihuat huethuet*" significance is present in the artistic representation of La Ciguanaba by the Chalatenango, El Salvador government. In this painting, La Ciguanaba's shapeshifting is in process as she is an old woman holding a young women's face mask. Adrian Recino (1918, p. 560) argues that La Ciguanaba's indigenous etymology translates her name to "*mujer desnuda*," or naked woman. Each of her early iterations describes her within these stereotypically gendered etymologies. Clara de Guevara (2010, p. 107) goes as far as to assert that La Ciguanaba embodies infidelity. Her name depicts negative connotations that label her a witch, sexualize her, and classify beauty by ageist and colorist standards. Unlike Karina Alma's retelling, which focuses on sexual violence and resistance, several Ciguanaba tales state that her ability to transform is a punishment for abandoning her husband and child Cipito (Clara de Guevara, 2010, p. 108). Salvadoran and Guatemalan scholars describe La Ciguanaba's afterlife form as a long-dark-haired, or dark-skinned woman who bathes herself in a river. Once a man approaches her, she taunts them; depending on the telling, she terrifies men by shapeshifting her face into a skull, horse head, or an old hag (Lara-Figueroa, 1984; Clara de Guevara, 2010; Chinchilla, 2017; Gomez, 2010). The Chalatenango painting and the concept art for the upcoming Sun and Moon Film "La Siguanaba: A Salvadoran Urban Legend" both offer visuals of these terrifying yet sexualized descriptions. In the Chalatenango visual, La Ciguanaba is sexualized, surrounded by another nude woman; she is a long-dark-haired old woman with long nails that exposes one breast. In the "La Siguanaba" concept art, she is mid-transformation from a woman to a horse skeleton, and La Ciguanaba is unclothed with her breasts shown in their profile. La Ciguanaba's sexualization and representation as an Indigenous or Ladina woman is not coincidental, as her sexualization connects to her racialization as an evil terror associated with the racial Other.

Epistemic Haunting and Latinx Feminist Folklore

Drawing on queer Latina feminist epistemologies, folklore, and hauntology, I term *epistemic haunting* as a form of haunting that reveals a deceased and living individual's suppressed knowledge and delegitimized knowledge to expose an ongoing injustice. Epistemic haunting is dualistic; it is in itself a form of knowledge, but it also reveals suppressed knowledge. Epistemic haunting's dialectic characteristics allow ghosts like La Llorona and La Ciguanaba to live through knowledge in a way that was contested in their life. Reyna, Jade, and Francia's experiences and memories of White supremacy, xenophobia, sexism, and transphobia are embedded in their epistemic hauntings. These oppressive power structures enact a form of social violence that suppresses their existence and experiential knowledge. American Studies scholar Lisa Cacho's (2019) "social death" demonstrates the consequences of denying humanity, as power structures deny living individuals resources. African Studies Scholar Ayo Coly (2019) establishes that the study of hauntology as a metaphor for repressed violence connects colonialism's hypervisibility with postcolonial invisibility with women of color's bodies. Drawing from Emma Perez's *Decolonial Imaginary* (1999, p. 59) as "the time lag between the colonial and the postcolonial," in epistemic hauntings, ghosts inhabit in-between spaces; they exist in-between the colonial and postcolonial, they are both visible and invisible, and both alive and dead. Ghosts are the haunted and the haunter. For Reyna, Jade, and Francia, their hauntings respond to the dehumanization they experienced and continue to experience. A response that has them navigating liminal spaces in life and death.

Knowledge is a significant factor in an epistemic haunting that enacts resistance in a dialectic form. Gordon (1997, p. xvii) notes that haunting aims to find "a method of knowledge production" to write and represent hauntings and "reveal and learn from subjugated knowledge." In epistemic hauntings, knowledge is alive, even if its creator has passed or the creator is not present, because it is engaging, even if subtly, with others in the world. Epistemic hauntings describe how knowledge denied to the ghost (as living marginalized individuals) comes back to reveal itself. As such, it is twofold; it is in itself a form of knowledge, but it also reveals suppressed knowledge. It centers haunting as knowledge because "haunting is a very particular way of knowing what has happened or is happening" (Gordon, 1997, p. 8). Considering the decolonial imaginary, in epistemic hauntings, knowledge also inhabits in-between spaces and in-between temporality because knowledge is engaging, faintly and explicitly, with the world. Knowledge is alive even if its creator cannot verbalize this knowledge directly.

LatIndigenous experiences alongside folkloric figures like La Ciguanaba offer an opportunity to deconstruct hauntings. Folkloric icons complicate feminism and hauntology, as they provide foundations for integrating Indigenous and Latina cultural figures into haunting theories. La Llorona, La Ciguanaba, and La Virgen de Guadalupe, among others, act as transnational symbols and knowledge towards framing Indigenous and Latinx social violence and epistemic hauntings. Several La Ciguanaba retellings depict her as an Indigenous or Ladina young woman working on a plantation as she challenges the plantation owner's sexual advances; aggravated by her resistance, he murders her (Alvarado, 2017, p. 108). In the afterlife, she haunts the river where she died, focusing on haunting promiscuous men who confront her. Embodying dualism, she shapeshifts from a beautiful woman to an old hag to frighten men who enact sexual violence against living women (Alvarado, 2017, p. 109). Each retelling describes La Ciguanaba within four characteristics: beauty, exile, haunting, and misogynists' terror (Alvarado, 2017, p. 99). US Central American theorist Karina Alma (2017, p. 111) demonstrates the importance of La Ciguanaba through her concept of "cigua resistance," which asserts that Salvadoran women's resistance parallels the resistance against gendered violence present in La Ciguanaba's folkloric haunting (Alvarado, 2017). Alma affirms that the term cigua spotlights "indigenous-mestiza women and as people indigenous to the Americas" and recenter *centroamericanas* who often do not have their own intellectual feminist spaces (Alvarado, 2017, p. 102). I apply cigua resistance to Avery Gordon's haunting to reiterate La Ciguanaba's spectrality and contemporary cultural significance. Recalling that, Gordon (1997, p. xviii) defines haunting as the instances by "which a repressed or unresolved social violence is [repetitively] making itself known," La Ciguanaba's haunting is both literal and metaphorical. Within her mythology, she haunts promiscuous men who replicate her historical colonizer's violence. She also enacts Gordon's haunting as she haunts El Salvador, the US, and Mexico through her myth's critique of heteropatriarchy and colonialism. As Alma (2017, p. 111) states, La Ciguanaba's haunting is "a signifier that refuses erasure." By asserting stereotypical characteristics such as passiveness and silence as strategies for her attack, she flips the script on heteropatriarchal standards.

La Ciguanaba has a multifaceted identity that impacts heteropatriarchal standards of femininity, beauty, sexuality, and inclusion within her existence. She also embodies what Emma Perez (1999, pp. 3–4) calls a "dialectics of doubling" as ways Latinas enact opposites within their actions and rhetoric as they establish their own "place and meaning" within a larger nationalistic framework. Dialectics of doubling is especially important when understanding how La Ciguanaba disrupts heteronormative ideals about knowledge and bodies. As Susan Stryker notes, "Epistemological concerns lie at the heart of transgender critique . . . [it] points the way to a different understanding of how bodies mean, how representation works, and what counts as legitimate knowledge. [sic]" (Beauchamp, 2019, p. 5). La Ciguanaba's folklore is knowledge that utilizes her body to reframe her physical expression and display resistance through deviance. Her deviance is present in her Indigenous Ladina identity and, as I demonstrate later, her queerness. One instance of defiance is Mayan Kaqchikel musician Sara Curruchich's (2021) music video for "La Siguanaba," which highlights the figures' resistance, as she sings *"Le llaman la Siguanaba, Le llaman la bruja, Le llaman animal, Por que lucha contra las violencias del sistema, Patriarchal."* Translated, *"They call her La Siguanaba, they call her the witch, they call her animal, because she fights against the patriarchal system's violence."* Singing part of the song in the Kaqchikel language, Curruchich spotlights violence against Indigenous Maya women while also placing La Ciguanaba as a figure for feminist resistance. In addition to La Ciguanaba's Indigenous feminist symbolism, queering La Ciguanaba through queer Latinx feminism expands her meaning. As a trans critique, La Ciguanaba is a framework that redefines racialized womanhood's sexuality, gender, and gender expression and roles. One example of La Ciguanaba's redefinition of womanhood is her dialectic framing as both an attractive passive woman and a menacing creature. She accomplishes this "menacing" action through her bodily autonomy. Her body is fluid, and her shapeshifting helps reveal her monster bodily expression as she wishes. La Cigunaba's identity is based on resistance to the larger narrative that glorifies colonialism and heteropatriarchy that sexualizes women. In acknowledging her bodily autonomy, we begin to understand the complexity and "in-betweens" within people's beings (Perez, 1999, p. 110). For La Ciguanaba, this complexity comes in her layered feminist and fear-provoking fluid identity and shapeshifter body. Her bodily autonomy helps highlight other Indigenous and Latina women's autonomy, even in environments that purposely and strategically enact violence against women, including Reyna, Jade, and Francia's resistance.

Archiving the Caravan and the "Lady in the Barrel"

In 1999, Hamid Tafaghodi moved into his new home on 67 Forest Drive in New York City.[1] Soon after, the new homeowner discovered a three hundred-and-forty-pound fifty-five-gallon barrel in his basement's crawl space. After several failed attempts to have sanitation workers move it, he decided to take matters into his own hands and discard it himself. He begrudgingly moved the heavy barrel from the basement's crawl space to the sidewalk. But before taking it to the sanitary station, he opened it. To his horror, inside, it was full of green slush and a human hand and shoe floating at the barrel's surface (*New York Times*, 1999). Tafaghodi called the police immediately, where forensic investigations uncovered that this hand, shoe, and the rest of the mummified pregnant body inside the barrel belonged to Salvadoran refugee Reyna Angelica Marroquin (*New York Times*, 1999). About thirty years prior, Reyna had migrated from El Salvador to the US, attempting to escape sexual violence and pursue economic opportunities (*New York Times*, 1999). Before disappearing in 1969, Reyna lived in New York City, working at a plastic flower molding company. Howard Elkins owned that company, and before selling the home in 1972, Elkins also owned the house at 67 Forest Drive (*New York Times*, 1999). He had lived in the home with his wife, children, and Reyna's body in a barrel for years (*New York Times*, 1999). For decades, Reyna haunted Elkins; in 1999, her presence was finally known.

I first heard Reyna Marroquin's name and story on a true crime podcast called *My Favorite Murder* on my one-and-a-half-hour drive home from my "Central American Memory-Making" class. Basing their narrative on a Wikipedia entry, the hosts began to talk about "The Lady in the Barrel." Newspapers had given Reyna the name "The Lady in the Barrel" when a Jane Doe's body was discovered inside a barrel. The ghost of Marroquin is embedded within popular media consumption. The rise of true crime may not seem explicitly related to LatIndigeneity, but Indigenous and women of color's deaths and survival stories, fill true crime podcasts and shows. LatIndigeneity permeates through diverse mainstream mediums, yet examinations and retellings often overlook these women's racialization and gendered violence (as a self-proclaimed feminist podcast, *My Favorite Murder* was an exception). As Reyna's narrative lingered in my mind (a sign of her epistemic haunting), the news was booming with headlines about the Central American Caravan. A group of LGBTQ+ Central American refugees traveled together from Central American countries (including El Salvador, Guatemala, and Honduras) to the US-Mexico border. During this time, the caravan crossed Mexico's southern borders and reached Tijuana. That same week, I also heard La Ciguanaba's folklore in Karina Alma's course for the first time. As a Mexican American Chicana, La Ciguanaba was not part of my cultural memory. However, her story still haunted me as I researched La Llorona, another Latina folkloric icon with which I was much more familiar. At the same time, Reyna's name continued to occupy my mind, but this time alongside La Ciguanaba. Reyna, La Ciguanaba, and the Caravan narratives embody LatIndigenous theory. They were not just spectral metaphors; LatIndigeneity centered these women's experiences, real-life deaths, and violent assaults. Their narratives also forefront epistemic hauntings as an intersectional framework that acknowledges that ghost's knowledge is often subtly found outside academic borders. Like La Ciguanaba's silence, Reyna's story was a subtle presence that lured me to a digital archival search for "Reyna Marroquin." An investigation that eventually led me to seek other Central American women's narratives. Because LGBTQ+, particularly trans women, spoke about their Central American Caravan experiences, I can highlight Jade and Francia's lives. A small utterance led me to a longer epistemic haunting trail of resistance and, eventually, all three Salvadoran women's names. I bring up this moment to give perspective on my preliminary methods and the historical narrative's construction.

Through archival research of *ProQuest's Historical Newspapers* digital archive, I analyze historical and contemporary periodicals from the *New York Times*, *Newsday*, and *CBS News* to highlight these Salvadoran women's epistemic hauntings. Within *ProQuest's Historical Newspapers*, I conducted a Boolean search for "Reyna Marroquin" and "Lady in the Barrel." To archive Jade and Francia's experiences, I initially searched for "Central American Caravan." Later I searched their names, with little trace present in the archives. Through a content textual analysis of news articles, I highlight these three Salvadoran women refugees' experiences, testimonies, and memories. I purposely use the term refugees to oppose the United States policy that deems Salvadorans solely undocumented immigrants and disregards US political interventions.

Evaluating these digital archives involves being aware they are historical constructions (L'Eplattenier, 2009, p. 68). I employ two methodologies to understand this historical construction and highlight intersectional marginalized narratives: literary scholar Maria Del Pilar Blanco's ghost-watching and Gender studies scholar Anne Cvetkovich's "archive of feeling." The archive is a physical site filled with the immaterial, including affect and memory (Cvetkovic, 2007, p. 7). To designate an archive, an "archive of feelings" means acknowledging and centering the emotions present in its artifacts (Cvetkovic, 2007). The archive of feelings is a haunted space that highlights a manifestation amid "noisy silences and seething absences" (Gordon, 1997, p. 200). Material artifacts create a "memory landscape," or the values, beliefs, and feelings found in a collection of physical objects (Assmann, 2011, pp. 111–12). When emotion is present in the archive, it acts as a ghost, signaling that an absence or a trace is present. Ghost-watching as a methodology involves highlighting these absences by vigilantly "reading perceptions of space within a given text" (del Pilar Blanco, 2012, p. 1). Gordon (1999, p. 200) notes, "To study social life, one must confront the ghostly aspects of it. This confrontation requires (or produces) a fundamental change in the way we know and make knowledge." Central American studies scholar Floridalma Boj Lopez (2017) demonstrates how archives preserve knowledge through "mobile archives" or archives that document Maya migrants' epistemologies and experiences in material that can move with them. Drawing from mobile archives, I can highlight the archive of feeling that moves with Reyna, Francia, and Jade, including their oral traditions. By ghost-watching *ProQuest's Historical Newspapers* digital archives, I read the archival artifacts with the understanding that ghosts hide in them and treat these ghosts as knowledge. As forms of knowledge, ghosts in the archive "exert power" and reveal emotion "independently of their human creators" (Tai et al., 2019, p. 5). It is important to note that although archives independently communicate knowledge, this does not mean this knowledge is independent of their racialized and gendered identities; the women's intersectional identities are attached to the archives' knowledge.

Sexual Hauntings in the Borderlands

To understand how Reyna, Francia, and Jade combat heteropatriarchy and colonialism, it's essential to explicate gender relations within El Salvador that cause Indigenous, Ladina, and queer women to migrate and the gendered and sexualized violence they face during migration.[2] Sociologist Leisy Abrego (2014) notes that the civil war, economic stability, and an escape from gendered violence are the main reasons Salvadoran women journey to the United States. She argues that migration is a matter of survival, noting that pre-1980s Salvadorans migrated for labor, and by the 1980s, state-sanctioned violence caused people to flee the country (Abrego, 2014, p. 27). Reasons for seeking asylum connect to a history of suppressive dictatorships and US imperialism. In the 1960s, General Maximiliano Hernandez Martinez's dictatorship repressed any form of organization and devastated El Salvador's economy (Alegria, 1986). From the 1970–80s, El Salvador was politically unstable, and

US political and economic intervention was set into motion to suppress communism within the state. The United States is still silent about intervention-initiated violence (Abrego, 2017, pp. 74–75). Economic and immigration policies, such as the limitations placed on visas and Temporary Protection Status, and the exploitative economic conditions caused by the Dominican Republic-Central American Free Trade Act perpetuated this outbreak of violence (Abrego, 2017, p. 14). Abrego (2017, p. 46) notes that the civil war's violence parallels today's gendered violence as many Salvadoran women seek refuge from sexual objectification and assault. The United Nations (2015, pp. 27–28) "Women on the Run" reports that trans women from El Salvador testified that they were sexually assaulted and humiliated with no state protection.

Reyna's life intertwines with the history of violence presented above. In an epistemic haunting, unresolved social violence interconnects temporality and space through knowledge. Reyna's epistemic haunting and migration enacts La Ciguanaba's exile characteristic. A physical and metaphorical exile as her death bars her from returning to El Salvador and living in the United States. Her exile is a trace that highlights her existence and her past before immigrating to the US. This past is part of a "communicative memory," or the everyday noninstitutional memories people communicate with, as her life entwines within the memories of many other individuals in El Salvador and the United States (Assmann, 2010, p. 111). Reyna Marroquin demonstrates her "cigua resistance" as she inhabits individuals' "obstinate memories," or lingering memories that people cannot forget (Osuna, 2017, p. 83). These obstinate memories signal an epistemic haunting. The memory itself is a source of knowledge about the violence Reyna faced. Her death revealed her memories. After her homicide investigation, reporters contacted Reyna's friend, Kathy Andrade, and located her family in El Salvador. Kathy and Reyna's family memories filled necessary absences in her haunting. With their memories, Reyna's story no longer begins with her death, and for her family in El Salvador, it no longer ends in mystery. Her haunting connects with LatIndigenous history as it begins with political violence against Indigenous and Ladino peoples in El Salvador. From the 1930s to the 1960s, General Maximiliano Hernandez Martinez's dictatorship led to Indigenous genocide and economic turmoil. During the 1960s, Reyna migrated to Long Island, New York, from El Salvador. Like many other Salvadoran women who migrate to escape gendered violence, Reyna had migrated to seek financial stability and leave her unfaithful, abusive husband. Reyna's "cigua resistance" reveals her epistemic haunting began before she came to the United States.

Like Reyna, trans women of color also seek refuge from the violence in their homelands but often face heteropatriarchal violence during their migrations into Mexico and the United States. In Mexico, Central Americans reside in what Chicana lesbian feminist scholar Gloria Anzaldua (1987, p. 25) calls a "borderlands," or liminal space where two or more worlds clash. Mexico's borderlands are a haunting space where Central Americans face a "cultural tyranny" in which paradigms attempt to assert Mexican culture as dominant (Anzaldua, 1987, p. 25). Snorton (2017) shifts trans away from a fixed gender and instead defines its ontology within movement and liminality as transness is created in difference. Transness as movement and form connects with La Ciguanaba's exile as a constriction from movement and demonstrates how her shapeshifting abilities are a way of becoming. As such, trans interconnects with other intersectional identities and cannot be analyzed independently (Snorton, 2017). Jade and Francia's transness is transitive, in movement, within their bodies and space as asylum seekers. It also means that their epistemic haunting is a trans haunting that shifts through time and space.

Many asylum seekers' memories of their migration through Mexico are filled with "exploitation and abuse" (Osuna, 2017, p. 84). Francia and Jade suffer from what Gloria Anzaldua calls the "fear of going home" as they confront the homophobia and transphobia that sees their gender and existence as a form of "loqueria" or craziness (Anzaldua, 1987, p. 41). Francia and Jade share La Ciguanaba's exile characteristic (Alvarado, 2017, p. 99). Central American women risk facing rape and other forms of sexual assault as men see their bodies as commodities (Abrego, 2017, pp. 78–9). As sexually objectified beings, Central American women are commodified and at risk of kidnapping and being forced into the sex trafficking industry (Vogt, 2013). In the United States, this commodification continues as Central American migrants work in exploitative conditions for low wages (Abrego, 2014, p. 11). The sexualized threats and abusive labor in El Salvador, Mexico, and the US are reminiscent of La Ciguanaba's commodification at the colonizers' hands.

Although Francia and Jade's narratives take place decades after Reyna's story, their memories repeat a haunting of sexual violence. Francia and Jade are refugees currently seeking asylum in the United States. Although their home countries did not legally banish them, dangerous conditions forced them to leave. As trans women, Francia and Jade's reasons for fleeing El Salvador align with the women's testimonies in the U.N.'s "Women on the Run." Jade recalls memories of her LGBTQ+ friends in El Salvador being murdered, forced into sex trafficking, and brutally assaulted (Del Real, 2018). For Jade, migration is a survival strategy and an attempt to live, as she discloses, "I decided to leave [El Salvador] because I didn't want to die" (Del Real, 2018). Even though they do not know each other, Francia's decision to leave El Salvador reflects the same violence Jade speaks about. Francia Camila asserts that she left El Salvador after working in the sex industry and receiving threats against her life (Ottoway & Daliwal, 2017). In their actions, as they suffer through and confront their "fear of going home," they reveal the transphobia and sexual violence haunting El Salvador and Mexico. They break through the United States and Mexico's silence on violence against trans women. For instance, Jade speaks to the sexual harassment she has faced on La Bestia (the train used in Mexico to travel north), stating, "We had to give our services so that they'd let us on. They were abusing us the whole way through" (Del Real, 2018). Jade alludes to sexual assault faced in Mexico when she asserts that LGBTQ+ refugees are coerced into sexual acts to gain access to La Bestia, one of the only forms of transportation northward during the trek. Additionally, she states that, like many other Central American LGBTQ+ refugees in town, "she has been accosted on the streets of Tijuana and harassed" (Del Real, 2018). Francia also remembers Mexico's transphobia during her time in Chiapas. Initially leaving El Salvador to escape the sex industry, Francia is a skilled beautician who was excluded from employment in a beauty salon in Chiapas due to transphobia. *Vice* reports, "She [Francia Camila] tried to work as a stylist in Chiapas, but said salons told her they 'only hire women,' so she turned back to sex work to survive" (Ottoway & Daliwal, 2017). In Chiapas, the epistemic haunting continued to deny her knowledge as a beautician and her humanity, resulting in Francia facing the same sexual violence she was fleeing in El Salvador.

Memory Tracing in Epistemic Hauntings

Memory helps signal epistemic hauntings. It links time together to trace the epistemic hauntings' repetitive nature and connection to La Ciguanaba's characteristics. More so, material artifacts capture and signal memories from epistemic hauntings. This materiality is present in the periodicals themselves. As primary and secondary sources, digital newspapers preserve memories. The newspapers are a form of knowledge, not just as informative journalism, but as a way ghosts (living and dead) make themselves known. These ghosts may not be communicating their direct perspectives and emotions, but traces of their experiences are present in the in-between spaces throughout the texts. As a result, these in-between spaces also transcend time to communicate a ghost's feelings to others.

The materials these periodicals highlight include the barrel that preserved Reyna Marroquin's body, a written note, and a phonebook. These materials are part of Marroquin's memory landscape and act as traces that unveil Reyna's death and her last few moments in life. By analyzing her preserved clothes inside the barrel, forensics investigations discovered she had been missing since 1969 (McQuisiton, 1999). Investigators also determined that Reyna was pregnant. Reyna had become pregnant with her boss Howard Elkins' child. Three decades before her body's discovery, Reyna had an affair with her boss Howard Elkins and became pregnant. She told Elkins about the pregnancy, and when she attempted to tell his wife about their affair, Elkins murdered Reyna for speaking her truth (*Metro News Briefs*, 2000). By expressing her truth, she enacted La Ciguanaba's fourth characteristic as a misogynist's terror. Reyna was a threat to Elkins' imagined heteropatriarchal world. Just as the plantation owner desired La Ciguanaba until her resistance, Reyna's voice was also an act of resistance that made her undesirable to Elkins. The barrel preserved this resistance alongside her body. Within Reyna's clothing, she held onto an address book where she stored her social security card, the phone numbers of her closest friends in the United States, and a note to Elkins. These objects make up her memory landscape. She is a ghost who travels through time using these artifacts. After three decades, this address book was still legible. Although some may consider Reyna's death evidence for her passivity, I argue that the autotopography, "or a collection of significant items that tie identity to a larger network and social meaning in life," is present in her address book and note (Gonzalez, 1995, pp. 133–34). They are signs of resistance. The address book held the phone number of Reyna's friend Kathy, who had worked at the same plastic flower molding company. Kathy knew about the affair and had been searching for Reyna since her disappearance. Her testimony led investigators to Elkins. The note in the address book was also crucial to Reyna voicing her truth. *CBS News* (2000) reports that the note to Elkins read, "Don't be mad, I told the truth." This statement asserts her subjectivity and experiences as knowledge and defies Elkin's heteropatriarchal expectations that she will remain silent. Even in life, she haunted her oppressor, like La Ciguanaba, who punishes promiscuous men; Reyna intended to expose Elkins' promiscuity and seek justice against his infidelity. Her existence demonstrates a similar fluidity to La Ciguanaba. Like the plantation owner who pursues her for his sexual gratification, Elkins treated Reyna as an object for sex and labor. Although some view her as a passive being, the note shows Reyna's duality as both the haunted and the haunter. After the police discovered the note, they interrogated Elkins, and shortly after, he committed suicide. The note shows how Reyna actively sought justice for her death, even if she was not alive to see this justice played out.

The barrel itself is also an affective material that preserves multifaceted emotions. The barrel was in Elkin's home basement and became a facet of his everyday life. Some accounts say that his children would use the barrel as a hiding place during hide-and-seek games. When Elkins moved, Reyna made herself repetitively known to strangers, such as the new homeowner, until they discovered the truth about her existence within the barrel and the reality of her death. The barrel held her remains and eventually filled the absent memories about her. Forensic investigations uncovered Reyna's identity through her memory landscape (*Metro News Briefs*, 2000). A memory landscape that surpassed several borders, as Reyna's mother, Ercilia, who resided in El Salvador, dreamt about her daughter in a barrel. After her case closed, *Newsday* reporters traveled to El Salvador to tell her family about her death. During this visit, Ercilia confessed that for years she dreamt that Reyna "was trapped inside a barrel. She was falling" (Corral et al., 1999). The barrel was a ghostly source of unconscious knowledge for Ercilia. Within the dreams, the barrel acted as a ghost transporting knowledge within the epistemic haunting. An epistemic haunting that was not limited to the physical barrel's presence but also included its imagery. The barrel's imagery was able to pass through physical borderlands and become a prominent presence in Reyna's family's minds for years. The barrel haunted Ercilia, a haunting that was trying to help her find her daughter.

Hometactics as Queer Survival

Reyna, Francia, and Jade navigate several physical and spectral borderlands as they negotiate between nations, heteropatriarchal norms, and the concept of home (Anzaldua, 1987, p. 25). For Reyna's epistemic haunting, these borderlands are a clash between the living and the dead, past and future, and resistance and white heteropatriarchy. Francia and Jade's experiences clash between transphobia and queer survival, danger and safety, and social death and dignified existence. Each woman sought to make the United States their home. A goal that connects to their desire to enact La Ciguanaba's beauty characteristic. While La Ciguanaba's folklore depicts beauty in relation to her youthful form, by queering La Ciguanaba, I acknowledge that her beauty lies in her ability to shapeshift, to express her being in whatever form she pleases, and to occupy different time and space when she wishes. Reyna's persistence to speak when Elkins expects her to be silent demonstrates her defiance and beauty as an expression of her truth. Although Jade and Francia seek refuge in the United States, they have made Mexico's borderlands a temporary home. Existing within liminality, they convey their gender identities and expressions within the current in-between space of Mexico. Gordon (1997) speaks to this complexity as she states that contradiction fills people's actions and memories. Their lives are complex and filled with contradiction because although they have made Mexico and the US their homes as ways to resist sexual violence in El Salvador, in Mexico and the United States, these women are confronted with transphobia, gendered harassment, and sexual violence. To resist this social violence, they enact their "cigua resistance" by "refus[ing] erasure" through "hometactics," or the everyday strategies Latinas use to make an uncomfortable setting a home (Alvarado, 2017; Ortega, 2016).

Reyna's hometactics focus on her aspirations during her lifetime. While Elkins saw her as immigrant labor (sexually and as an employee at his factory), the individuals in her address book affirm Marroquin's desires and resistance to heteropatriarchy away from Elkins' hostile presence. Kathy adds complexity to Reyna's existence. Acknowledging Reyna's desires reframes her away from passivity, as she becomes more than just a murder victim, factory worker, or mistress, but instead is humanized. Reyna's hopes and dreams are highlighted, as Kathy states that Reyna came to the United States to become a fashion designer (Corral et al., 1999). The image of Reyna as an aspiring fashion designer is prevalent in Andrade's memory, alongside other valuable experiences with her friend. Elkins does not define her. Instead, her family and friends' memories establish that, like La Ciguanaba, she is a human who existed before she was the missing "Lady in the Barrel."

Jade and Francia have resisted violence by enacting "hometactics" (Ortega, 2016, pp. 202–3), even when navigating dangerous borderlands. Francia and Jade's hometactics initially seem like passive actions, but like the Ciguanaba, they resist and, at times, make themselves known in their silence. Whereas Jade and Francia's rhetoric demonstrates a passivity to their endured violence, their actions are hometactics are survival strategies that create a home. Although Francia has experienced violence in Mexico, obstinate memories of El Salvador's violence still haunt her, jokily telling individuals who believe Tijuana is dangerous, "You should see El Salvador." Francia's beautician work in Tijuana functions as a hometactic (Ottoway & Daliwal, 2017). Francia very literally and metaphorically enacts La Ciguanaba's beauty. As a customer and a beautician, the beauty salon functions as a space where El Salvador and Mexico's violence momentarily halt. Francia can "close her eyes," relax, and experience self-care in the salon. (Ottoway & Daliwal, 2017). Amid Mexico's transphobia, Jade finds home in el Jardin de las Mariposas, a Tijuana LGBTQ+ rehabilitation center that has functioned as a shelter for LGBTQ+ refugees (Del Real, 2018). Residing in the Jardin de la Mariposas is a hometactic for Jade, where she can feel safe for a moment. The center also allows Jade time to establish her next hometactic as she contemplates whether she should remain in Mexico or seek a new home in the United States. For both Jade and Francia, El Salvador's repetitive violence and their resilience play crucial roles in their epistemic hauntings. Though the memories of sexual violence haunt them, as ghosts, they also haunt. Their hometactics appear as ghostly hauntings. Francia and Jade's actions remind El Salvador, the United States, and Mexico that state-sanctioned violence is still occurring and that there are still many ghosts to uncover. Their narratives serve as a reminder of refugees' existence and resilience to survive this violence.

Ciguanabas' Call to Haunt

Jade and Francia exist decades apart from Reyna and centuries away from La Ciguanaba's legend, yet each woman's existence interweaves a transnational LatIndigenous epistemic haunting. Their memories and archives are threaded together by their "cigua resistance" and the individuals that witness this resistance. The growth of popular media has allowed these ghostly women to share their narratives with a broader audience. As such, LatIndigeneity is not just a theory that exists in the abstract. Like the ghost, it is a living entity that exists inside the bodies and spirits that exist amongst true-crime podcasts, newspaper articles, and social media posts.

These Ciguanabas' actions and memories enact a LatIndigenous resistance reminiscent of the La Ciguanaba's characteristics—beauty, exile, haunting, and terror—while also demonstrating that the folkloric icon's transformation is a queer way of being. Jade, Francia, and Reyna exist in-between temporality and space while navigating contradictions, traces, and suppressed knowledge. Materiality is at the center of their mobility as they move through borderlands through their archives. Their existence demonstrates these Ciguanabas' ability to speak past violence and past death to haunt the nations that enact violence against them. While Jade, Francia, and Reyna's epistemic hauntings are not as well-known as La Ciguanaba's myth, they exist. As a result, they leave small traces, memories, and archives that make them known, even when violence claims they do not exist. Ciguanabas' memories and experiences have significant implications for the borderlands they inhabit and the heteropatriarchal landscapes they defy as they attempt to validate their existence. Popular media and mainstream texts, including journalism and creative writing, offer the opportunity to highlight stories that are left in society's shadows. For academia, this means there is a call to acknowledge and deconstruct popular mediums for the in-between spaces and times where more ghosts may live.

Notes

1. This is a trigger warning for this section as the details of Reyna's murder are quite gruesome and violent.

2. This is a vast and in-depth transnational history and it is significant to state that within this paper, I will not do justice the complexity of political, gendered, and sexualized relations as I attempt to condense both historical and contemporary reasons for LGBTQ+ individuals and women's reasons for asylum.

References

Abrego, L. (2017). On Silences: Salvadoran refugees then and now. *Latino Studies* 15, 73–85.

Abrego, L. (2014). *Sacrificing Families: Navigating Laws, Labor, and Love Across Borders.* Stanford University Press.

Alegria, C. (1986). The Two Cultures of El Salvador, *The Massachusetts Review* 27(3–4), 493–502.

Alvarado, K. (2017). A Gynealogy of Cigua Resistance: La Ciguanaba, Prudencia Ayala, and Leticia Hernandez-Linares in Conversation in *U.S. Central Americans: Reconstructing Memories, Struggles, and Communities of Resistance.* Edited by Karina O. Alvarado, Alicia Ivonne Estrada, and Ester E. Hernandez. University of Arizona Press.

Alvarado, K. (2013). An interdisciplinary reading of Chicana/o and (U.S.) Central American cross-cultural narrations. *Latino Studies,* 11(3), 366–87. https://doi.org/10.1057/lst.2013.13.

Anzaldua, G. (1987). *Borderlands/La Frontera: The New Mestiza.* Aunt lute books.

Assmann, J. (2010). Communicative and Cultural Memory in *A Companion to Cultural Memory Studies.* Edited by Astrid Erll and Ansgar Nunning. De Gruyter.

Boj Lopez, F. (2017). Mobile archives of indigeneity: Building La Comunidad Ixim through organizing in the Maya diaspora. *Latino Studies,* 15(2), 201–18. https://doi.org/10.1057 /s41276-017-0056-0.

Cacho, L. (2012). *Social Death: Racialized Rightlessness and the Criminalization of the Unprotected.* New York University Press.

CBS News Staff. (March 8, 2000). The Clue in the Drum: A Plastic Flower Stem Leads to a Killer, *CBS News.* https://www.cbsnews.com/news/the-clue-in-the-drum/.

Chinchilla Mazariegos, O. F. (2017). *Art and myth of the ancient Maya.* Yale University Press.

Corral, O. et al., (October 2, 1999). I had a Dream . . . She Was Trapped Inside a Barrel/ Mother of slain women mourns for long-lost daughter. *Newsday.* https://www.newsday.com/news /i-had-adream-she-was-trapped-inside-a-barrel-mother-of-slain-woman-mourns-for -long-lost-daughter-1.379952#.

Cvetkovich, A. (2003). *An Archive of Feelings: Trauma, Sexuality, and Lesbian Public Cultures.* Duke University Press.

de Guevara, C. C. (2010). Tradición oral salvadoreña. Mestizaje, religión y valores. *Universidad Tecnológica de El Salvador,* 102–13.

Del Real, J. (2018). They Were Abusing Us the Whole Way: A Tough Path for Gay and Trans Migrants. *New York Times.* https://www.nytimes.com/2018/07/11/us/lgbt-migrants-abuse.html.

Freccero, C. (2013). "Queer Spectralities: Haunting of the Past" *The Spectralities Reader: Ghosts and Haunting Contemporary Cultural Theory*. Ed. Maria Del Pilar Blanco and Esther Peeren. Bloomsbury Press.

Gómez Garrido, L. M. (2010). Cuentos y leyendas inmigrantes. Duendes, fantasmas, brujas, diablos, santos, bandidos, y otros seres inquietos e inquietantes de Hispanoamérica y de algún misterioso lugar más by José Manuel Pedrosa, Silvia Espinal, Jesús Herrera, José Zaragoza, Alfonso Romero, Ana Lucía Camposeco, Carmelo Lacayo, Orlando Mejía, Patricia Martínez, Andry Ratsimandresy, Agathe Rakotojoelimaria, Óscar Abenójar, Claudia Carranza, Cristina Castillo, Susana Gala, Sara Galán, Sergio González, Ema Nishida and Dolores Randriamalandy. *Nueva Revista de Filología Hispánica, 58*(2), 745–47.

Gonzalez, J. (1995). Autotopographies in *Prosthetic Territories: Politics and Hypertechnologies*. Edited by Gabriel Brahm and Mark Driscoll. Westview Press.

Gordon, A. (1997). *Ghostly Matters: Haunting and the Sociological Imagination*, University of Minnesota Press.

Lara-Figueroa, C. (1984). *Leyendas y Casos de La Tradicion Oral De La Cuidad De Guatemala* (Vol. 3). Editorial Universitaria De Guatemala.

McNay, M. (2009). Absent Memory, Family Secrets, Narrative Inheritance, *Qualitative Inquiry* 15(7), 1178–88.

McQuisiton, J. (1999). Body in Barrel is Believed to be Women Who Vanished in '69, *The New York Times. ProQuest Historical Newspapers*.

Metro News Briefs. (2000). Dead Woman's Ex-Boss was Father of Her Baby. *The New York Times. ProQuest Historical Newspapers*.

"New Homeowner Finds Body of Pregnant Woman in Barrel." (1999). *The New York Times. ProQuest Historical Newspapers*.

Ortego, M. (2016). *In-Between: Latina Feminist Phenomenology, Multiplicity, and the Self*. SUNY Press.

Osuna, S. (2017). Obstinate Transnational Memories: How Oral Histories Shape Salvadoran-Mexican Subjectivities in *U.S. Central Americans: Reconstructing Memories, Struggles, and Communities of Resistance*. edited by Karina O. Alvarado, Alicia Ivonne Estrada, and Ester E. Hernandez, University of Arizona Press.

Ottoway, A., and Daliwal, M. (2017). How Two Trans Salvadoran Migrants Found Peace in Tijuana. *Vice*. https://www.vice.com/en_us/article/ne3y7z/how-two-trans-salvadoran-migrants-found-peace-in-tijuana.

Perez, E. (1999). *The Decolonial Imaginary: Writing Chicanas into History*. Bloomington: Indiana University Press.

Recinos, A. (1916). Algunas Observaciones Sobre el Folk-Lore de Guatemala. *The Journal of American Folklore, 29*(114), 559. https://doi.org/10.2307/534391.

Rodriguez Diaz, R. (2000). *La muerte y la literatura: Más allá de 2000 en El Salvador*. 429–32.

Snorton, C. R. (2017). *Black on both sides: A racial history of trans identity*. University of Minnesota Press.

UNHCR. (2015). *Women on the Run: Firsthand Accounts of Refugees Fleeing El Salvador, Guatemala, Honduras, and Mexico*, Washington D.C: United Nations High Commissioner for Refugees.

Vogt, W. (2013). Crossing Mexico: Structural Violence and the commodification of undocumented Central American migrants. *American Ethnologist* 40(4), 764–80.

CHAPTER 6

"Entre la Santa y la Muerte"
Liminality and Empowerment in Mexico's Santa Muerte

Luisa Fernanda Grijalva-Maza

She is a skeleton with jewelry, wigs, party dresses, or robes adorned with local seeds and plants. *She* has a scythe in one hand and a globe in the other. For some, *she* is a grotesque and monstrous image. For others, *she* is a beautiful saint that walks alongside them as a companion in the present. *She* is an understanding friend that promises death but also life (Figure 6.1). *She* is Santa Muerte (Holy Death or Saint Death). This popular Mexican saint made her first public appearance in 2001 when Enriqueta Romero decided to display her altar to Santa Muerte outside her house in Tepito, Mexico City (Hernández Hernández, 2016, p. 22). Little did she know that amidst the violence, illegal commerce, insecurity, and criminality of Tepito, her altar would become a site of reunion, prayer, devotion, love, and utmost respect for the now-famous Santa Muerte.

Even though Mexico's constitution upholds freedom of religion, a triangle of power (the Mexican state and military, the Catholic church, and the media) has deployed diverse symbolic, political, and religious strategies to marginalize and *bury* the female death. She is related to the Devil by the Catholic Church, connected to narco cartels by the media, and military force destroys her altars.[1] This harsh response to La Santísima suggests she poses a threat to the power structures in Mexico.[2] The beginning of the *public* cult can be traced to marginalized areas of Mexico. However, many researchers that have studied Santa Muerte emphasize that her followers come from all walks of life. Therefore, her devotion is not composed uniquely of the poorest parts of society or criminals. In this sense, La Niña Blanca has served the purpose of advocating for the vulnerable and marginalized (Fragoso, 2011, p. 16)—Felipe Gaytán Alcalá refers to her as the Saint among the damned (2008, p. 41). Authors such as R. Andrew Chestnut, Matgorzata Oleszkiewics-Peralba, and Kate Kingsbury have noted the empowering force Santa Muerte has on her followers. Indeed, the empowerment of the "other" can become a threat to the Mexican elites. Nevertheless, followers are not necessarily joining together to instigate a revolution against the Mexican state or form political parties to bring down and substitute the power structures in Mexico.

Unlike several Indigenous communities in Mexico that have been infantilized and discriminated against because of their demand for spiritual autonomy (Marcos, 2014, p. 148), it is not clear that Santa Muerte is engendering a specific spirituality or identity completely divergent from the hegemonic logic of the state and Catholicism. The non-oppositional nature of La Santa then leads to the question, what kind of empowerment is engendered by Santa Muerte, and why does it make the Mexican power structures tremble?

The paradoxical nature of Santa Muerte resides in that she is composed of a mix of indigenous beliefs of death, medieval Catholicism, Cuban Santería, witchcraft, and other traditions that pertain to the different contexts and people that are devoted to her. Yet, she is not against the Catholic church, as most of her devotees declare themselves to be Catholic. The fact that La Santa's composition depends on her location and the individuals that worship her implies there is no agreement on the precise traditions she encompasses, or the time and location of her origin, or the specific norms she promotes. In this sense, identity in Santa Muerte is not fixed. On the contrary, it flows, moves, changes, and cannot be defined because she materializes the experience of what I term *liminal hybridity* in Mexico[3]—a result of coloniality and identity politics. The logic engendered by La Santísima is the product of her hybridity (after all, she is a mestiza) and a liminal movement that does not promote the need to constitute a determined identity. Her mestizaje—the mix of indigenous veneration of death and the Catholic iconography of death—make her a contemporary *LatIndigenous* logic that does not prescribe the consolidation of identity but instead embodies the power of encounters, movement, and becomings.

Following the above, the general argument of the present chapter is that Santa Muerte, as a female death, materializes the transgressive potentiality of *liminal hybridity*. It is not only that she transgresses the limits of identity imposed and policed by the structures of political and economic power in Mexican society, but also that her relationship with her followers is much closer, lived, embodied, and mirrored than those of Catholic Saints, which allows La Santa to represent the empowerment of the liminal mestizos. She is feared by the State, the Church, and the media because she is a haunting reminder of the horrors of coloniality, modernity, and identity. Most of all, she is feared because she threatens with a potential empowerment that is constantly moving, changing—an empowerment that moves in liminality and, therefore, cannot be fully targeted for destruction.

From Rite of Passage to Permanent Liminality: The Crux of the Noncivilized Mestizo in Mexico

It is crucial to look beyond the economic and political crises of the 1990s to understand the conditions of possibility that engendered the popularity of Santa Muerte. We are forced to look at the profoundly ethnoracialized structures that dominate Mexico, the legacy of colonization, oppression, and slavery that continues to impact the everyday, particularly in the form of the *mestizo* (hybrid). (Alcalá González & Bussing López, 2020, pp. 2–3).

As Aníbal Quijano notes, among the many strategies of European colonization, one of the most important was the imposition of a "mystified image of their own patters of producing knowledge and meaning" (2007, p. 169). With time, colonizers began partially including the dominated into their patterns and institutions of power to transform European culture into an aspiration (2007, p. 169). Quijano's work is crucial to understand that the end of colonization did not bring the end of these power relations or the seduction of European culture in Latin America, including the produced discursive relation between this European ideal and "whiteness."

In the case of Mexico, colonial power relations created an assortment of identities that derived from the complex construction of mestizaje (the mixing of indigenous peoples, the colonizers, enslaved African people that were brought during the colonization of Latin America, etc.). During la Colonia, charts were painted to categorize, catalog, and control the different products of mestizaje (hybridity), assigning them names and hierarchical positions.[4] Second only to the white Spanish colonizer was the mestizo, the result of the mix between a white Spanish and an Indigenous person (in some cases "white" or whiter than the Indigenous parent, or not). This category would prove to be paradigmatic in social and political structures since the independence of Mexico, especially considering the allure of European culture imposed during La Colonia.[5]

Hybridity (mestizaje) became the center of a political ideology that dominated after the Mexican Revolution in the 1920s, permeating the social and political logic to this day. What Olivia Gall calls "mestizofilia" was born of a project by José Vasconcelos (2004, p. 242), a prominent Mexican politician of the 1920s, whereby he composed a social and political agenda that would lead the Latin American mestizo to become the most civilized and developed race.[6] The mestizo would unite all races through hybridity to become the only universal and fraternal race (Vasconcelos, 2012, p. 17). For Revolutionary Mexico, national identity was born with mestizaje. However, this process was not only defined by biological mixing. A mestizo is a complex concept that includes a cultural, political, and social composition. A variety of public policies were implemented under the guidance of Vasconcelos to create a defined mestizo identity: education policies that concentrated on publishing and teaching the Greek classics and European writers; immigration policies that gave clear preferences to white and European populations; cultural programs in the arts, etc. (Manrique, 2016, pp. 5–7). That is, the mestizo population of Mexico was not yet the ideal race. As Manrique argues, "Vasconcelos viewed the mestizo as rising to the status of a cosmic race as long as he became that which he was not: Europeanized, educated, and cultured" (2016, p. 7). Vasconcelos' policies sedimented through the construction of a reality that permeated all sociocultural sectors in Mexico, a reality whereby to be Mexican is to be a mestizo, a reality that let to subsume difference "under an ideal of progressive whitening" (Gall, 2004, p. 243). Of course, this process was not only related to the generation of lighter skin color to the extent of being considered white but also to a particular culture that recognized its Indigenous past while leaving it behind and tending towards a Europeanized status.[7]

Liminality appears in the passage from undesired hybridity to the ideal state of mestizaje. As Matgorzata Oleszkiewics-Peralba explains, liminality refers to passages from one undesirable state to a desirable one (2015, pp. 3–4). The liminal is the in-between state of being, implying a process of transition that is happening outside the normative limits of identity (2015, pp. 3–4). For Tally Jr., liminality is more complex. "It implies an in-between experience of place (with guarded limits) and space (the outside). Therefore, liminality is also related to "threshold," or the point of entry to place, the possibility of transgressing the boundaries of place (Tally Jr., 2016, p. xi).

As designed in Vasconcelos' project, Mexican hybridity had to move through liminality to reach "civilized" hybridity. Yet, as Tally Jr. notes, the liminal can potentially reveal the discursive and produced nature of the limits of identity and race, that is, that identity is the result of unequal relations of power and not nature.[8] For example, Abril Saldaña Tejeda notes that domestic workers in Mexico, independent of their ethnic origin or skin color, are racialized as others because of their employment and the historical and colonialist relation between domestic work and Indigenous ethnicity (2013, p. 74).[9]

These cases show that the Raza Cósmica's limits depend on the group that decides the characteristics that count to be excluded from or included among the elite ranks.[10] In the Mexican case, liminality is not a temporary passage but a permanent reality of mixing in the in-between space and place, always reaching for the ideal while never really getting there—*liminal hybridity*.

In this sense, la Raza Cósmica, as any normative and discursive identity, produced an in-between place and space where "uncivilized" mestizos are eternally transitioning towards an identity that is contingent and dependent on relations of power. Furthermore, the permanency of the liminal process generated encounters with marginalized groups without any apparent possibility to transition; for example, Indigenous peoples, returned migrants, communities of African descent, migration flows from Central America, peoples in extreme poverty, prisoners, etc. The Cosmic Race opened an in-between where heterogeneity is moving, encountering, and becoming while engendering the conditions of possibility for the encounter of death and the feminine—La Santa Muerte.

La Santa Muerte is not only a female saint but also a saint that embodies liminal hybridity, which can explain some of her most important traits or lack thereof. Santa Muerte is a mestiza—a hybrid—that integrates pre-Columbian indigenous devotion to death, African traditions that arrived in Mexico through the slave trade during colonization, Catholic religion, Cuban Santería, witchcraft, and others (Hernández Hernández, 2016, p. 22). This heterogeneity has made it difficult to pinpoint an absolute origin of Santa Muerte (2016, p. 22). Her movement and transformation from place to place, from altar to altar, and person to person limit the possibility of ever producing a finalized identity. As a mestiza without absolute origin and identity, her institutionalization has been impossible (Flores Martos, 2008, p. 56). There have been a few attempts to create an institutionalized Church of Santa Muerte. However, followers of La Niña Blanca have resisted. That is, La Santa answers to no one, not the State, Church, or any power structure for that matter (Oleszkiewics-Peralba, 2015, p. 106).

Because of this lack of origin, identity, and institutionalization, Santa Muerte cannot be a symbol of opposition, which would require a stable and structured identity. In fact, most of her followers identify themselves as Catholic, and some even ask the permission of the Catholic God to invoke Santa Muerte (Gaytán Alcalá, 2008, p. 43). Given that she flows in liminality, she is also not against the State, as many of her followers are politicians or part of state police forces (2008, p. 41). This fluidity makes her even more puzzling: she does not have a determined identity, and she is also not an opposition symbol. What, then, is the kind of empowerment she is promoting?

Monster, Saint, and Cannibal: The Empowerment of Liminal Hybridity

La Madrina is puzzling because the attempts to find her absolute origin have failed. The items that characterize her (the skeleton, the robe, the scythe, the globe, the hourglass, the balance) can be traced back to the figure of death—the Grim Reaper—that appeared during the Black Plague in Europe (Reyes Ruiz, 2011, p. 52). Although the Grim Reaper is not a female, the figuration of death reached Latin America with Catholic colonization. Claudia Reyes Ruiz notes that several images of death can be traced to the eighteenth century in Mexico (2011, p. 53). However, none were female and can only be considered predecessors of what we now identify as La Santa Muerte. By the 1950s, small cards with Santa Muerte appeared in different parts of Mexico. The local belief was that she had the power to reunite lovers or travelers with their families, as well as protect prisoners against enemies, proving that the veneration of the female death had been brewing among families for decades, only appearing publicly until 2001 when her popularity exploded (Hernández Hernández, 2016, p. 22).

Her long and confusing history and her liminal hybridity make her empowerment even more puzzling. Yet, La Niña Blanca is precisely the embodiment of empowerment that results from the experience of liminal hybridity. That is, a life of lack, ambiguity, and movement.

It is not only that Santa Muerte is a mestiza. Liminality is crucial for the empowerment that she is engendering. Let me explain this further. Santa Muerte is not the only divine entity that is a hybrid or mestiza in Mexico. La Virgen de Guadalupe (the Mexican Virgin Mary, who is part of the symbols of national identity) is also a mestiza. However, given that she is a product of the Catholic Church during colonial times, la Virgen de Guadalupe responds to the moral rules of Catholicism and discriminates against those that oppose that normativity. On the contrary, the liminal existence of Santa Muerte does not tie her to any figure of authority or normative code. She does not discriminate against anyone (gender, color, ethnicity, social class, moral standing)[11]—she is death; she comes to everyone without judgment (Kingsbury, 2020, p. 7), which has allowed the exponential increase of her followers.

Lack of moral norm is the condition of the possibility to transgress limits of all kinds—for example, those of traditional gender roles. Whereas la Virgen de Guadalupe fits the norms of Catholic womanhood, Santa Muerte is not married, is not a virgin, and can enjoy the pleasures prohibited to women by Catholic morality (Kingsbury, 2020, p. 8). Followers shower La Santa with gifts such as alcohol, cigarettes, chocolates, expensive jewelry, money, or anything she might enjoy (see Figure 6.2).

La Huesuda also transgresses the traditional limits of the relationship with authority figures. While Catholic saints and powerful state personalities are in a position of admiration and aspiration (and fear), authors including Yllescas Illescas and Kingsbury note that devotees have a bodily and mirror relationship with Santa Muerte. The devotion to La Santa is a relationship, a connection, an encounter, where followers dress La Santa as they dress themselves, they give her gifts that they enjoy, they dance with her in local events, they see themselves reflected in la Santa at the same time that she reflects herself and her power on them (Yllescas Illescas, 2016, p. 68).

Followers project on La Santa their fears, the violence they experience, the difficulties of living on the edge of the state, the realities of coloniality, the marginalization of neoliberal systems, the effects of patriarchy, and Santa Muerte reflects on them the strength the devotees believe she has (Kingsbury, 2020, p. 18). In this sense, Santa Muerte is also a reflection of the evils of coloniality, which might explain the constant horror she generates among specific sectors of the population—Santa Muerte is a contemporary figure of the Latin American grotesque. As López Get argues, the Latin American grotesque is a movement that seeks to represent the events of horror, disgust, and fear that happen in Latin America (such as rape, abuse, poverty, and violence) as a form of denunciation of the state and power (2015, p. 88). The mirrored and symbiotic relationship between Santa Muerte and her followers permit her to be not only death as such but the reflection of all the violence, discrimination, marginalization, and abuse her devotees experience on the part of the state, the elites, the Catholic Church. In this double twist of la Huesuda's powers, she is created in the image of her followers and then reflects strength on them, generating a cycle of double empowerment (Kingsbury, 2020, p. 9).

These cycles are also possible precisely because of la Santa's mestizaje. Her hybridity is not only the result of the encounters in liminality; there are elements of her that come from the structures of power that are now attacking her, giving her additional powers. Flores Martos has identified that altars become popular as they respond to the needs and demands of their followers. That is, the commercialization of figures, prayers, candles, incense, and other relevant objects is not the product of an institutionalized creed, but of what people want, by supply and demand of the market (2008, p. 60). She is displacing Catholic saints (people go to her instead of the Catholic church), the state justice system (prisoners trust her more than lawyers), and she is using the market while gobbling up its powers to become herself more powerful, making her now a transnational figure that moves with migrants towards the Río Grande—she is a cannibal (2008, pp. 61–62). It is not the case that Santa Muerte is against the Catholic Church or the State, or even neoliberalism; she is not a figure of war against these structures. Nevertheless, she is a grotesque and cannibal figure that devours their power, increasing her followers and empowering them in the process. In contrast, the power of the state and the Church decreases regarding the production of identity and its limits.

The Female Death That Cannot Be Buried

The strategies deployed to bury La Santa have further failed because she is the encounter of death and the female. Although Santa Muerte encompasses elements from Mictecacíhuatl, the Aztec goddess of Mictlán (the ninth level of the underworld) who cares for the bones of the dead, La Santa is also a product of the images that were brought to Latin America through the violence of colonization. In this sense, it is possible to argue that her empowering nature is a response to how women have been culturally produced and treated in Western societies by patriarchal structures such as the state, the Catholic Church, and the capitalist mode of production.

Elisabeth Bronfen argues that Western cultural productions have historically coupled women and death, not only because women have been the "other" of order and stability but because both women and death are representations of liminality. Given that women "are associated with the *polluting* world of biology, with the timebound individual, with *corrupting flesh*, with the *putrescence* of the corpse, with 'bad' death . . . By vanquishing Woman, death is vanquished and viceversa" (1992, p. 199). To effectively vanquish death and the feminine, burial is necessary—the symbolism of a tombstone as a staple of continuity and order—which is fundamentally a masculine activity. However, this is not possible with Santa Muerte precisely because she is female but is not a living woman, she is a skeleton. She is death and cannot be killed, cannot be buried.

Furthermore, in the Mexican Santa Muerte, there is an *encounter* of the female and death in liminal hybridity and, as a result, a myriad of becomings. That is, a double capture derived from an encounter, whereby the entities form a connection where they are moving and changing (Deleuze & Parnet, 1987, p. 2). In the case of Santa Muerte, the feminine is not only a representation of death; she is an encounter of the feminine with death and a double capture that produces a connection where both death and the feminine are moving, flowing, and changing.

The encounters in liminality are multiple. In the same way, Santa Muerte is an encounter of the feminine and death; she encounters others as well—migrants, noncivilized mestizos, indigenous cultures, communities of African descent, members of the LGBTQ+ community, women, etc. The becomings are endless. Considering that liminality in Mexico is not a temporary transition, it could be said that the monstrous, the, and the corrupt, as representations of what lingers in-between space and place encounter with Santa Muerte producing relations that permanently haunt the realities and effects of the Cosmic Race. This haunting is even more terrifying because it shifts, flows, and changes, as does Santa Muerte. As I mentioned, she has no defined origin or identity because she is in a flow of encounters; she responds to no figure of authority. Yllescas Illescas notes Santa Muerte is attractive because there is a lack of orthodoxy, and the imagination of her followers is represented in the varied practices, rituals, and connections with her—practices that are not imposed but only circulated, generating even more encounters (2016, p. 65).

As liminality in Mexico is permanent, so are the hauntings of la Santa. In contrast to the Western practice of masculine burials to put the chaos of women and death to rest, Santa Muerte cannot be buried, not only because she is death but because she is flowing and changing in a permanent liminality that cannot be stopped.

Concluding Remarks

Santa Muerte comprises many elements that make her horrifying and a threat to the policing structures of Mexican identity. She is hybrid and liminal. She is death, and she is feminine. She is a cannibal, and she is grotesque. She is a critique of identity that cannot be formalized, finished, or killed. While identity formation has long been criticized, the horror that Santa Muerte generates lies in that she is the embodiment of a realization and a potentiality of the LatIndigenous: *identity is not the end of the story nor the objective.* Santa Muerte is a reminder that there is potential and power in moving within permanent liminality through the figure of the hybrid. The subtleties of liminal hybridity are found even in the term LatIndigeneity itself, a coupling or mix of multiple identities that transgress the hegemonic idealization of the Indigenous and the Latino. In the interstices opened by the term lies

Figure 6.1. Maestuoso Altar de la Santa Muerte en Puebla, Mexico, photo by Luisa Fernanda Grijalva-Maza.

the potentiality of movement of liminal hybridity–subjectivities that oscillate between identities producing knowledge and creating new and changing ways of existing in this world. This is knowledge produced in liminality, knowledge that moves, oscillates, and thereby eludes the attacks that come from power structures while contesting the hegemonic definitions and limits of identity politics and knowledge production.

Santa Muerte transforms the formal and heavily guarded limits of identity, sedimented by the State and the Catholic Church, into systematically transgressed and cannibalized thresholds. She is the haunting presence of the colonial horrors contemporary societies uphold as the necessary evil of progress and modernization but that, at the same time, we try to forget when materialized in the lives of many marginalized peoples. The haunting presence not only creates disgust and horror because she is a reminder of the past that is in the present but because Santa Muerte devours the power of those that try to police the limits of place, normativity, and safety while empowering the downtrodden, who might, in a turn of events, devour those structures as well. It is no wonder the Mexican state and the Catholic Church try to repress Santa Muerte—she represents LatIndigenous potentiality, spirituality, and a logic that does not demand identity but instead flows through emergent practices.

Figure 6.2. Gifts to Santa Muerte, photo by Luisa Fernanda Grijalva-Maza.

Notes

1. In 2009, the Mexican military destroyed thirty-four altars of Santa Muerte outside Nuevo Laredo, Tamaulipas (La Redacció, 2009).Local authorities justified the raid by stating that Santa Muerte is a saint of Cartel del Golfo.

2. Santa Muerte is also called La Santa, Santísima, Niña Blanca, La Huesuda, La Madrina, etc.

3. In her study of feminine divinities in different regions of the Global South, Matgorzata Oleszkiewics-Peralba notes that Santa Muerte is, in fact, a liminal figure. I draw from Oleszkiewics-Peralba's work and look to understand the productive nature of an encounter between hybridity and liminality.

4. For more images and information about these charts, Las Castas, https://mediateca.inah .gob.mx/islandora_74/islandora/object/pintura%3A2123.

5. To this day, the saying "hay que mejorar la raza" ("we have to improve the race") continues to be expressed in Mexico as the wish to marry "up" (in skin color, education, and socioeconomic position).

6. José Vasconcelos was minister of Education and dean of UNAM in the 1920s.

7. Although Vasconcelos favored artistic productions that exalted our Indigenous past (i.e., representations of Indigenous cultures in the work of Diego Rivera or Alfaro Siqueiros), he also considered that one of the most important obstacles to reach the idealized mestizo was the fact that Indigenous populations had not mixed completely with Spanish blood and culture (Vasconcelos, 2012, pp. 8–12).

8. Authors including Derrida, Butler, Laclau, García Canclini, Bhabba have shown that identity is a discursive production founded on unequal relations of power.

9. In contemporary Mexico, the term "whitexican" is used in social media to allude and ridicule the discriminatory and ignorant behavior of the privileged and powerful sectors of society (a word that plays with the words "white" and "Mexican") (Almanza, 2019).

10. Increasing immigration, transnational adoption, globalization, have shown that race and ethnicity are political categories that function to organize society and institutionalize oppression (Brubaker, 2016, p. 5).

11. For example, there is an important number of altars to Santa Muerte that are led by transexual or transgender people (Yllescas Illescas, 2016, p. 65).

References

Alcalá González, A., & Bussing López, I. (2020). Introduction. In *Doubles and Hybrids in Latin American Gothic*, 1–16. Routledge, Taylor and Francis Group.

Bronfen, E. (1992). *Over Her Dead Body: Death Femininity and the Aesthetic*. Manchester University Press.

Brubaker, R. (2016). The Dolezal affair: Race, gender, and the micropolitics of identity. *Ethnic and Racial Studies*, 39(3), 1–35.

Deleuze, G., & Parnet, C. (1987). *Dialogues* (H. Tomlinson & B. Habberjam, Trans.). Columbia University Press.

Flores Martos, J. A. (2008). Transformismos y Transculturación de un Culto Novomestizo Emergente: La Santa Muerte Mexicana. In M. Cornejo, M. Cantón, & R. Llera (Eds.), *Teorías y Prácticas Emergentes en Antropología de la Religión* (pp. 55–76). Ankulegi.

Fragoso, P. (2011). De la "calavera domada" a la subversión santificada. La Santa Muerte, un nuevo imaginario religioso en México. *El Cotidiano*, 169, 5–16.

Gall, O. (2004). Identidad, exclusión y racismo: Reflexiones teóricas y sobre México. *Revista Mexicana de Sociología*, 66(2), 221–59.

Gaytán Alcalá, F. (2008). Santa entre los Malditos. Culto a la Santa Muerte en el México del Siglo XXI. *LiminaR. Estudios Sociales y Humanísticos*, 6(1), 40–51.

Hernández Hernández, A. (2016). Introducción: La Santa Muerte. Espacios, cultos y devociones. In A. Hernández Hernández (Ed.), *La Santa Muerte. Espacios, cultos y devociones*. El Colegio de la Frontera Norte A.C., El Colegio de San Luis.

Kingsbury, K. (2020). Death is Women's Work: Santa Muerte, a Folk Saint and Her Female Followers. *International Journal of Latin American Religions*. https://doi.org/10.1007/s41603-020-00106-2.

La Redacción. (2009, March 24). Derriba Ejército 34 altares dedicados a la Santa Muerte. *Revista Proceso*. https://www.proceso.com.mx/nacional/2009/3/24/derriba-ejercito-34-altares-dedicados-la-santa-muerte-13917.html.

López Get, A. (2015). Lo Grotesco y el Arte Contemporáneo Latinoamericano. *Reflexiones*, 94(1), 81–96.

Manrique, L. (2016). Dreaming of a cosmic race: José Vasconcelos and the politics of race in Mexico, 1920s–1930s. *Cogent Arts & Humanities*, 3(1), 1–13.

Marcos, S. (2014). La espiritualidad de las mujeres indígenas mesoamericanas: Descolonizando las creencias religiosas. In Y. Espinosa Miñoso, D. Gómez Correal, & K. Ochoa Muñoz (Eds.), *Tejiendo de otro modo: Feminismo, epistemología y apuestas decoloniales en Abya Yala* (pp. 143–60). Editorial Universidad del Cauca.

Oleszkiewics-Peralba, M. (2015). *Fierce Femenine Divinities of Eurasia and Latin America: Baba Yaga, Kālī, Pombagira, and Santa Muerte*. Palgrave MacMillan.

Quijano, A. (2007). COLONIALITY AND MODERNITY/RATIONALITY. *Cultural Studies*, 21(2–3), 168–78.

Reyes Ruiz, C. (2011). Historia y actualidad del culto a la Santa Muerte. *El Cotidiano*, 169, 51–57.

Saldaña Tejeda, A. (2013). Racismo, proximidad y mestizaje: El caso de las mujeres en el servicio doméstico en México. *Trayectorias*, 15(37), 73–89.

Tally Jr., R. T. (2016). Forward: "A Utopia of the In-Between," or, Limning the Liminal. In *Landscapes of Liminality: Between Space and Place* (pp. ix–xv). Rowman and Littlefield.

Vasconcelos, J. (2012). *La Raza Cósmica* (6th ed.). Editorial Porrúa.

Yllescas Illescas, J. A. (2016). La Santa Muerte ¿Un culto en consolidación? In A. Hernández Hernández (Ed.), *La Santa Muerte: Espacios, Cultos y Devociones* (pp. 65–84). El Colegio de la Frontera Norte A.C., El Colegio de San Luis.

CHAPTER 7

La Coyota Perejundia

Moises Gonzales

On June 13, during the feast of San Antonio, located in the Sandía mountains of central New Mexico east of Albuquerque, a group of children gathered along with communities in the village of San Antonio in the Merced de Cañón de Carnué land grant community.[1] Every year the children would watch with excitement the *Ensaya* (dance teaching) *real de los Matachines*. La Viejita Adilia Garcia asked a group of children, why are you all so excited to see the *danzantes*? Many children answered with excitement, "someday I am going to be a danzante. One child answered, "I can't wait to see *la Perejundia-la abuela* (our spirit grandmother) because she is going to give me candy." The elder Adilia answered and began to tell the ancient story of la coyota perjejundia, "many of you have seen la Perejundia during the Matachines Dance at the *fiestas* of San Antonio, San Miguel de Carnué, and San Lorenzo de Cañoncito. She makes us all laugh, gives us candy, and best of all she gives us loving hugs." Our *abuelitos*, our grandparents, used to say it is a blessing to receive a candy as a gift from la Perejundia because she only visits once a year during the feast day. The feast day and la danza is the most special time of the year. It is when all the families from the sierra (mountain communities) get together, and we visit with *primos* (relatives) we haven't seen in a while, such as our family in Colorado. Once in a while, even our primos, *los manitos* (New Mexicans living in nearby states), drive all the way from California and Colorado to come for the big feast. We are told that after the feast day, when all the *familia* has enjoyed the time they have spent together, and the danzantes have finished the procession of putting the Santo back in the church, la Perejundia goes back home to live in her small adobe *chantito* on the top of South Sandía Peak.

Figure 7.1. La Perejundia rests, surrounded by Matachines dancers. San Antonio de Padua fiesta, New Mexico. Courtesy Miguel A. Gandert.

We call the place she lives during the rest of the year as el ponte del Venado, Deer Peak. La Perejundia lives there because it is the highest point in all of La Merced, and from here, she can see Carnuel, San Antonio, and Cañoncito. Yes, from the Poniente del Venado, she can protect, look after, as well as even instigate movidas to make sure we are all taken care of in el Cañón de Carnué. The only thing la Perejundia asks in return for her work during the year is that we all take care of los viejitos, *la comunidad* y *cada uno al otro*. She wants us all to remember our *querencia*, our deep love of home, place, and one another.

La Perejunidia also used to be called la Coyota Perejundia. Let me tell you how this came to be. She is known as a coyota because she was *un india genízara* of Tiwa-Piro pueblo background. Se dice que su abuela left the original pueblo of Carnué during the 1680 Pueblo Revolt along with some of the Tiwas from Isleta pueblo. Several generations later, la Coyota Perejundia was living in the genízaro village of Valencia near Los Lunas and Isleta Pueblo. She wanted to come to la sierra to be back where her ancient abuelas and bis-abuelas came from, and mostly she wanted to be close to their spirits. When the land grant was being resettled after being abandoned because of the raids by nomadic tribes in 1819, la Coyota Perejundia joined to help rebuild San Miguel de Carnué, and she eventually settled within the walled village of San Antonio de Padua. Las viejitas in La Merced always debate and argue what her real name was. They argue whether it was Manuela Padilla, Juliana

Figure 7.2. La Coyota Abuela descending from the Sierra Sandía for her yearly visit for the fiesta de San Antonio. Image of artist and writer Moises Gonzales.

Gutíerrez, María Juana García, or Jacinta Delgado, although it really doesn't matter because we all come from la Coyota Perejunidia . . . She is the *tátara abuela*, the great grandmother to all of us . . . de todo nosotros. . . .

During the early years of establishing the village of San Antonio de Padua, la Coyota became important to sustaining La Merced, *la acequia y la tierra*. She was known as *la curandera*, the traditional healer, and she knew the purpose of all the herbs for healing and where to gather the herbs from around la sierra. She would gather *la cota, la yerba buena, oshá, la tuna de cholla, and harvest sal del lago seco de los Tompiros*, known as Las Salinas today. She would gather *uña de gato* that she would harvest as far as La Placita de La Madera on the north side of the Sandía mountains. In the old days, after the feast of San Miguel de Carnué on September 29, all the able men would leave for the buffalo hunts on the Llano Estacado and would not return until Noche Buena on Christmas Eve. Los Ciboleros (buffalo hunters) would hunt buffalo for months to bring back Carne seca, and more importantly, the buffalo hides used for *tewas* (moccasins) for the whole village, chimales (rawhide war shields), *gamuza* or finely tanned leggings and shirts for the men, skirts, blouses, and shawls for the women. Even the bones were made into buttons and knife handles.

During the early winter months, when the men of the village were gone on buffalo hunts, the village of San Antonio was attacked during the most violent raids by *las naciones* de los apaches, yutas, caiguas, y navajoses. La Coyota Perejundia and all the women would defend the walled villages with a *macana* or club. La Coyota was one of the most fearless woman warriors who would stand on top of the *torreón* violently swinging her macana with

Figure 7.3. La Coyota Abuela Warrior, defending the village from Apache Raids. Artist Moises Gonzales.

her right hand and the elk antler spear in her left hand, defending los viejitos and protecting the children from being taken captive to join other tribes and never to be seen again. It was said that one time, she was so mad that the Apaches were camped on top of the Cerrito Centinela for three days preparing for a raid that she rolled a large *tinaja* pot full of boiling *manteca* grease from frying sopapillas several hundred yards, which exploded at the base of the Cerrito. The small band of Apaches ran off down through the Vallecito de San Antonio and escaped back to the Llano Estacado.

Eventually, the men returned from the llano in time for the celebration of Santo Niño y la Navidad. This was a joyful time with food and the la danza of los Matachines. *El Monarca*, the head dancer, would dance with a special pair of tewas to honor the Santo Niño in thanks for the return of the men and the safety of the women, children, and elderly back home. The people prayed for the return of the cautivos that may have been taken that year. La Coyota Perejundia had El Abuelo visit each of the homes on Noche Buena and spank the children as a blessing and have them dance the *comanchitos* to honor *Santo Niño*. They danced in lines before his altar while these *versos* were sung.

Hey Ya Na . . . Hey ya ni yo
Hey Ya Na . . . Hey ya ni yo

Aquí estoy, Santo Niñito
para cumplir mi promesa,
este Grupo de Comanchitos
te vienen a acompañar

Figure 7.4. El Abuelo and los Comancheros hunting the Buffalo on the Llano Estacado. Artist Moises Gonzales.

Hey Ya Na . . . Hey ya ni yo
Hey Ya Na . . . Hey ya ni yo

Sometimes El Abuelo would get grumpy on *Noche Buena* because he was tired from the buffalo hunts, conducting the business of La Merced all year, as well as tending to the preparation of the *morada* chapel for the upcoming *cuaresma*, the Lenten season, but la Coyota Perejundia reminded him of his *obligación* and *la tarea por la querencia del Las Placitas de Carnué*.

When the Americanos came in 1848, everything changed. There were fewer buffalo on the *Llano Estacado*, and a small group of yutas told stories of the Jicarilla Apaches being held in jails near Mora up north at a place called Fort Union. And down south, los navajoses were held in *corrales* and cages in Bosque Redondo. Small bands of comanches allied with the village of San Antonio dropped off the elderly and children and said they would return if they could outrun the United States army. Los viejitos dicen que los comanches *nunca regresaron por sus niños*. Since their relatives never returned, these comanches were adopted into the village of San Antonio. A small group of apaches settled in El Rito de Coyota, Coyota Springs, as they call it today. La familia Herrera de los apaches still live there on La Merced.

When the Americans came, El Abuelo was in a fight to keep the *ejido* (communal lands) de La Merced and villages intact because they wanted to take everything the village owned. El Abuelo made countless trips to Washington, DC in order to save the land for the community. Finally, after fifty years of fighting for the land, the US Supreme Court ruled that 80 percent of the land would become Forest Service and federal land. The *americanos* fenced off the majority of the land grant from the livestock of the community and kicked out the *borregas, cabras, y vacas* that sustained us. The forest now belonged to outsiders who didn't even know how to take care of it. They fought every wildfire, and the forest got overgrown and sick. And *El Abuelo* spent all his time at the *sala del pueblo* (community land grant hall), fighting *el gobierno* for the community rights to water, land, and culture. La Coyota Perejundia agreed that *El Abuelo* needed to spend most of his time fighting for the rights of La Merced. One day the government came in with bulldozers and tractors to build a large highway through La Merced. The government workers flattened the acequia, the orchards, and the corn fields. La Coyota Perejundia had enough. She told *El Abuelo* to stay fighting los americanos, and she was going to move into the sierra to protect la querencia de Carnué from on high in the spirit world. She ran into her old house in San Antonio and reached into a large *petaca*, and grabbed her dusty macana and elk antler used in the *Comanchería* wars to fight as a Coyota genízara women warrior again. She put on her tewas and shawl, covered her face with fringe from a matachín cupil to be anonymous, and grabbed her medicine bag filled with uña de gato to fight evil and those that do harm to the Cañón de Carnué. She told *El abuelo* she would be in her adobe chantito on top of el Ponte del Venado watching over her grandchildren, but that she would visit them to dance, hug them and give them blessings on the feast of San Antonio, San Miguel, and San Lorenzo. Now at very old age, she also uses her macana and elk antler as canes to walk up the steep mountain. When she has to fight, her warrior genízara woman strength brings her back from the spirit world.

Los viejitos dicen que on very windy days or nights, la Coyota Perejundia wages a spiritual battle to protect la querencia de Carnué, the community, and most of all, her *nietos*, her grandchildren. It is her way of letting us know she is fighting the la "Floresta" (the Forest Service), el gobierno, and all things that work against the future of La Merced. So with her macana and elk horn swinging full force as in her youth and with the fire throwing una de gato flying out of her palm, la Coyota Perejundia will keep us all safe and protect us. They say she is always blowing up the cell phone towers on Cedro Peak with her flame-throwing uña de gato because she understands the problems that come with new technology. She gets upset when she comes down to the village from the ponte del Venado for the fiesta to dance los Matachines, and she sees all the teenagers and adults on their cell phones rather than sharing time with family and community to receive her blessings. She also hates the cell towers at the sala del pueblo,

Figure 7.5. La Coyota Abuela Ascends to the Sierra Sandía to watch her grandchildren for the next year as La Danza de Los Matachines comes to an end for the Fiesta de San Antonio de Carnué. Artist Moises Gonzales.

but she doesn't blow them up because the land grant needs the money from the towers to help pay for the fiestas as well as the land taxes for La Merced.

So next year, when you see la Coyota Perejundia at the fiesta, give her a big hug and let *El abuelo* know you are thankful. Let her know that you are thankful for making us safe for the year and for protecting la querencia de Carnué. If you pay real close attention, at the end of the fiesta when los danzantes are putting up the santo for the next year, look up towards la sierra, and you might see la Coyota Perejundia making her way up the mountain with her macana and elk horn in hand while she looks at you one last time. Don't be sad, remember she will return next year for the fiesta and how joyous it will be to spend time as a family again. Maybe our primos *los manitos* will make it home again for the fiesta all the way from California next year.

Note

1. Genizaro Community land grants were established by Governor Tomás Vélez Cachupín as providing opportunity for Genízaros to acquire land, but also serving a purpose to the colony. Governor Cachupín believed that establishing community land grants for Genízaros was a way to move this landless Indigenous population living in servitude into land ownership. "During those years, Genízaros were living, not only in Abiquiu but also neighboring Ojo Caliente, in Santa Fe, Trampas, Ranchos de Taos, [and] Carnue(l)." (Gonzales, 2020, p. 252).

CHAPTER 8

Iconografía Prohibida / Forbidden Iconography

Lizzeth Tecuatl Cuaxiloa

As a Nahua and Cholultecan artist, my work tries to recover the visual arts and expression of the Cholula people and their roots as a great pottery center in the last five centuries before the conquest. My work presents a reflection that recovers, through abstract and figurative drawings on ceramics, of the Nahua, Mayan, and Zapotec communities.

Truillot (1995) stated that "some Europeans and their colonized students saw in this alleged absence of rules the infantile freedom that they came to associate with savagery, while others saw in it one more proof of the inferiority of nonwhites. We now know that both sides were wrong; grammar functions in all languages" (p.7).

Likewise, the Spanish took advantage of their great skills in handling and knowledge in pottery and forced the Cholula people to reproduce alien and unknown ceramic designs. In conditions very close to slavery, the Cholula people were forced to create what is now known as Talavera. This project developed from the reflection on the importance of contemporary colonialism and how it affects daily life in present-day Mesoamerican indigenous communities.

These ceramic pieces are inspired by the graphic work of historian Alfredo Lopez Austin (2015), a historian who analyzes Mesoamerican religion and worldview. According to him, the Mesoamerican iconography was of vital importance as it was part of its religious rituals and agricultural activities. They were based on their own anthropomorphic and zoomorphic images and the divinization of time, which were the core of Mesoamerica.

Figure 8.1. *Suciedad (Filthiness)*. Zapotec Iconography. Ink over ceramic tile (2018). Photo by Lizzeth Tecuatl Cuaxiloa.

Figure 8.2. *Corazón (Heart)*. Zapotec Iconography. Ink over ceramic tile (2018). Photo by Lizzeth Tecuatl Cuaxiloa.

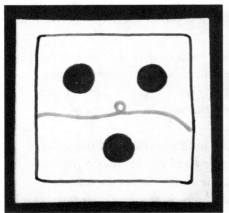

Figure 8.3. *Señor (Man)*. Mayan Iconography. Ink over ceramic tile (2019). Photo by Lizzeth Tecuatl Cuaxiloa.

Figure 8.4. *Muerte (Death)*. Nahua Iconography. Ink over ceramic tile (2019). Photo by Lizzeth Tecuatl Cuaxiloa.

In my work, I claim these images and provide a reinterpretation both figuratively and abstractedly. I aim to make iconographic traditions visible and digestible to the general public and not only to those within academia. Ceramics are the means of artistic expression that links history and culture of almost all the peoples of the world. Through these ceramic pieces, I hope that indigenous communities that do not have access to the written records can get closer or be curious about their indigenous roots that have been neglected, trampled on, and forgotten over the years.

These pieces are made on enameled ceramics, with each symbol illustrated with traditional colors. The clay is the appropriation of the earth and represents the beauty and fragility of the subject itself. It is, in turn, practically indestructible. However, it breaks easily, but there is always a piece, a moment in time, that has precious information.

As a Nahua woman, my art gives me permission to situate myself politically in a historical, social, and political space that has been historically denied and silenced to indigenous people. My work is a form of empowerment that allows me to speak about my own experience about colonialism, ethnocide, racism, machismo, genocide, and other forms of oppression that indigenous peoples have been subjected to for more than five hundred years. It is an honor to be able to bring memory and resistance to my people.

References

López Austin, A. (2015). *Las razones del mito: la cosmovisión mesoamericana.* Ediciones Era.

Trouillot, M. R. (2017). *Silenciando el pasado: El poder y la producción de la Historia.* Editorial Comares.

CHAPTER 9

Making a Living

Saul Ramirez

In 1848, after the signing of the Treaty of Guadalupe Hidalgo, effectively ending the Mexican-American War, the Mesilla Valley would be split by the warring parties. After the Treaty, the land once named La Sierra de los Mansos by tribe that has occupied the Mesilla Valley since long before colonization, today known as the Piro-Manso-Tiwa Tribe who are the preserveres and keepers of the local traditions, histories, and memories vital to this Valley. Having the longest standing petition for federal recognition to still go unrecognized, the Piro-Manso-Tiwa tribe remains faithfully aware of the complex ancestries and migrations which they represent, and it is with this ambivalence that I began this document. The document takes an interesting shape as the archive gives it shape; here emerges the map as the Modern landscape, as a tool for handling and controlling the land, which takes a shape other than that given by the land. In the Southwest, it was the treaty of Guadalupe Hidalgo which would split the Valley along the Rio Grande, cutting between La Sierra de los Mansos to create the Town of Mesilla and the City of Las Cruces at this border crossing where two new nations would be born. The Civil War would break out less than twenty years after the end of this first expansionist war which the US began for the purposes expanding the military occupation of this landscape, a settler colonialism that would throw the local life into disarray (Ray John De Aragon). After the territories changed status, its occupants also changed legal citizenship status, and many had to choose to be either Mexican or American citizens and many locals decided to move to the Town of Mesilla to remain Mexican. There were many disputes in the landscape whose irritation would only exacerbate after the arrival of the Anglo-Americans. Disputes began to

Figure 9.1. View of installation in the Annex from the second floor. Photo by Saul Ramirez.

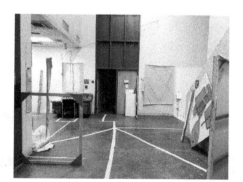

Figure 9.2. View of the installation in the Annex from the eastern entrance. Photo by Saul Ramirez.

Figure 9.3. Installation detail: video tucked behind staircase. Photo by Saul Ramirez.

break out contesting the borders of lands granted by the Spanish occupation, and later, the Mexican grant settlements after the Mexican Independence. The contemporary towns of Las Cruces and Mesilla would be settled beginning with the Doña Ana Bend Colony Grant of 1839, in which the Mexican government granted various "empty" lands along El Camino Real to its citizens to gain better control of the fertile trade economy that existed in the Mesilla Valley. For many of the following years, there was a constant flow of

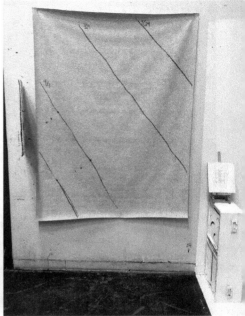

Figure 9.4. Installation detail: Staircase with painted path.   Figure 9.5. Installation Detail: Sun dial. Photo by Saul Ramire
Photo by Saul Ramirez.

migration between the people of Chihuahua, El Paso, and Las Cruces which continues today and which also flowed well into the lower and upper parts of the American continent (Owen, 1999, pp. 15–32). It would be 1850 when New Mexico was annexed into the United States, causing yet another series of disputes over the encroaching US presence. At first, the state was proposed as a slave territory which didn't hold locally due to the fact that slavery had been illegal in the Mesilla valley since 1829 when it was a part of Mexico. This gestured that New Mexico would be loyal to the Union in some regard, although many of its southern and eastern towns had strong Confederate ties because of their proximity to Texas, whose occupation started the Mexican-American War in the first place. In the 1860s, secessionist soldiers succeeded in occupying the Mesilla Valley, along with Southern Arizona as a part of the Confederacy and Mesilla served as its capital. What made this possible were the 1854 negotiations between James Gadsden with Mexican President Antonio Lopez de Santa Anna to purchase the lands of southern Arizona and New Mexico under the suggestion of Senator James Davis, who would later become the first President of the Confederacy, pushing the border south swallowing the town of Mesilla into the annexation of the territories, and in 1854

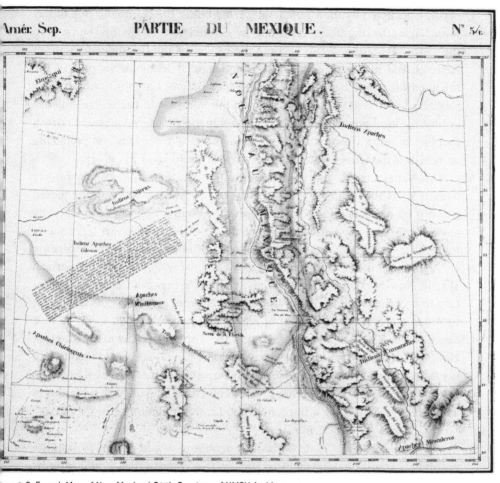

Amér: Sep.   PARTIE   DU   MEXIQUE.   N° 54.

ure 9.6. French Map of New Mexico (1825): Courtesy of NMSU Archives.

the Mexican flag would be ceremoniously taken down, and the United States flag would be raised (Owen, 1999, pp. 35–38).

Gadsden had been a South Carolina Railroad Company executive and was trusted in striking a deal that would allow for the expansion of a transcontinental railroad from the southern states crossing El Paso and Las Cruces, could give the Confederacy passage West under the Rocky Mountains into Arizona, competing with the Union's northern railroads through Santa Fe. Right before the war, the Mesilla Valley experienced an economic boom with the trading and mining communities that set up shop here (Owen, 1999, p. 34). In the 1860s, after the start of the Civil War, many US Army officers in New Mexico would defect to the Confederacy, and the Mesilla Valley would become occupied by the Confederate Army under the command of Colonel John Baylor, having been welcomed by Confederate sympathizers. In 1861, the Town of Mesilla would become the capital of the Confederate State of Arizona, and his harsh occupation would quickly lose him support in the town. Baylor would battle with Union General James Carleton, who was also welcomed at first as a relief from Baylor, but both would use severe violence against the local population as a tactical tool in their warfare, General Carleton specifically using violence against the Indigenous populations and practicing scorched earth tactics as a tool in his warfare (Owen, 1999, pp. 38–47).

This Valley's quick and violent annexation is a history that has scarcely been told; as Ray John De Aragon shows, New Mexico was not conquered without blood as is often said, but rather through a violence motivated by expansionist and capitalist enterprises of US citizens which was reflected by the military tactics they used in the region. The soldiers fought according to their aims, and as De Aragon says, "it was during the Mexican-American War in New Mexico that approaches specifically meant to bring a population to its knees were tried and tested" (De Aragon, 2019, p. 98). It is difficult to not look at these maps without seeing the ambivalence of violence hidden underneath its production. Much of the Tribe, as well as many Mexican Nationals, all Nuevo Mexicanos, would become heavily displaced throughout the following decades as a result of this occupation, and as our local historian Jerry D. Thompson says, "Perhaps nowhere in New Mexico was the military as oppressive and as big a burden on the local population as in the Mesilla Valley" (Thompson, 2008, p. 84).

After the Civil war ended, Mesilla's economy would return to stability around its traditional agriculture and trade economy that would now be connected to the railroads beginning in 1881. By the time these railroads arrived, there was already great community fervor around public education, and in the Mesilla Valley, the community worked hard to establish institutions of education beginning in the late 1870s; a passion that was so intense that the counties of Dona Ana, Lincoln, Grant and Sierra even threatened to secede from New Mexico into a new territory called Sierra, "which would have schooling as its first priority" (Owen, 1999, pp. 70–72). Many leaders emerged in Las Cruces who passionately worked to develop public education for the state of New Mexico, such as Simon Newman, Guadalupe Ascarate, Jacinto Armijo, Martin Amador, and Martin Lohman, and many of them would serve in various civic positions throughout the state to successfully spearhead early education bills at the State level throughout the 1880s. Despite this work at the State, the local difficulties of propping up

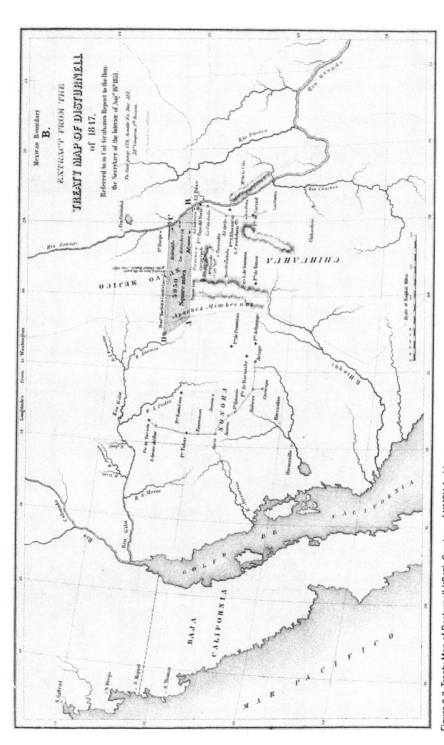

Figure 9.7. Treaty Map of Desturnell (1847): Courtesy of NMSU Archives.

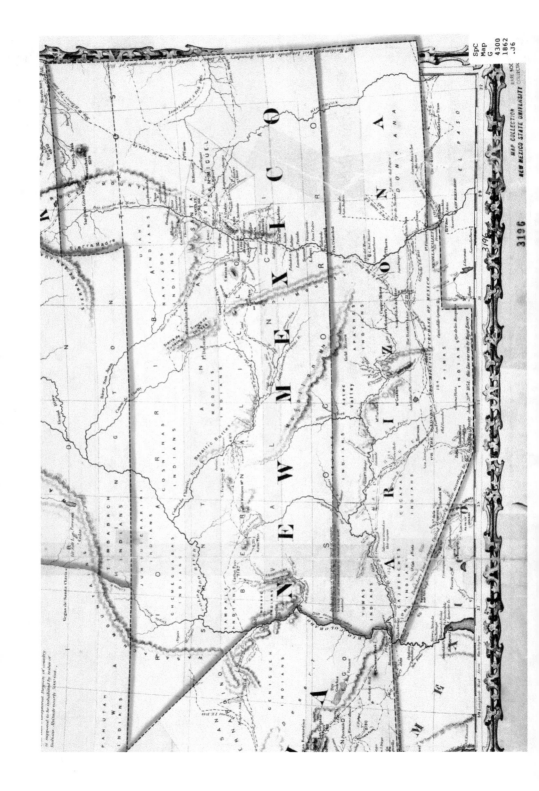

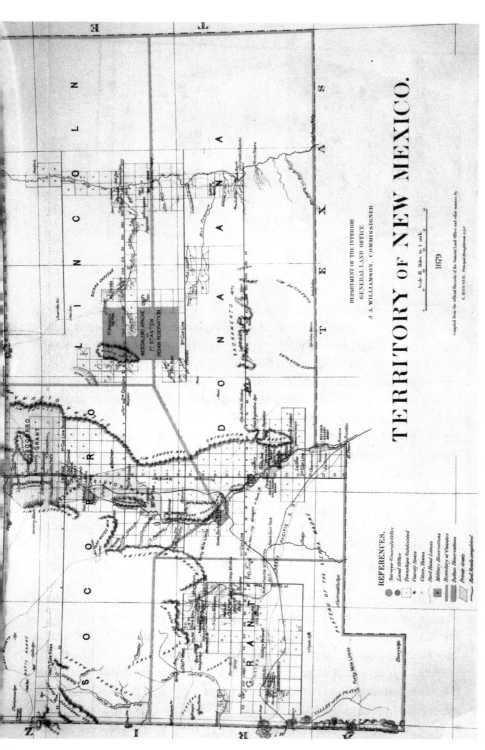

Figure 9.9. J. A. Williamson Map of the Territory of New Mexico (1879): Courtesy of NMSU Archives.

Figure 9.10. Hiram Hadley in front of the first College (1889): Courtesy of the NMSU Archives.

new public schools were tremendous as many of these early schools were too expensive for locals to afford, as well as the church schools would lobby against them, leading early attempts to fail (Owen, 1999, pp. 74–80). It wasn't until the late 1880s that Hiram Hadley, a Quaker man in his fifties, arrived in the Mesilla Valley after his son who moved for medical reasons; having already established three very respected schools in other states, he took charge of reorganizing local efforts towards public education by helping the young city lobby to the state for grants to purchase land to open an Agricultural School. In 1888, Las Cruces College opened to the public. The first college was housed in a small, abandoned building on the corner of Amador and Alameda, teaching elementary, college preparation, and business with the young students being taught at South Ward School (Owen, 1999, p. 50). Under the leadership of Hiram Hadley and Albert Fountain, the town successfully lobbied for funds to build their new agricultural college under the Morillo Act of 1862 and the Hatch Act of 1872, granting them land and funds for the establishment of a variety of public institutions in the states and territories (Van Citters, 2009, p. 1). Fountain would give a passionate address at the House as a part of the legislature that would help the development of public education and equal educational opportunities between sexes and territories (Owen, 1999, pp. 74–80).

"Although agricultural and mechanical arts composed the primary curricula, the newly founded college in Las Cruces also taught liberal arts" (Van Citters, 2009, p. 10) but it was uncertain where this was located. D. W. Williams Hall was built in 1938 as part of a New Deal grant; it was originally built as a gymnasium

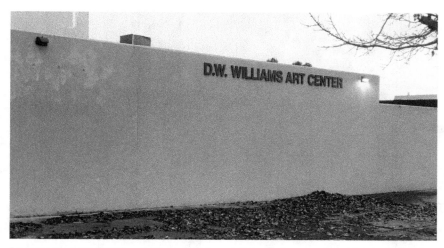

Figure 9.11. Front of D. W. Williams Hall facing North towards University Ave. ca. 2018–19. Photo by Saul Ramirez.

named after Dan Williams, who was the President of the Board of Regents from at the time. A sports enthusiast, Dan Williams wanted his name on the building and would personally persuade the governor of New Mexico to allow him to name the building after him. In 1973, after athletics was fully vacated for the Pan American Center (built in 1968), the building would be remodeled and become transformed into our campus art building (Grumet, p. 339).

Patricia Grumet's *The Buildings of New Mexico State University: NMSU's Building History Vol.1* offers a blurry reproduction from an old newspaper article from the 1930s which advertised: "The Proposal for the projected remodeling of Williams Gymnasium, submitted in 1972 after it was learned the building would be vacated by physical education, states, 'Need for Facilities: Art' is now located in an 1894 two story building which has the second floor boarded up as unsafe, in barracks buildings and in a quonset hut" (Grumet, p. 333).

Williams Hall was poorly designed for the task it had been given; asbestos could be found in the original part of the building; luckily, the Annex where I installed my work was the new part added to Williams Hall in 1983 and was occupiable. *The New Mexico State University Heritage Preservation Plan* excludes Williams Hall as historically significant altogether, with the building only being mentioned once in the document in reference to various construction projects that were happening in the late 1930s and merely as a side note (Van Citters, 2009, p. 22). What this signifies is really that this building lacked value worth preserving.

I reflect here on what art was worth as a space to the university and maybe even in our city as a whole, seen on the building's various forms of inadequacy

Figure 9.12. Installation detail: Locus of the painted path. Photo by Saul Ramirez.

Figure 9.13. Installation detail: Frame gesture. Photo by Saul Ramirez.

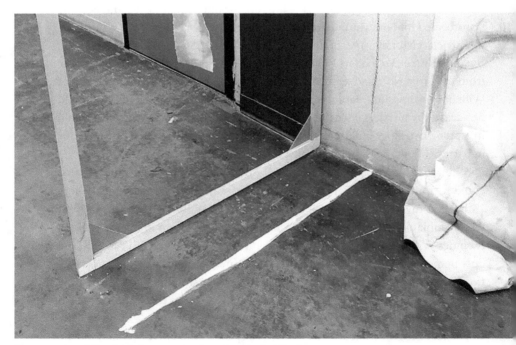

Figure 9.14. Installation detail: Frame gesture floor. Photo by Saul Ramirez.

ure 9.15. Installation detail: Gesture on frame gesture. Photo by Saul Ramirez.

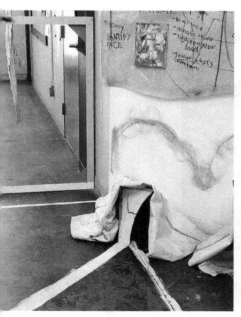

ure 9.16. Installation detail: Propositional cave and path.
to by Saul Ramirez.

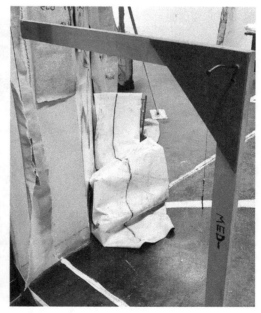

Figure 9.17. Installation detail: Frame gesture, looking
towards the cave and path intersect. Photo by Saul Ramirez.

Figure 9.18. Installation detail: Path turning the corner on the second floor. Photo by Saul Ramirez.

Figure 9.19. Installation detail: Architectural Decay, mixed media sculpture, 4′x4′x2′ along a corner of the path on the second floor. Photo by Saul Ramirez.

Figure 9.20. Installation detail: Path splitting on the second floor. Photo by Saul Ramirez.

Figure 9.21. Installation detail: Path turning the corner on the second floor. Photo by Saul Ramirez.

Figure 9.22. Installation detail: Path snaking north on the second floor. Photo by Saul Ramirez.

Figure 9.23. Installation view: Huitzilopochtli's Carriage (A Map of New Mexico), oil on canvas, 5′x4′ at the end of the path going downstairs towards the northern entrance. Photo by Saul Ramirez.

Figure 9.24. Installation view of the Ascetic's cave. Photo by Saul Ramirez.

Figure 9.25. Installation view of the gallery paintings: (left to right) Desert Speech, oil on canvas, 18"x24", A Manner of Transcribing Clouds, triptych, oil on dyed cotton, and Prometheus' Fire (A Method for Building), Oil on Canvas, 4'x4'. Photo by Saul Ramirez.

and decay I remember when I studied there can be read in the context of a depreciation of the arts by the local and national community. This came to represent other dysfunctions in our institutions with its many symptoms of collapse. There was no issue in scheduling the building for demolition in the summer of 2019 and my BFA show, *Reveries*, alongside the MFA show, *discontinuum*, were the last to take place in that old gymnasium.

I became a student in 2013, and the space was barely capable of housing its own functions. It was a palpable nuisance to all of us who studied there. The demolition of the building would only come about as a result of an intense campaign taken up by the entire department, from students to teachers to administrative staff, in the efforts to pass the General Obligation Bond C in 2016, which allocated $22.5 million for the construction of new art facilities on campus; Williams hall would be scheduled to be demolished the summer of 2019, and this became an opportunity for me to engage the building directly with my work.

I began marking the decay, the biggest symptom being its physical division. The annex where I made and exhibited my work was isolated on the other side of the building where the front office, University Art Gallery and the

ure 9.26. Installation detail: Path from the Annex to the   Figure 9.27. Installation detail: Ascetic's library. Photo by
cond floor. Photo by Saul Ramirez.   Saul Ramirez.

sculpture and ceramic studios were; funnily enough, the side with the annex
was where most people accessed the building since it faced campus as well as
a large parking lot the front office facing the main road. Visitors would stop by
and often ask me, or other students and teachers who taught on that side, for
directions to the office, and I would break out into a performance of pointing
and describing how they could circle around through the patio or if they're
able, by going up the stairs, and circle back down the other side.

As part of a critique, I spoke about turning the room I was allowed to use
as a studio into an installation where I would enact a migration between
the gallery and the annex; when the problem of the ableist structure of the
building, I had to rethink the relationship between my work and my audience in the space. I sought to mitigate the issue by emphasizing the failure
of the space and decided to paint white lines on the floor with a paint made
of a mix of gesso and chalk which led from one side to the other via two
different paths. But because the path which led to the gallery had to pass
through the sidewalk of a business on campus, (and I also failed to ask
permission to do it), I was asked to clean the chalk line with the threat of
not being allowed graduate if I couldn't. The work was about my active

presence in "my studio" for the majority of the semester, mostly for two very practical reasons. The first was that the previous semester, my financial aid ran out and I could no longer afford to take any unnecessary credits. I had finished all my studio credits and so I had no space to work; I set up in a small "unused" room in the annex which led to two other rooms (the grad kitchen and the gallery photo room which people needed to access) where I began to work on objects which I would display in the room and outside in the annex. I was mostly I my chair writing, picturing, building, slowly moving the installations outside into the annex where a ritual of internalization and externalization took place; I was able to interact with people, connect with them and ask them to connect with me. And because my request for gallery space did not meet my needs for migrating my work there gave me the second reason to stay, leaving my studio as an installation in the annex. In the Gallery, I hung a series of abstract, formalist paintings which I had finished the semester prior which had become an exhaust of my economy, a type of waste.

As I worked, the building became an extension of my body, like a dark, cavernous mirror where I would get in touch with its economy, with its channels of value, its paths of desire, and an expression that plugs me into the architecture.

It was as much a public engagement for me as it was a private claim for territory. It was an attempt at recognizing something ambiguous and ambivalent in me as the building encases us in rooms that become little homes for our practice, a place to find our artistic affirmations that folded into social ones.

I used the space to propose some questions:

1. How does one start?

I propped up my ideas,
                I counted

up
what I had
                An examined critique of myself

                                A reevaluation (to classify
                                what was there and what
                                wasn't)

2. How does one continue?

I moved (orbited and spun
in place) a story
I found the cycles of my
creative economy, the
churning of its things:
moved, displaced, managed
like a home, what my
body was yearning for
all along

ETYMOLOGIAS: ECONOMIA
Greek, oikos+nemien
(home)+(management)

CUERPO
Latin, corpus
Proto-Indo-European, *kwerp-
(body, form, appearance, person,
life)

CIENCIA
Latin, scientia
(knowledge, expertness)

ARTE
Latin, ars
(artwork, practical skill)

PROPOSICION
Latin, proositionem, pro+ponere
(a setting forth, statement,
presentation, representation)

processed by architectures

en otras lenguas

Figure 9.28. Generative Geometry, diptych, oil on raw canvas. Photo by Saul Ramirez.

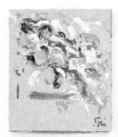

Figure 9.29. A Manner of Transcribing Clouds, triptych, oil on dyed cotton. Photo by Saul Ramirez.

Figure 9.30. Huitzilopochtli's Carriage (A Map of New Mexico), oil on canvas, 5'x4'. Photo by Saul Ramirez.

Figure 9.31. Installation view from the southern entrance. Photo by Saul Ramirez.

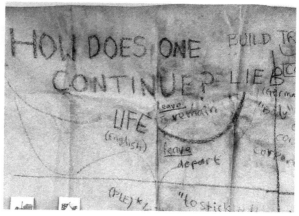

Figure 9.32. Installation detail: Proposition wall with scraps and half of Generative Geometry diptych. Photo by Saul Ramirez.

Figure 9.33. Installation detail: Proposition wall with etymology notes and question, "HOW DOES ONE CONTINUE?" Photo by Saul Ramirez.

Figure 9.34. Installation detail: Proposition wall with scraps, framed photograph, and etymological notes. Photo by Saul Ramirez.

Figure 9.35. Installation detail: Symbol of architectural power made of a doorframe fragment. Photo by Saul Ramirez.

I marked my presence

lines

trajectories

locations

con ciencia

I followed faithfully

yo tengo fe en mi procesco

y este edificio, segregated by its own functions, *las marque*

these rooms of laughing light

        cascading over walls
        speaking into being

organizations of
material and space.

boundaries that
motivate a desire to
transcend its organs

traps of
its mediums

        and compositions

In my occupation, space pushed up tightly against my skin, pressures of geometry which I had to navigate; I give it a name, to the land, a measure. I became the dense and opaque accumulation of organs plugged directly into this environment. This building functions as a supplement for my presence in the movements that it sheltered as it guided them, hopefully somewhere better.

El movimiento es una apertura, boca y ojo; soft edge becoming a hard line, transitioning through them in the subtle forms of violence and generosity to which this possibility belongs.

Me occupe.

Poseida, todo se exterioriza, gestos son mapas, tensions the institution hangs on: tensiones de privilegio, tensiones de fuerza; made of currencies, a flow it maintains in its withholding, machines of a disempowerment they were built to eradicate.

In working in the annex, I recognized that I was given an allowance; I was *granted* a space to occupy and work, which reflected my indebted condition. At times felt like I was *taking advantage of the institution*. Power and its acknowledgments are entangled things. Desire and promise filled these halls in the diluted forms of dream and fantasy; I mean, what else could art be for? What else could education be for? These walls were safety and refuge, but they were also the stubborn concrete that stifles my roots. There was an empty room I was looking to fill, mimetic connections which I was eager to make——so many forgotten histories that I may have never had access to, stories I may never have cared for had I been elsewhere, which makes me wonder what I've lost in being here instead. My mother often reminds me how much better it is to be on this side of the border and that I should be grateful; when she hears my critiques of this country, she believes I am not, and so I have been made aware of another flesh which the edge of my words was running against.

This place was my resource (*mi recurso*), my mode of operation. I am still paying the university the money I came to owe them because I ran out of financial aid; my degree is still on hold, but that's economics, I guess; even beyond this fact, there was nothing I've gained that came without debt; nothing came without all those forms of generosity and love I've received *el amor de nihez*, a love I have continued to receive in the genuine patience and attention given to me by my peers and mentors—my friends and family who have allowed me to take excessively ambiguous amounts of space and time in the search of some excessively ambiguous desire which could be going nowhere. *Con su fe, me confundo.*

Figure 9.36. Installation detail: Ascetic's cave in the Annex and the staircase. Photo by Saul Ramirez.

Figure 9.37. Installation detail: Path leading towards the avenue of the dead. Photo by Saul Ramirez.

Figure 9.38. Installation view of the Ascetic's room. Photo by Saul Ramirez.

Figure 9.39. View of Sun Dial installation with sun beam crossing it. Photo by Saul Ramirez.

Figure 9.40. View of the Annex staircase with beams of light crossing it. Photo by Saul Ramirez.

Figure 9.41. Light from the windows projecting against t staircase. Photo by Saul Ramirez.

Figure 9.42. Installation detail: Path fork with cave, frame sture, and avenue of the dead. Photo by Saul Ramirez.

Figure 9.43. Installation detail: Path forking towards the eastern entrance. Photo by Saul Ramirez.

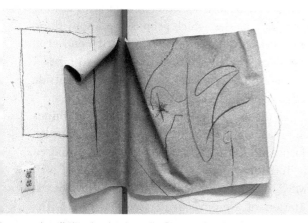

ure 9.44. Installation sketches in studio. Photo by Saul Ramirez.

Figure 9.45. Installation sketches in studio. Photo by Saul Ramirez.

ure 9.46. Installation sketches in studio. to by Saul Ramirez.

Figure 9.47. Installation sketches in studio. Photo by Saul Ramirez.

Figure 9.48. Installation detail: Ascetic's study, symbol of architectural power. Photo by Saul Ramirez.

Moving downward, making things felt like a desperate search for something impossible; I opened up into many points like a cactus; hardened against the drought; I desired to make my mom proud, to impress my peers and professors, to honor my friends and loved ones as well as to honor myself and take pleasure in my work. I desired so much for release and catharsis, but at the end of the show, after I took it all down, I sank into a long depression, feeling that my labor was unfruitful and empty; I could not understand where I was or where I was going. I longed for something more; I longed to go back to some mythical place deep in my body. I desired deeply to go home.

Maybe this is why I began to look at maps: a search for a place and for a way to manage these excesses. The world around me becomes a series of measures, facts, and anthropological detachments. I dug into libraries seeking comfort in the ascetic simplicity of its aisles, which promised me something real beyond the walls of the university, something ancient. At the end of it, I began to doubt the very umbilical functions they were meant to take—I doubted the feasibility of applying my desires to the organs of society outside these walls, and I doubted I could have an art career.

Such is the silence lurking in the establishment of an institution; things that are covered over and left invisible for the sanitation of its cosmic order. Erasures, like the names of Jacob and Bertha Schanblin, whose one hundred acres of land was sold to the Territory of New Mexico for "one dollar," as it says in the deed allowing NMSU to be established in 1889 as the "Agricultural College and Agricultural Station of New Mexico" (Grumet, p. 13). The Schanblin name seems to appear nowhere in the landscape today, now like the name of Dan W. Williams returns to the earth with his building, like the many names of the Manso people whose names are still audible when the wind kicks up the dust.

Forgotten agreements, names, and languages sink beneath the present tense of our earthy ambitions, and it has me saying prayers in foreign tongues so I can justify myself. All I desired was a beautiful interaction (in that decaying space I lived in), the way a child desires attention from an absent father (or an overworking mother). I am still at odds with myself and those mythologies at the foundation of my being; I still mourn those things that my body was constructed on top of. In full awareness of its certain and necessary death, I tried to honor the life and spirit of this building the way it honored mine once by housing it, even if I did so a little inadequately.

No se que sangre cone por mis venas.

No se de que tierra estoy hecha. No se mi genero, no cosco mi patria; no se de mi padre ni de lo que quiero comer.

Yo se que este edificio fue armado de ladrillos de cemento. Como cemento son mis deudas, imposible de pagar, escritas en letra latinas, dichas en lenguas europeas.

Yo habito estos cuartos como mi espiritu habita mi cuerpo: como el material que ocupa el espacio y que el tiempo derrumba.

Aqui yo escribo estas letritas para reconocerme; escribo este documentito para acordarme, para dejar mi marca y para que me acuerden: en estas paredes vacias y en estos cuartitos secos dejare la prueba de mi existencia echo arena.

Yo se que esto va a desaparecer con los pasos del sol, con el rostro del edificio y la estructura de mi memoria. Enves de cemento quisiera usar ladrillo de adobe pero quedo pocho, vacio, y fragmentado. Para regresar a mi patria necesito hallar mi lengua materna;yo tome una close de espanol mi ultimo semestre; fue una decision practica para graduarme rapido per tambien era para poder practicar a leer y escribir en espanol.

Por primera vez, le empece a decir a mi mama que somos indigenas sin tribu; nos queda es recordar nuestras lenguas mas antiguas. Un nuevo recurso para mi practica artistica que se hico negocio academico e economico. Busco abundancias lejanas, amores viejos y valores eternos en mis archivos corporales.

Calling myself "Native" opens up my heart like a wound as deep as my dislocations, a gap that bleeds when I would sit in a Native American Art History class with the guilty feeling that it was not my history I was learning, that I was an outsider looking in. I was born in El Paso and grew up in Juarez and Albuquerque, and came here to study in this strange, ambivalent town, and I found myself lost, drawing on concrete floors, not realizing I should be breaking through them instead, that they were in the way of the

Figure 9.49. Installation detail: Frame gesture, charcoal sign. Photo by Saul Ramirez.

Figure 9.50. Installation detail: The ascetic's desk. Photo by Saul Ramirez.

Figure 9.51. Installation detail: Corner altar in Ascetic's cave. Photo by Saul Ramirez.

Figure 9.52. Installation detail: Corner altar in Ascetic's cave. Photo by Saul Ramirez.

Figure 9.53. Installation detail: Corner altar in Ascetic's cave. Photo by Saul Ramirez.

Figure 9.54. Installation detail: Corner altar in Ascetic's cave. Photo by Saul Ramirez.

Figure 9.55. Installation detail: Path and wall gestures on the second floor. Photo by Saul Ramirez.

Figure 9.56. Installation detail: Path and wall gestures on the second floor. Photo by Saul Ramirez.

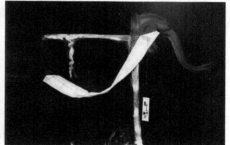

Figure 9.57. Installation detail: Path and wall gestures on the second floor. Photo by Saul Ramirez.

Figure 9.58. Installation detail: Path and wall gestures on the second floor. Photo by Saul Ramirez.

Figure 9.59. *Corner Altar in Ascetic's Cave*, mixed media installation, 6'x4'x3'. Photo by Saul Ramirez.

Figure 9.60. *White Fire,* Mixed media installation, 4'x3'x3'. Photo by Saul Ramirez.

Figure 9.61. Annex staircase with the evening sun com-   Figure 9.62. Light in the Annex in the evening.
ing in through the windows. Photo by Saul Ramirez.   Photo by Saul Ramirez.

roots I was searching for. I have felt at home and unsettled here. As I weave
this narrative, I hope not to cover other significant things that get pushed
down by dual forces of desire and shame: empty memories built out of the
distance which has grown in mi propia familia due to border crossings,
deaths, and economic conditions. The distances I've traversed in my departures, departures from home in the form of academic classisms, which I
confuse with the desire for progress (whatever that may be). Those splits
produced in those moments like when mi propia madre casually called
homophobia and misogyny a part of nuestra cultura. What do I leave,
what leaves with me? I am haunted by those things I cannot know; gaps
that develop in the process of coming out to myself as lo que sea, strange
identities that mark and measure the distances I make to keep myself safe
from other's gaze; gaps that are measured out in legal documents and blood
quantums which say better than myself who I am. There is so much to be
said about what Latinidad erases from Indigeneity, and this document is
only a beginning.

References

De Aragon, R. J. (2019). *New Mexico in the Mexican-American War*, The History Press.

Disturnell, J. Extract from the Treaty Map of Disturnell of 1847, from US Senate Executive Document 121, 32nd Congress, 1st Session. Philadelphia: P. S. Duval, 1851. New Mexico State University Library Special Collections, G3701, F2 1851 .G73.

Grumet, P. *The Buildings of New Mexico State University: NMSU's Building History vol.1.*, New Mexico State University Space Facility Management.

Johnson & Ward. *Johnson's California, Territories of New Mexico and Utah*. New York: Johnson and Ward, 1862. New Mexico State University Library Special Collections, G4300 1862 J6.

Owen, G. R. (1999). *Las Cruces New Mexico 1849–1999: Multicultural Crossroads*, Red Sky Publishing Co.

Roeser, C. Territory of New Mexico. Washington, D.C.: General Land Office, 1879. New Mexico State University Library Special Collections, G4320 1879, U5.

Thompson, J. D. (2008). *New Mexico Territory During the Civil War*, University of New Mexico Press.

Van Citters, K., Cherry, E., Dodge, W. A., & Sawyer, T. L. (2009). *New Mexico State University Heritage Preservation Plan Vol. 1*, Van Citters Historic Preservation.

Vandermaelen, P. Partie du Mexique, No. 54, from Vandermaelen's Atlas Universel. Brussels: Ph. Vandermaelen, 1825. New Mexico State University Library Special Collections, G4320 1825, V3.

PART II

Hazme Caso: Memoir, Poetry, and Stories

CHAPTER 10

Curse of the Zamora Girls
Unveiling Familial Ghost Stories for Survival

Bianca Tonantzin Zamora

Your body remembers
The whispers of the muxeres who came before you
They are the songs of the Zamora girls—cautionary tales
The mamis, primas, tías, abuelas, and bisabuelas
Their memories live in your body too.
In your hair
In your bones
In your dreams
Your hxstories move with the wind and surpass fronteras

Your body remembers
How the Zamora girls saved you when you were alone with men
You felt a magic lift you as ran out of the room
Ran and hid the way they did in Mexico years ago
When dozens of men came to their homes
Hungry with guns and horses and rape
Ready to claim blood and brides
They hid under the floorboards
And were passed through neighboring towns for survival

Your body remembers
How men in family albums are monsters painted pretty in fairytales
How the Bracero Program was a racialized and gendered war that left
    womxn famished

How your great-great-grandfather kidnapped young girls like you
How their blood was shed among mountains, and everyone knew
How the curse of the Zamora girls and the howls of las lloronas would follow
    for generations
How when you dance, the scent of Papa Salvador's sins stains the floor
How you, too, taste so much blood

Your body remembers.
How comadres nurtured bruises behind closed doors
How the Zamora girls begged *to never let a man treat you like mierda*
How you would be the one to break the curse
How you would be *mejor sola que mal acompañada*
How you would be smarter because their cuentos warned you
How you would not be like your mami with hands crushing her throat,
Like your aunties who were shoved in closets with guns in their faces,
Like your grandmother whose bloody body was left on the floor to rot
Like your great-grandmother who ran and escaped those men on horses

Your body screams:
Do not set foot in the revolving door!
You're a Brown, beautiful, brilliant, bold, queer baddie
And still . . . so foolish
To think that the revolving door would burn to a crisp
To forget that ghosts move across borders and generations
That these stories are rooted in colonial violence
How you, too, were called "whore" by the one you loved
You, too, dance with the memories
And they live in your flesh

My love, let your body remember and never forget
The power that runs through the Zamora girls
That grueling fires also mean bountiful rebirths
That you come from a lineage of luchadoras
That your tongue and song and joy and pen are your greatest weapons
That you hold magic in your palms and can rewrite the story
That you, too, dream with the Zamora girls
Dream of possibilities of a new womxnhood—of a new system

Of a mundo where colonial curses and cabrones find home in the grave.

CHAPTER 11

And He Whispered, "Yolanda, Yolanda"

Spencer R. Herrera

This is a story about a family and
as there is a ghost involved, you
might call it a ghost story. But every family is a ghost story. The dead sit
at our tables long after they have gone.
—MITCH ALBOM (P. 6)

Papa was a rollin' stone/
Wherever he laid his hat was his home.
—THE TEMPTATIONS

The border has a way of erasing history. When erasing it proves too difficult, altering it will do just fine. The changing of border markers and land ownership and the movement of people in all directions create multiple histories which defy the idea of an "official history." Having one official history to explain many different points of view often fails in answering key questions about the past because recorded history does not always match collective memory. Those who distort or forget history say we crossed the border. Those who remember it say the border crossed us. The discrepancy lies in our inability to agree on how we name things. One map names the river that demarcates half of the southern border between the US and México, the Río Grande. Another calls it el Río Bravo. The Apache, Diné, and Pueblo people surely have their own name for it in their respective languages. So many names for one body of water that, for stretches between El Paso and southern New Mexico, sits as a dry bed of sand for half of the year. There could not be a better metaphor for US-México border history than a river with more names than the depth of feet. Yet every year, people drown in it, underestimating its swirling current and pockets of dark, deep water. History is not unsimilar; it can seem simple and calm on the surface, but complexities and undercurrents run deep.

Texas is not a lone star state, as it's often portrayed in popular culture. On the contrary, official Texas history claims that six flags have flown over Texas (Spain, México, France, the Republic of Texas, the Confederacy, and the United States of America). Such official history, however, is as muddy as the waters of the Río Grande, serving as a tool to colonize the historical record and the people who have lived in this region for generations. The perpetuators of a mythical official history want us to forget that border people in south Texas and northern México were once a nation unto themselves. The writers of official history purposely omit that there was once a seventh flag that flew over Texas: The Republic of the Río Grande, which included the states of Coahuila y Texas, Nuevo León, and Tamaulipas with its capital along the Río Grande in Laredo. What could be a bigger ghost story than a people without history? What could be more haunting than an entire nation of Chicanos, Mexicanos, and Indigenous communities who were erased from existence?

Ghosts are something that we imagine to exist but lack the evidence to prove that they do. Herein lies our conflict: If we are unaware of our people's history, then it is next to impossible to imagine how we existed precolonization before we became Mexican Americans. In truth, we did not cross the border, nor did it cross us. We are the border. It lies within us. People, not maps, define nations and imagined communities. As the myth of Aztlán tells us, one day, the people who inhabited that land will return to reclaim what was theirs. This process begins with reclaiming our stories. Many of our elders learned to conceal their family's traumas to protect their loved ones from the pain they bore and witnessed. Their stories *are* ghost stories. For ghosts are not just disembodied souls but disembodied stories. If our spirit relatives haunt us upon their return it is not to invoke fear but to provoke our memories of them. They want their stories told, for their untold history is what haunts them and us. As such, it is our job to recover these stories before they are lost to erasure. To fail to recover these stories is to succumb to the last step of colonization. For without stories, we have no identity that is unique to us.

The process of decolonization begins within the family by asking our elders to remember and share with us, albeit painfully, the stories that define them. We cannot give up the ghost of colonization until we engage with the ghosts that call out to us. And when they call, we must answer. This is what my mother did years ago when my grandfather's ghost called out to her. Like

Figure 11.1. Consuelo Mejía.
Courtesy Spencer R. Herrera.

most ghost stories, the story is not just about the ghost's appearance but what makes their presence haunting. In my family's case, it was the years of so much buried painful history that further colonized our existence. This story is my attempt to remember and reclaim our presence in this country, on both sides of the border, where we have always belonged. Decolonization begins at home within the confines of our stories.

This ghost story, although taking place in 1993, has roots that weave through generations of family history. If family stories are ghost stories and decolonization begins in the home, then there is no one in my family who reminds me more of home than my grandmother, Consuelo Mejía Salazar. Unfortunately, however, Grandma wasn't much of a storyteller. But how I wish she were, for she had some stories to tell. Maybe that is why she preferred not to reflect on the past, because it would force her to remember too many memories of pain and suffering. So instead of reminiscing about yesteryear, when a loved one would visit, she would simply ask, "Are you hungry?" Just as you started to reply, she would rock herself off her favorite chair with a view to the front porch, and straight to the stove, she would go, saying, "let me warm you

Figure 11.2. Agustín Caffarel. Courtesy Spencer R. Herrera.

up something to eat." There were always beans and rice, often accompanied by carne guisada or fideo con pollo. As long as she was cooking and feeding you or playing the piano and singing church hymns, or watching her favorite novela, then she didn't have to engage in storytelling about the past.

Over the years, as the family stories leaked out from a tío or distant primo, I began to understand why my grandmother preferred to leave the past behind. For many Chicano families like mine who suffered through poverty, discrimination, and intra- and extrafamilial violence, family history was not to be cherished and remembered but rather slowly forgotten through the passage of time and with each dying elder. There was too much pain for them to look back. It was better to look forward.

Many years after my grandfather had passed away, and wanting to know more about who my grandparents were, I asked my grandmother how she and my grandfather met. She kept her answer short, "we met at a dance." Nudging her for more details, I asked why they got married. She did not have to reflect long, easily recalling her youth, talking about herself in the third person as my grandmother often did, "Grandma used to like to dance a lot. And your grandfather, he was a good dancer. That's why I got married to him, I wanted to dance all my life." And they did get married, and the dancing continued, although he did so without her. Grandpa even won a dance contest at the famous Pan American Ballroom in Houston's Northside neighborhood. The prize—a sewing machine, which he took home to his wife, where she cooked, cleaned, and

Figure 11.3. Consuelo and Lino Salazar. Courtesy Spencer R. Herrera.

looked after their children. Her dream of dancing all of her life never materialized. Hidden in those day-to-day routines of raising a family were many
memories that most in my family prefer to leave unspoken. But I have memories, too, and they have led me to slowly uncover some of my family's secrets,
especially those surrounding my maternal grandfather Lino Salazar.

As a young man in his twenties, my grandfather served as a merchant
marine. His work took him across the Atlantic Ocean to different port cities. He eventually made his way back to Galveston, Texas, the island where
my grandmother was born and raised. At one point in time, Galveston was
the largest city in Texas, with a thriving port industry. Galveston is where
my grandparents met, married, and started a family. They had six children.
The first child, Jorge, was stillborn. My grandmother (his mother) and
great-grandmother had him buried in the historic Broadway Cemetery in
Galveston. All of my grandparents' children, including baby Jorge, were given
my grandfather's last name of Salazar.

Grandpa, although thoroughly Mexicano, did not have the typical build
or appearance of the average Mexican man per the public imagination. He
was roughly six feet tall, with a slim build, and had a light olive complexion. I once remember, when I was an adolescent, him telling me that he was
French. At the time, I did not make much of his comment as I did not know
about the French occupation of México and subsequent French immigration and presence in the state of Veracruz. It would be several years later

when I would become interested in my family's history and origin and how they influenced my Chicano identity.

A few years after my grandfather had mentioned to me that he was French, I went on a trip with my grandmother to Puebla to visit relatives. While there, I remember different people asking my grandmother, "¿Cómo está Agustín?" and "Cómo le va a Agustín?" I knew of no Agustín in my family, and so I asked my grandmother who was this Agustín about whom people were inquiring. She simply replied, "That's your grandfather," and left it at that. Naturally, more thoughts of curiosity and questions came to mind. "But I thought his name was Lino," I said confusingly, prodding her for more information. My grandmother, too reluctant to provide enough words to compose a story, simply said that when he came to the US, he took the name of Lino Salazar so he could work legally in the country without fear of being deported. Over time and through conversations with several relatives, including my grandfather when he was alive, and through my own research, I slowly began to uncover hidden information about my grandfather's secret past.

My grandfather was born in Orizaba, Veracruz. His birth name was Agustín Caffarel Escudero. His father, also named Agustín Caffarel, was originally from the "Bassen Alps" region of southeastern France, according to the SS *Monterey* ship manifest on which the elder Agustín boarded in Veracruz and crossed through Ellis Island on a return trip to France in the year 1919. With the stories, documents, and origin of the last name all serving as evidence, it is likely that they were Catalan from the French side of that region shared with Spain.

In order to live and work in the US, my grandfather, Agustín Caffarel Escudero, assumed the identity of Lino Salazar. None of his children ever knew this history. It remained a family secret that was probably withheld from them to protect them from any legal problems. They all bore the last name Salazar never knowing they were actually Caffarel. Although my grandfather passed away some time ago, he now has great-grandchildren with the name of Salazar.

I learned many things during my childhood and adolescence about my Mexican culture and identity from my grandfather, although not by direct teachings, but through quiet observation and a lot of listening. I learned that México is a nation full of regional identities and that each of them contributes to the creation of a beautiful country rich in culture and history to which we Chicanos are connected and belong. Every time we went out to eat at a Mexican restaurant, my grandfather remade that connection with the strangers who served us. My grandfather loved to speak to the meseras in Spanish

LIST OR MANIFEST OF ALIEN PASSENGERS FOR THE UNITED [STATES]

List ___

ALL ALIENS arriving at a port of continental United States from a foreign port or a port of the insular possessions of the United States, and all aliens arriving at a port of said insular possessions from a foreign port, a port of continental United States. This (said) sheet is for the listing of

S. S. _____ MONTEREY

Passengers sailing from Vera Cruz, Mexico _____ June 28th 1919 _____, 191__

No.	Family name	Given name	Age	Sex	Head-tax status	Calling or occupation	Able to — Read / Read what language	Nationality (Country of which citizen or subject)	Race or people	Last permanent residence Country / City or town	The name and complete address of nearest relative or friend in country whence alien came	Final destination State / City or town
1	BODY	WILLIAM A.	45	M S	MERCHANT	Yes English	Yes England	English	Mexico Vera Cruz	AGUILA OIL CO. 17 Moreno St. Vera Cruz, Mex.	Eng. Southampton
2	CAFFAREL	AGUSTIN	50	M M	MERCHANT	Yes French	Yes France	French	Mexico Orizaba	Pedro Caffarel, Brother Orizaba, Mexico	France
3	CAFFAREL	MARIA	26	F M		Yes French	Yes France	French	Mexico Orizaba	Eith Husband # 2	France
4	CARRETANY	ALBERTO	38	M M		Yes	Yes Spain	Spanish	Mexico Mexico City	Residence 64 Mesones 156, Mexico City, Spain	
5	CAMARGO	JOSEFINA	30	F S	SERVANT	Yes Spanish	Yes Mexico	Mexican	Mexico Mexico City	Mrs. A. L. De Camargo, Mother Balderteina 136, Mexico City	N.Y. New York
6	FLORES	MARIA D.B.	25	F	DRESSMAKER	Yes Spanish	Yes Mexico	Mexican	Mexico Mexico City	Jose Ballesteras, Brother Estanco Hombres 35, Mexico City	N.Y. New York
7	PARDO	ALFONSO S.	35	M S	REPORTER	Yes Spanish	Yes Mexico	Mexican	Mexico Mexico City	Rosa Pardo, Mother	N.Y. New York
8	PETISME	SALVADOR	39	M M	MERCHANT	Yes	Yes Spain	Spanish	Mexico Mexico City	Residence 71 Bel Pino 273 Mex. City	N.Y. New York
9	PETISME	VIOLET G.	34	F M		Yes Spanish	Yes Spain	Spanish	Mexico Mexico City	Alfonso Herrera, Mexico City	N.Y. New York
10	PETISME	SALVADOR	6	M S		No	No Spain	Spanish	Mexico Mexico City	Eith Husband #8	N.Y. New York
11	PETISME	JORGE	4	M S		No	No Spain	Spanish	Mexico Mexico City	Eith Parents # 8 & 9	N.Y. New York
12	PETISME	EMMA	6	F S		No	No Spain	Spanish	Mexico Mexico City	Eith Parents # 8 & 9	N.Y. New York
13	RODRIGUEZ	OTON	29	M S	MERCHANT	Yes Spanish	Yes Spain	Spanish	Mexico Tezapa	Agustin R. Oberino, Brother 3 Lobrc To. Tepaspa, Mex.	N.Y. New York
14	RIVERA	DOLORES C.	32	F M		Yes Spanish	Yes Mexico	Mexican	Mexico Tampico	Mrs. C. M. Cortina, Mother Tampico, Mexico	Can. Torontork
15	RIVERA	GUADALUPE	2	F S		No	No Mexico	Mexican	Mexico Tampico	Eith Mother # 14	Can. Torontork
16	SANCHEZ	ISABEL	23	F S	NURSE	Yes Spanish	Yes Mexico	Mexican	Mexico Tampico	Eith Mrs. Rivera, # 14	Can. Torontork
17	TAYLOR	JOHN T.	57	M M	MASTER	Yes English	Yes England	English	Mexico Vera Cruz	Industrial Co. of Orizaba, Vera Cruz	Eng. Liverpool
18	TAYLOR	JANE	57	F M		Yes English	Yes England	English	Mexico Vera Cruz	Eith Husband # 17	Eng. Liverpool

and ask them what part of México they were from. He would always comment on how beautiful that part of the country was. He loved his homeland
and missed it dearly. If he could not be there, he at least wanted to be among
its people and talk with them in their native language about the places, food,
and culture that make it their home with a tenderness in their words that
showed their desire to someday return to their querencia.

But Grandpa was not one to just reminisce about the memories of his
homeland. Grandpa had been a traveler his entire adult life. He loved to visit
new places, which he did as a young man in the Merchant Marines. After
marrying my grandmother, he took a job that did not require him to go
abroad but still afforded him the opportunity to travel. He became a trucker
for Yellow Freight Lines. But in 1971, as the story goes, he slipped getting out
of the tub and broke his hip. Long haul trucking and dancing, for that matter,
were no longer part of his life. Unable to work with a hip that never healed
but progressively deteriorated over time, he collected social security and scant
retirement benefits. He went from being a strong working man to an old man
who used a cane and later a walker, with too brief of a transition between
those periods in his life.

Like many family secrets of deep pain and tragedy, the story of Grandpa
breaking his hip after slipping in the tub was just a cover story told to me
by my mother to satisfy my inquisitive mind and help ease the untold truth
disappear into erasure. The story made sense, and I never questioned it as a
child. However, Grandpa's hip injury, although real, was not bone related but
neurological. Trauma has a way of reaching back into the brain's synapses and
dispersing the pain to other areas of the body when one part of the body cannot bare the load by itself. It is like that with family, too. Although one person
may bear the brunt of the physical and emotional pain, the pain resonates
with the entire family. With Chicano families, the pain can be generational,
the scar tissue never healing, only reopening new wounds inflicted by learned
behavior. This is why my mother did not tell me the truth. Maybe my generation would be different, she hoped. Maybe we could finally put this ghost to
rest. Unfortunately, although the physical pain is short, the forgetting is long.

In truth, Grandpa never broke his hip. The pain was deeper than that. As
the stories go, Grandpa was hell to live with when he was younger. The late-
night borracheras at the dance halls and cantinas, the next day hangovers, and
old-school, macho ways made home life unstable and many times unbearable
and unsafe. The marriage between my grandmother and grandfather was not
an "until death do us part" matrimony, at least in the intended form. Going
to the cantinas on a Friday night in search of your husband to get money for

groceries before he blew his paycheck on booze and women was bad enough. But the physically and mentally abusive relationship with his wife and children took a heavy toll on all of them.

It was not uncommon that Grandpa would become belligerent with his wife and children after he started drinking. But one night, in particular, would change him and the family forever. Grandpa was not the causal drinker. When he drank, he drank hard, and with the drinking came whatever demons that haunted him. They did not give a damn if he tried to leave Agustín behind in a previous life in México. Terrorizing Lino and those he loved would do just fine.

The drinking often unleashed violence. Sometimes it was verbal assaults lofted toward my grandmother. Other times it was whoever was home among the three sons and two daughters, but usually the males. But this night's rampage started earlier in the week. It began over an unsettled argument between my grandmother and grandfather surrounding the tragic and mysterious death of my great-grandmother, my grandmother's mother. My grandmother's pain, due to the sudden loss of her mother, was immense. And my grandfather's deeper descent into an alcohol-induced rage was unbearable.

Beer-drinking binges were a slow-motion event. But when he started with his favorite, Oso Negro Vodka, the family knew the matter would be a serious one. Fueled by hard liquor followed by beer after the bottle of vodka was empty, the argument between the two quickly escalated into a violent confrontation. Grandpa, devoid of the ability to make good decisions, became belligerent and broke a beer bottle, and chased Grandma out the back door. Thankfully, she escaped without physical harm. But their children, who now ranged from adolescents to young adults, could no longer bear the familial violence. They loved their mother dearly, and they did not want to see her get hurt any further.

The middle child, nicknamed Spook because he was born on Halloween, looked nothing like the rest of the family. The two oldest siblings were dark-skinned, but at least they bore a family resemblance. The younger two were light-skinned, and one had green eyes. Lighter skin and "colored" eyes have long been prized over dark features in México. Spook was the darkest of his siblings and took on the traits of the Afro-Mestizo of la sangre veracruzana. He even sported an afro in high school, which he was attending when the incident occurred. Make no mistake, Mexican culture can be just as racist as in the US, whether against Indigenous people, the darker complexion mestizos, or the Afro-Mexicanos. Spook grew up with this, even being called the "n-word" of the house by his own family on occasion when fights broke out amongst the siblings.

After seeing his mother being chased out the back door by his father, Spook left the house to escape the violence. But inside, his anger boiled. He was tired of his father's violent ways, and tonight would be the last time he would tolerate it. He left for a friend's house, where he managed to get a .410 shotgun. After returning home later that night, he was confronted by his father. His father began to whip him for disobeying his order to not return home late. Spook then retrieved the gun and threatened his father with it. The scene unfolded in the living room in front of the family. Grandpa's only words were, "Don't do it, son." But he did. Spook shot his father from close range. The shotgun spray hit him directly in the face, taking out an eye and also hitting the top of his forehead. The ambulance soon came for my grandfather and took him away. Then the SWAT team came for my uncle. They had the house surrounded with their guns drawn. My father, who was dating my mother at the time and was recently honorably discharged from the Air Force after serving as a Military Police Officer in the Vietnam War, offered to go inside the house and convince Spook to turn himself in. Fortunately, my father was successful in convincing Spook to surrender. However, after coming out of the house, the police tackled both my father and my uncle to the ground, saying they were unsure of what they were going to do.

A gunshot to the face from close range would kill most men on the spot. But my grandfather was no ordinary man. His head was just too damn thick for the shotgun pellets to pierce his skull. He survived, although with a small, visible dent in his forehead and a new glass eye. He did not press charges against his son. Spook's actions probably saved his mother's life. Surprisingly, Grandma remained married to my grandfather, at least for the time being. After her last child graduated from high school, she filed for divorce. The incident ended his drinking days, but his life and health would never be the same.

As expected, due to the injuries, Grandpa suffered terrible headaches on a daily basis. The neurological damage also caused him to develop a limp that radiated from his hip. As he got older and his chronic headaches and hip worsened, along with his pain-induced temper, nobody would take him in except for my mother, his eldest daughter. For years, from my childhood through my sophomore year in college, my grandfather lived with us in our two-bedroom wood frame house in an old Polish and Czech neighborhood in Houston's Northside. Grandpa would sleep in the room that my brother and I shared. He was a smoker. At night I would see the orange glow of his cigarette light up the room for a quick smoke. The cube-sized air purifier that sat next to his dentures in a glass of water helped relieve some of the smoke from the small bedroom we shared. But more than anything, I think my brother and

I were too tired to be bothered by cigarette smoke. What awakened us more than the smoke was the sound of him peeing in the middle of the night. The bad hip impeded him from getting out of bed with ease. So instead, he would pee in a used milk gallon jug that he kept on the floor next to his bed. It was the job of my brother or me to empty it out in the toilet. Since neither of us ever wanted to do it, we usually waited until the jug was almost full. Although we took turns emptying it, we also argued about who was the last one to do it and that it was the other's turn again. This argument was never settled.

Grandpa would get up early in the morning and borrow my mother's car before she left for work to drive to the corner store to buy the newspaper. He loved to read the paper outside in the front yard, drinking instant coffee and smoking cigarettes out in the open air, so my mom would not yell at him about burning the house down. After school, he would then give me some money to go to the store and buy a gallon of milk and cigarettes. I would ride my Huffy down the street to Clayton's, the neighborhood store, and ask the clerk for a carton of Vantage regulars. "They're for my grandfather," I would say. There were no questions or suspicious looks, they handed over the carton of cigarettes every time.

Having Grandpa live with us and share a room with my brother and me was tolerable at first, but after a few months, it did begin to wear on us. This is especially true when he would run out of money each month as he waited for his next social security check. It was like a little miracle when his check finally arrived in the mail. Grandpa usually took my mother and my brother, and me out to eat. One of our favorite places was down the street at the corner of Airline and Parker Rd., Charlie's Hamburger's, with their "over two dozen sold" sign arching over the entrance. Every now and then, we ventured out of the neighborhood for a special treat. Once we went to a Chinese restaurant. After the meal, we each ate our fortune cookies and read our fortunes aloud. I asked Grandpa what his fortune said. With his mouth full and cookie crumbs sprinkled around his lips, he replied, "What fortune?" We all had a good laugh knowing that Grandpa ate the cookie whole and that his fortune would become a Chinese secret. The beginning of his check cycle was a good time. We had extra groceries, we ate out, and Grandpa had his meds.

Grandpa took different painkillers to help him deal with his chronic headaches and neurological injuries he sustained from being shot in the head. The meds helped, but they were not a cure. And the stronger, more effective meds that he preferred to take he could not buy in the US. For that, he would have to go to México. Fortunately, for Grandpa, despite his bad hip, he still loved to travel. And México was only a bus ride away. He knew that after six months or so of living in our cramped two-bedroom house that his welcome would begin to wear thin. So after his stint with us and another check came in the mail, it was off to México he would go, where he could live comfortably even with limited resources, and more importantly, where he felt at home in his querencia mexicana.

Every six months or so off, he would go to México, usually to his home state of Veracruz. There he would stay in a hotel where he could pay for someone to cook and take care of him. In México, he was Don Lino, living a good life amongst his people. Plus, to help him deal with his chronic pains, he could buy his non-FDA-approved painkillers straight from the Mexican pharmacist. And the stronger the drugs, the better. This pattern of living with us for half a year or so and then living in México for another long stretch began when I was young and went on through my high school years and part of college. Although for one summer, he did live with our neighbors across the street, Calvin, a one-armed, old Irishman, and his wife Katy, who walked as if she were struck by polio as a child. He was forced to move out of our home when my mother became furious with him after he threw a cigarette out the kitchen window, which ignited a small fire along the back of the wood-frame house. It did not help that his headaches, and consequently, his mood swings, were getting worse. After receiving one of his checks in the mail, he took a taxi to buy his meds somewhere in Houston. The taxicab dropped him off in the street in front of the house. My brother, on his way home from school, found him lying in the ditch, passed out, high off the meds, and then helped him inside. He had to stay with us; nobody else could or would take care of him like we did.

Eventually, he would return to his tierra mexicana, as was his custom. Although Houston was where he had family who would give him a home, his heart belonged to México. México was like a mother who always called for her son to come home. In 1993, she called one more time. And like a good son, he followed through on his mother's request.

When my grandfather passed away, he died alone in a rented room in Orizaba, Veracruz. It was from that faraway place one night when his spirit came calling back for us. When my mother got the call early one morning, she knew something had happened and that it concerned her father. The night before, as she lay in bed, she heard a noise awaken her in her already uneasy state of sleep. She heard my grandfather's walker slowly shuffling down the hallway approaching her bedroom and then his voice whispering out to her, calling her by name, "Yolanda, Yolanda." She did not dream or imagine it. My brother heard it, too. His call was real and urgent.

My grandfather may have died alone in a rented room, but we were comforted knowing that he died amongst his people. It is said that someone is never really gone as long as we remember his or her name. "No nos olviden," these voices cry out to us. It is a Mexican custom to never leave the body alone after the person has died. Someone must stay with the body to protect it. Who knows from what, but it is a last reminder that family must be there for each other, even as we cross over to the afterlife. My grandfather's body was cared for until my mother and brother could arrive in Orizaba and have him properly buried. She did not forget him. He was still her "daddy." We could not let his memory die in solitude despite the pain he caused his family over so many years. We would not forget that we are connected to a past, a place, and a people who gave us everything we needed to, in turn, create a future generation who could do the same for us and for our children. We are all bound together, one by one, promising to never forget from whence we came. By doing so, we can rebuild a family structure, generation by generation, that is safe and loving by undoing the pain heaped upon us through colonization.

Years later, my family and I would visit my grandfather's grave in the cemetery in the hills outside of Orizaba. The plot was difficult to find. Mexican graveyards are seldom manicured like American ones. It is the duty of the family to maintain the plot and keep it neat. After finding it, we cleaned it up and made plans to provide a nicer headstone so that we could better locate it next time. There was a sense of relief that we found his plot amongst what seemed to be a maze of poorly marked ones. Sitting in the quiet existence and soft breeze running through the wildflowers and overgrown grass, it was peaceful to just rest and be thankful that we found what we had been searching for, the resting place of my grandfather: born Agustín Caffarel Escudero in 1926, died Lino Salazar in 1993.

My grandfather's life had not been an easy one. And those whom he loved and who tried to love him back, in many ways, had it harder, for they had no escape from whatever demons that haunted him. In the end, I think my grandmother and their children forgave him, each in their own way and in their own time. Forgiveness is the saving grace that helps bring closure to our families' intergenerational trauma. But it is the storytelling that puts our ghosts to rest. Their presence no longer haunts us once we learn how to keep their spirits alive.

References

Albom, M. (2006). *For One More Day*. Little Brown.

Whitefield, N. and Strong, B. (1971). "Papa Was a Rollin' Stone" [Recorded by The Temptations]. On *All Directions* [LP]. Detroit, MI: Gordy. (1972)

CHAPTER 12

Mi Abuelita y Los Rosarios

Arturo "Velaz" Muñoz

It's sunrise with a hint of *café.*
A slick streak of burnt *tortilla* smoke
    makes its way out the front screen door.
Abuelita has been too focused on her *rosario*
                tending the wrinkles of her hands.
    She begs to the heavens to keep me safe
      as I leave to roam the streets, tatted on the homies' chest,
the streets we identify with and claim   with more pride
          than the pride we have on our own last name.

My *abuelita's* cries to *diosito* stopped on my tracks, so I turned to the sky.
    Although the sun shines,
              my mind is too concerned
      on what would be the words
   or date engraved on the tombstone I'll one day lay.
It causes me pain to think of the possibility
    of *Abuelita* attending her *nieto's* funeral.

I tug on my *rosario*, pulling it out from between my long sleeve
           and extra large shirt.
    I've never been religious, but seeing *abuelita's* faith
leads me to find peace in this cross.
    I give it a kiss imagining I was giving *Abuelita* a kiss goodbye.
A homie shouldn't be showing feelings, holding back my tears
        as I yearn to tell her how much I love her.

As I close the door and hit the sidewalk,
   I noticed the smell of *Abuelita's velas* fade away.
I only hear the sizzle of *Abuelita's* tears hit the *comal.*
   I hope she knows I love her,
         I hope her prayers are heard.
I hope that I return to see my family again.

I reach the corner of my block,
   and I'm forced to forget the few memories of my childhood,
   forced to place my *abuelita* in the back of my mind.
       Once I step any further,
          I am no longer seen as her grandson,
  I am no longer who the neighbors saw grow up,
        And, in the eyes of the 5–0, I'm not even human;
        Instead, I deserve to be caged.
So, deeper I pray, I pray, and I pray.
       Deeper and deeper I hide my feelings.

I look up to the sky one more time, with rage;
   for all the ways I have been forced to be
           what I am not;
   for having to endure the need to survive;
   for having to be the villain
       when my barrio has done more good
         for my community than the juras have.

I hide my rosario beneath both my shirts.
   I hide my eyes behind my dark sunglasses.
   I hide everything but my rage,
       as I am no longer my *abuelita's chiquiado.*
I am now one of the homies, one entire new familia
       having to be creative in the ways
  we provide for those at home,
       for the loved one who pray for our return.

CHAPTER 13

Los Aullidos de las Madres

Sarah Amira de la Garza

It was another windy day in Marzo. Mamá was wearing a scarf firmly around her head, and she had made sure my hair was tightly pulled up into a moño, making me feel as if each hair was doing its best not to come out of my scalp. The vientos always come in March, and with them, the wind, the dust, the sounds, the feelings on the flesh and in the soul, the whipping strands of hair slapping our faces if they were not tied down. The Chihuahuan desert is known for these winds every spring, and Tía Flor used to draw wavy lines into the earth and blow dust from her hand to show me what was happening. I never knew Tata "el Jefe" or Don Antonio, Flor's father, because he had not come with the women and children after great wars against the people of the earth. But I heard the madrinas talking one time when I was pretending to be asleep, and they said that he had gone to fight the gringos from el norte, and he and the other men disappeared into the rising clouds of dust during a windy day in Marzo, and they never came back.

"Cierren las ventanas!" Mamá would yell, running through the house, slamming shut all the windows, and latching them, too, as if the extra locking of the windows was needed protection from the dust headed towards town and the homes. Then everyone would wait. Las tormentas de arena, or "los vientos malvados," as Mama Petra called them, would give everyone a chance to prepare—*if* they were paying attention, if they were watching the horizons. We should always watch the horizon. We would wait. And that is when we could hear the voices of the ancianos, los aullidos de las madres. Mama Petra said she would come and tell me secrets in the aullidos after she was gone, that this is why we should not leave the tierras of our ancestors—because when the vientos come, "el miedo te despierta, y te recuerdas quien eres—quienes somos—no te vayas, mijita," she would say. But I left.

Tía Flor would guide the family to watch the horizon from her place of silence, with her long dark hair hanging straight, wearing one of the long white cotton gowns she wore every day and every night. She could not hear or speak, but somehow, she knew when the aullidos began. The high shrieking sounds, somewhere between the sound of a whistle and faraway cries of someone being carried away, would start around the same time that the grains of sand would hit the glass. Flor would smile big and laugh silently, her face the way someone looks when a relative you have not seen shows up at your door. Then she would join the aullidos—one long thin arm outstretched, she moved barefoot into the bare spot in the middle of the room. She would begin to turn slowly, picking up speed until she was whirring around, spinning, never lowering her arm, her index finger tracing the horizon while she wailed in a way that sounded like someone learning to howl. We watched in silence, frightened in the places where we were weak, but in that inner space where the antepasados lived in us, we opened our hearts to the song of the truths. "Sin la canción de las madres," Mama Petra would tell us, "la vida ya nó nos pertenece." She would walk Flor to her cot afterward, where Flor would fall into a deep sleep.

Flor spent most of her time in the small aluminum cot nestled in the side room where she rested, and each day, she would put on a clean, stiff white cotton gown that had been washed and then hung to dry in the hot sun on the clothesline. Tía Flor was deaf and mute, so she didn't use words with the language everyone used. But she made señas, signals, and sounds that emitted from her throat in her most desperate moments. You had to look into her eyes to connect to her meaning—she taught me how to do this. And sometimes, she would laugh. She had many laughs. And when she would get the family's attention as she drew their eyes to the horizon when the thunder beings were rolling in, she would laugh silently as if she was seeing something very good. She would see everyone watching the horizon, and as if she had somehow reunited us all with the spirits only she could see, she would spin one more time, laughing loudly, then pound on her chest with tears running down her cheeks until someone ran to her and held her, walking her slowly back inside, to her cot. She never seemed to feel the stones or thorns strewn on the desert earth when she walked on them. I tried to do that, but my feet hurt too much. Even today, I try. Mama Petra said that because we could hear through our ears, we had lost the ability to hear through our feet or to speak in the dust, like Tía Flor. I have always wanted to hear through my feet and have tried to learn how to speak in the dust. But I never learned; I opted for other learning.

When the vientos came towards el pueblo, they would rise up high into the sky on the horizon, carrying the dust from far away, looking like a cloud with no fluffy edges. Mama Petra said no one should sweep the dust that the vientos left for us until we knew what it came to tell us. Tía Flor would trace Lipan images in the dust, making small cooing sounds as if she was telling a story or explaining something. She would look at the family to make sure we saw, and if you got close enough to her when she was doing this, she would grab you by the arm or leg and bring you over, take your hand and hold your index finger, showing how to trace the symbols. This would satisfy her greatly. And she would laugh, but the kind of laugh that sounds like love. To this day, I do not like to brush away the dust that comes from a storm, and I feel the anguish in my heart that my feet and my hands are deaf and mute.

✦———————✦

They say the dust in Batopilas had gold in it, that even the adobe in the walls of the buildings was full of gold because of this. The river flowed through the barranca and reached the place they called La Lluvia de Oro because of the way the gold seemed to flow like rain to make people rich. And in Batopilas, this meant that, of course, they would have to bring electricity here. No more candles, no more smelly kerosene lanterns. Not in Batopilas. No, they would replace the street lanterns with light bulbs. Doña Raquel did not like this. It meant that people would notice when she lit the two candles she lit every Friday evening before sunset like her mother before her had taught her. The electricity that flowed through the long cables and wires under the ground, inside the walls, and above their heads was like the eyes of the Inquisition, making sure the Shabbat candles would stand out if lit in the dark while all around, no one was using candles, as they showed off their electric lights. It had to be dark, and in the canyon, sunset was very dark. It was not right to turn on the electric lights.

The Rarámuri women and girls who cleaned her house would hide and watch every Friday as Raquel would take two new candles into the back bedroom, where the lights were not on. They moved quietly; the sounds of their movement muffled by the thick layers of their cotton skirts. They called her the *mukira naik eyerúame*, meaning woman of the fire in the moon, because she talked with the fire in the dark. And they prayed that if their grandchildren and grandchildren's grandchildren must be *chabochi*, that they would be of the blood of this woman. One day, this would come to be true. I am a *chabochi*, more white than of the earth.

In time, as it became more and more difficult to hide away on Friday nights, Doña Raquel lit the candles in her mind, and she would bring the light to her soul. Even the singing would draw attention to her. She would sing a wordless melody she learned from her mother, who learned it from her mother before her, as she imagined the candles, their light, closing her eyes to hold the image to her soul.

In time, Doña Raquel sang the melody to herself in her mind, and her daughter, and her daughter's daughter, and the daughters to come never learned to light the candles. It was said that when Doña Raquel died, she was singing the wordless melody and lifted her arms, drawing in the light from the heavens to her soul. But it was the prayers of the Rarámuri women that found themselves blown into the dust that traveled out of the canyon to blow across the Chihuahuan desert, along with her great-granddaughter, who would soon prefer to live the life of a *chabochi*, carrying the earth of their ancestors into foreign lands.

"It happened again. I was asleep—or thought I was asleep—and I could hear them," I shared.

"Them? What do you mean by 'them,' Susana?" My psychiatrist looked up at me with a facial expression that said she believed that I had no thoughts in my head and that I was just curious, but I knew it meant that if I shared what was happening to me, I would be considered possibly severely mentally ill, would be diagnosed, medicated . . . I felt trapped within this awareness that I was afraid of the person I was paying to help me.

"The crickets," I began to share, then changed my mind, "there are a lot of crickets getting into my house lately," I lied, spinning a story so I could pretend my reason for coming in was insomnia and not the sounds of whistling wind and lingering wailing I had been hearing. Not just crickets. Why in the world had I thought that a psychiatrist, of all people, would be a trustworthy confidant? I left the office with a prescription for enough Ambien to keep me asleep for the rest of the year.

A cricket sang from beneath the bushes as I walked by, and I felt that I was being watched.

España está tan lejos. Spain is across the ocean; it takes many weeks to get there.

No matter how many times Luz said this, it had no real meaning to her other than that Fernando would not be coming back to her for months, maybe even over a year. She had never been on a ship and had no idea what it was even to travel beyond the city of Chihuahua. She had never even seen an ocean, never visited el mar. For her, the trip out of the canyon, where she and her mother and her mother's mother had lived for their entire lives, was the first time she glimpsed her home from outside it. Aided by burros and a team of experienced Rarámuri guides, they traveled through the sierra and ultimately to the capital of Ciudad de Chihuahua; the trip seemed interminable and took forever. She envied the Rarámuri, who looked so unbothered and at ease, despite the fact they were walking the entire way. The idea of traveling beyond Chihuahua was so unfathomable that she opted to pretend that it made sense to her.

My great-grandmother Luz consoled herself with the memories of Baseseachi, the romantic waterfalls, el Serro de la Bufa, the breathtaking bluff overlooking the canyon, and the trips she had taken with Fernando, despite all warnings from her mother and her inner voice, that it was not wise. But Fernando was handsome, wealthy, from Spain, and he had looked her way! "Esos ojos azules—no wonder you were named Luz!" He bewitched—no, he seduced—no, he courted her . . . that is what Luz told herself as she held her large pregnant belly and began to tell others that she was married to him. When the daughter was born, she named her with his surname. Fernando was not there; he had gone back to Spain.

"He'll be here soon—he has to cross the ocean—it is very far . . ."

Only during her labor was she able to express the truth of the feelings inside of her, and even then, no one knew the source of her anguish was much deeper than the contractions pushing his daughter, Incarnación, out into the world of gold, electricity, and fascination with the foreign, returning to Batopilas where her mother, Raquel, awaited them. She prayed for her daughter and her daughter's daughter and the daughters of all her grandchildren— that they would learn to live without the silence of being a woman.

Her daughter would be named Incarnación, and her granddaughter would be named Suspiro. And Suspiro would change that name to Susana out of a desire to fit into the world that she lived in. I am Suspiro, Susana, and these stories were never told to me, but they lived inside me somewhere with just enough force to haunt me.

✦————✦

I clutched at my belly as I slept, writhing in my bed, before the sound of my own wailing from deep within woke me up. I could feel the vibrations in my throat mingle with the terror that was creeping through my body and holding my face stiff. As soon as I woke up, I felt for what should have been the smooth and soft threads of the expensive sheets I had put on my bed, but instead, I felt the rough, dry powdery feeling of . . . dirt. How did the dirt get on my bed? I ran my hands desperately on what should have been the surface of the mattress, but all I could feel was fine dry dirt that was covering my fingers with dust. Where was I? There was a golden light shining on the dust, revealing patterns in the dirt that I had just brushed aside—but wait! Where was the light coming from? It was the middle of the night! "Susana," I said to myself, "Wake up. Wake up!"

I looked up and was not ready for what I saw. The windows were open, and I could feel my hair blowing across my cheeks, and my voice was stuck in my throat, or somewhere my breath could not reach. As much as I wanted to scream, I could not. Then I saw where the light was coming from.

My bed was surrounded by a large circle of candles, the kind that Nana used to burn on her dresser—the holy kind in long, tall jars. These didn't have any pictures of Santos on them, and they were all white, and they were not standing on anything! It was like they were just there, in the air, but all set out in a huge circle that even went behind my bed—and my bed was against the wall—but there was no wall, and I was not on my bed. I was on hard, dry, dusty earth. This had to be a dream—but I knew I was awake. And I could smell the melting wax.

The smell of burning wax was just like the one I had smelled the times I had visited Nana as a child and spent the night. Nana burned candles all night long on the altar on her dresser. But there was no dresser here; everything in my room had been replaced by the golden color of the dirt and the flickering shadows from the candles floating around me.

Then I saw her. She was dressed in a white night gown that reached to her calves, and she had long gray braids. She was floating above the candles and walking towards me. She twirled around in a circle with her right arm outstretched and stopped right in front of me, extending her arm to me. I could still not make a sound, and I felt as if no air could enter my lungs.

All I could do was try to back away, and I felt the dirt beneath my hands. It was real. And so was this woman. Her eyes were the color of dark chocolate, with her mouth fixed in what looked partly like a nurturing smile, equally as if she were smirking at me with disdain, then laughing at me with her eyes as she turned and pointed to the space in front of her where an infant lay, covered in a blanket of dust. "Mira, Suspiro," she said. "Míralo. El niño que nunca tendrás."

Just as quickly as it had all appeared, it was suddenly all gone—the candles, the woman, the baby. All that remained was the smell of the burned candles and an image etched on my dusty sheets as if it had been burned. I tried again to shout, but nothing would come out of my mouth—I moved my fingers over the burned etching and noticed the curtains flapping from the wind blowing outside.

Finally, I gasped, wanting to cry but still unable to make a sound, breathing heavily to catch my breath. I fell on my side in the bed, curled up into a fetal position, my cheek pressing into the image in the dust and hearing the sound of the wind. The child that I would never have. That is what she showed me. But who had she been?

$$\text{✦}\text{———}\text{✦}$$

"Rosita, these curls on your head get tangled if you do not braid your hair when you go to sleep!" Marina told her daughter, tugging her daughter's dark brown hair tightly, causing Doña Clarita to wince but saying nothing. Marina pulled out the small comb from Rosita's hair and handed it to Clarita. Rosita was no longer a child; in fact, she was married and expecting her sixth child any day now. Doña Clarita was her grandmother. Rosita's belly was large, and her older sisters stood nearby in the kitchen preparing dinner while she allowed their mother to continue.

The baby would be born, a beautiful boy, surely to bring some joy and hope to Ignacio, her husband, and his mother. Only three years earlier, the baby's grandfather, José, had died after drinking a cup of Irish coffee he'd been offered by a fellow rancher. The coffee had been made with water that had been boiled with oleander in it, and when the doctor went to the ranch where José had been given the coffee, the batch of boiled branches lay in a clump not far from the fire where the water had been boiled. The family lost their land and farming businesses when the Irish and Anglo immigrants to their Texas hometown seized the opportunity of Don José's death to rush a demand for a full deed to all the waterfront parcels of land in exchange for the agreements he had made with them. Someone signed Doña Clarita's name as an "X," and they took claim over the properties. The grief and loss hung over their family like a dark grey storm cloud that never released the rain during a draught.

Ignacio and Rosita had a lovely family and a start to a new stability on the remaining property their two families had negotiated for their wedding. But they weren't expecting Rosita to suffer severely after the birth of the baby boy, dying only months after he was born. Nor were they expecting that a local Anglo merchant would suddenly shoot Ignacio and kill him while the child was less than a year old. Some people told stories of Doña Clarita sobbing by the springs that had only years before offered so much hope to her family they had moved here. Marina offered to care for the children, but in her grief and conviction that these springs were cursed, Doña Clarita refused and took the children with her to another small town with less water, less people, and where the grief could be allowed to fade in silence.

The sound of her cries by the waters of the springs where her husband and son had staked their families' futures was said to be indistinguishable from those of La Llorona. Every cry she had suppressed while alive now filled the night. That's what they said, anyway. And apparently, Doña Clarita was the grandmother of my great-grandmother. So much I didn't know.

The night of the candles and the visit by that woman had been several months ago, but it had affected me greatly. I couldn't sleep, and the terror of the images—were they only images?—kept me from closing my eyes again every time I woke up. These images, these sounds, these cries, and scenes of anguish that were visiting me now every night, were becoming familiar. It wasn't just the one woman now, but many of them. Each night, they came with another message. I didn't want to even think the words. But I couldn't help it—they were reverberating inside me. And every time I said my name, "Susana," I would hear them all chiding me, "That is not you. Tu no eres Susana. Eres Suspiro!" They were not inside me as if they were my thoughts, but somehow coming out of my very being from someplace inside me that was both near and far away at the same time. Yes, I knew their voices now. I was haunted by all I had never learned, all I did not know about who I was.

I looked at the open bottle of Ambien on my nightstand, next to my cell phone, which kept dinging with the sound of email and text messages I was neglecting. I had been unable to take even one. Just this morning, my older cousin Marisa had come knocking on my door looking for me, calling out my name, "Susana! Susana, wake up! Susana?" I lay still until she could hear the sound of Marisa's steps walking away. I wanted to say to her, "Don't you know that I am not Susana." But I said nothing and let her leave. That was not wise. I had not gone to my office for several days this week, and I knew that if I didn't contact someone soon, they would find a way to break into my home to look for me. So much drama. I lay down against the dust which now remained on my bed after the visits. It was beginning to comfort me.

There were heaps of paper strewn all over my bed, and I reached over them to reach for my phone. After a rather awkward and not fully truthful conversation with the director of my department about the "flu" that I had been dealing with, I sat up and swung my legs over the edge of the bed, and started to get ready to go teach the two classes that met later that afternoon. I pulled the sheets up over the papers, but not before pausing for a moment to look at them. They were covered with the design that the woman had drawn on my sheets.

✦ ——————— ✦

"Suspiro. María Celestina Suspiro," Zulema told the nurse who asked her if she had decided upon a name for her newborn baby. Zulema spelled it carefully and asked to see the forms before the nurse left the room. Zulema was a very devoted Catholic, and she wanted the name to mean something. Marcos, her husband, and the baby's father, was a cultural Catholic; he was Catholic because he was Mexican, and the Church was important to all the holidays and traditions, but he practiced the ways of the earth. He told Zulema that whatever she wanted to name the child was fine—as long as they connected the name to the gifts of the earth. Zulema was afraid of doing something pagan, so she tried to find names that would satisfy him while also not making God angry.

Zulema named her daughter after the heavenly mother Mary and Celestina because that was a way to say the sky or heaven, then added the name Suspiro because she knew that her life would never be the same after becoming a mother, and something told her that this daughter would suffer. Suspiro, a sigh. Zulema never called her María or Celestina; Susana had always been just Suspiro to her. Susana hated her name—that's why she never corrected the teachers who decided to call her Susana, because it was easier for them. It hurt her mother, but how could Susana tell her mother that she hated having a Mexican name that the teachers didn't like? And over the years, Susana had become the magic name that would erase her world as the teachers became her masters.

When Zulema died, Susana showed up less than an hour before her mother's last breath. She was busy with a student's thesis defense; you couldn't cancel *that* . . . Zulema smiled weakly when she saw her rush into her hospital room.

"Suspiro . . . llegaste," she said, using all the energy she had to speak and smile weakly.

Susana walked to her bedside and took her hand. "Mami, it's *Susana*."

"Sí," Zulema's mouth formed a sad, understanding, closed smile, then her face became animated, her eyes wide open, adding with force, "Don't forget to close the windows. Ay, viene la tierra!" Then she was gone. The nurse had not heard Zulema, but he was busy slamming windows shut in the next room, and the wind could be heard shrieking as the small particles of dust hit the window.

That night, there was no storm in the area, but Susana's windows also shrieked, and she woke the next morning to small mounds of melted candle wax on top of dust that had somehow blown into her room.

✢————————✢

Susana turned down requests for her participation in projects that she thought were made to her simply because of her ethnicity. She let people call her Susan and didn't tell them that her name was actually Suspiro, which means "a sigh," and that really, it embarrassed her to tell the story—after all, didn't she get her education so she could leave all the Mexican stories behind? Sometimes she just got so tired of the stories that tied her to so many people, so many traditions, so many things in history that . . . well, that made her *sigh*.

Her father said she thought she was too good for her own people; that if she was too good for her own people, then she was too good for herself! Her mother knew all of this was true. It hurt her, but she felt that the Madre María had told her to give her the name Suspiro because her life was going to be one of desesperación. Zulema and Marcos told her all the stories, even if she didn't seem to be listening. "En el desierto, las semillas nunca mueren, siempre esperando la agua," Marcos said at the end of each story. Sometimes he called Suspiro his little semilla. Zulema often wondered if she should have listened to Marcos and given her daughter a name of the earth. Susana lived her life desperate to prove she was better than she was, that she had somehow become better than her history, the history she didn't know. Desesperada, a life of sighs. But the seeds were there, awaiting the water. Her father used to say, "al final, no se puede averiguar con las verdades de la tierra."

As much as she played the part of Susana, Suspiro knew the truth. And Suspiro knew that somehow that was why the lady drew the marks on her dusty sheets. Suspiro knew, but she didn't want to know. She didn't want to hear the sound of her own thoughts—like the sound of crickets, hidden but unavoidable.

She was working late on Friday night in her office on a manuscript, spending time working on the bibliography, the part of the written work that could help make you seem like a serious scholar. When the phone rang, it startled her, and she jumped, accidentally deleting the full entry she had just spent time formatting.

"Shit!" she yelled as she brought the phone to her ear, "Hello. This is Susana. May I help you?" It was after 10:00 p.m.; she probably shouldn't have offered to help the caller. She waited.

"Susana? This is Verna, your neighbor from across the street. I hope you don't mind that I called you at work, but I just had to try and find you, and I remembered you work at the university, and I thought maybe, just maybe, you would be at your office . . . " she rambled. Susana interrupted her impatiently.

"Yes? Verna, how are you? What is the matter?" Susana was trying to retype the deleted bibliographic entry while she spoke.

"There's something wrong at your house, ma'am," Verna said, continuing, "there's a waterfall coming out of the second-floor window." Susana lived in a small two-story townhouse duplex.

"A waterfall?" Susana asked, accidentally deleting the entry, yet again. "What do you mean, a waterfall?!"

"Well, it's water, ma'am, and it's coming out the window in a huge stream," Verna responded, "but that's not all. I think there's somebody inside your house. We thought it was you, so we tried to get you to come to the door, but then I noticed your car was gone, and I told everyone, no, she took her car, she's not there, and I said, why don't I try to find her at work . . . "

"Verna," Susana began, looking at her manuscript and realizing it would not be done tonight, and then thought better about engaging Verna in more conversation. "I'll be right home. Thank you." And she hung up, closed her files, grabbed her bag, and headed for home. A waterfall?

By the time she got home, the fire department had already been called and had managed to turn off the water to her home, so Susana never got to see the waterfall. The fire captain told her that they had no idea what could have caused such a large water leak. "We usually don't see things like this except in the middle of a serious cold front, but seeing as it's late spring right now, that's not the problem. We don't recommend that you go inside your house, ma'am, seeing as the water could be everywhere, and we had to turn off your power seeing as you could accidentally go getting yourself electrocuted." The house was completely dark.

"Well, can I at least go in and get some clean clothes and an overnight bag if I'm careful?" she asked. He said yes, and gave her a flashlight, wished her luck.

"I hope you have insurance," he said as he and the fire crew drove off noisily in the large red truck.

Susana made it upstairs and saw how all her furniture had been pushed up against the wall where the windows had shattered, apparently from the force of the water pressure. The small items that had been on her nightstand and dresser, the counter in the bathroom, were on the floor, where they had floated on the water. The flooring squished from the water trapped under the tiles. She pointed the flashlight in the bathroom and screamed as the lights in the bathroom and bedroom began flashing. Hadn't the fire captain said that they turned the power *off*? She grabbed the bottom of her blouse and used it to flick the light switch, but when she did, nothing happened to the lights.

The lights continued to flash, not all at once, but at different times, so that parts of the rooms were dark while others were lit. She went in the bathroom to grab her toiletries and makeup, her toothbrush . . . and stopped dead in her tracks as she saw the mirror had something in it, what looked like the reflection of two candle sticks burning. She turned to look behind her, but there were no candles. The sound of an old woman's voice chanting in a language she didn't understand drew her attention, and deep inside the mirror was a woman with gray braids and a veil over her head, running her hands over the top of the candles like she was trying to bring their light to her.

Susana looked more closely, and as the woman's hands drew near to her own face, the light shone on it just as the woman looked up through the mirror straight at Susana's face and sighed very loudly. Susana's heart was racing, and she backed up towards the bathroom door, turning to see again the image she had seen in her bedroom weeks before! Candles suspended in midair in a large circle, and the wet tile completely dry and covered in thick dust. On the floor was the woman in the white night gown but this time without the braids, and she was younger, with long, loose dark hair, crouched on her knees, drawing symbols in the dust with her finger. She said nothing, but she heard loudly, "Eres de la tierra y no te puedes escapar!" She vanished, but her reflection remained in the bathroom mirror. The sound of the wind howling around the house and dust blowing against the windowpanes was filling her head. Susana turned the flashlight to see what the woman was drawing, but instead, the light shone directly on the woman's face as she looked up at her and moaned a loud and heartrending sigh. She heard the woman's voice wailing from behind the mirror; she was crying out her name, "Suspiro. . . . . . . Suspiro . . ."

Susana dropped the bag of items she had been collecting on the dusty floor, turning to run for the stairs, and just as she got to the top of the stairs, she saw two women walking up the stairs—they were dressed in late nineteenth-century clothing, and one seemed to be dressed as a nurse, and she had NO FACE. The other was holding what appeared to be a newborn baby swaddled in her arms and appeared to be the mother of the child. She looked up at Susana, and her face looked forlorn as she sighed loudly, holding the baby up to her with both arms. The baby was covered in dust. Again, she heard, "eres de la tierra, y no te puedes escapar!"

There was nowhere to go, and the sound of the women sighing grew while the old woman in the mirror chanted and wailed her name ever more loudly. She looked in the mirror and saw crowds of Rarámuri women running towards her but frozen in space behind the older woman, chanting loudly, "*Mukira nait ereyúame.*" Finally, when she could no longer handle the fear of being trapped in such a terrifying situation, Susana let out a moan from the depths of her being as if she were trying to escape from her very own life. All the women began to wail with her loudly as she felt the floor shake, and her wails grew deeper, less frightened and more sorrowful, full of grief, deeper and more resonant.

The lights stopped flashing, and all was silent. The women were no longer visible, but Susana felt their presence more strongly. She had dropped the flashlight but had no desire to look for it and walked carefully towards the stairs. She took each step slowly and cautiously, and as she approached the bottom stairs, her foot got caught in something that caused her to trip and fly against the far wall of the landing. She reached down to remove it from her shoe, only to find it was the baby's blanket! She lost her calm and screamed, running, rushing to her car, grabbing her keys from her pocket to open the door. She rapidly got in, sat down, locked the doors, and collapsed onto the steering wheel in tears while the sound of wind and dust whirling around her car picked up. She heard herself chant deep inside herself, "Soy de la tierra, y no me puedo escapar," and she let out a deep, loud sigh.

It had been two months since the flooding of her townhouse, and the reconstruction of the floors and walls was taking a lot longer than the contractors had initially estimated. Susana had told no one what had happened, but her coworkers and friends all could tell she was greatly traumatized by "the flooding." She couldn't tell them. What would she *say?*

Since the spring semester had ended, she thought it would be good for her to take a break and get away from where everything had happened. Even after the house was reconstructed, she was sure she could not live there again. So, she thought she would take the opportunity to go visit the springs of her mother's hometown and get away from the university. After everything that had happened, she found that her work was not as important to her either. She submitted the manuscript with an incomplete bibliography, and it was published, and it made no difference whatsoever to anyone. She found herself sighing a lot every day, and each time she sighed, she was partially relieved and equally triggered and reminded of the events.

She had moved the papers with the symbols to her office before the flood, and she had taken to doodling and drawing the signs on them as a way to calm herself. Lately, she found herself chanting tunes with no words as she did so. She folded the baby blanket and used it as a makeshift cushion while she sat on the floor. Everywhere she sat, dust would settle.

Susana eventually took a journey to El Ojo, her mother's hometown. She drove the long way across the high desert from the airport several hundreds of miles away, and she was hungry. It was midday, and she was hungry, so she stopped at a neighborhood grocery to pick up some food for the small kitchen in the house she had reserved for her retreat here. She had rented the house the owner had told her was walking distance from the location of the ojo, the source of the largest of the springs that had since dried due to unsustainable irrigation practices. The town was named after it. She had no family that she knew left in the town, and like so many of the small villages and towns in the southwest, it had been gentrified, largely populated by artists and retirees who came here from far away, who enjoyed the isolation and the stories of the days when it had been an oasis in the desert. She felt a longing in her heart that she was not familiar with, as if she should be able to lay claim to the place but had nothing to say. Her life had succeeded in accomplishing for her what the tourism had done to El Ojo, erasing the stories of people like her ancestors Petra, Rosita, Marina, and Clarita, Luz, and Incarnación, and her great-aunt Flor, the prayers of the Rarámuri for her great-great-great-grandmother Raquel, and the messages in the dust and voices in the wind.

After she put her bags in the house, she filled her water bottle and set off to walk as the sun was descending a couple of hours before sunset. She headed for the park that was located at the site of the once-flowing springs—the man at the grocery had told her that the trees were still fed by the water of the springs that were located deep beneath the earth but not high enough to fill the pools again.

At the edge of the large hole that had been the eye of the springs, there were many large flowering oleander bushes. Susana had never seen oleanders, and she picked several branches with blossoming flowers and immersed them in the water she was carrying. She watched her step as she edged her way to a small rocky ledge to sit and feel the breeze blowing in from the south, slowing and sitting herself down as she moved a few large rocks to even out the place she chose to sit. A small metal hair comb caked with mud and with many rusty spots on it caught her eye, and she picked it up. This is a good time to rest, she thought to herself. It is a good time to take a break, to come home. She heard the sound of gravel crunching under someone's steps near her.

An old woman wearing a head scarf and dressed all in black was walking towards her and greeted her with a small lifting of her chin and a smile on a face that looked like it had spent far too much time grieving and had nothing but love left to give. Susana felt moved to perform an act of kindness and got up and approached her, selecting a branch of the flowering oleander to offer her.

"Ma'am, Señora?" she started, realizing that perhaps the woman spoke only Spanish. Susana hoped not, as her Spanish was very bad. But she could at least start with a greeting that showed some respect, she thought. The woman looked up. She greeted Susana in English mixed with Spanish.

She spoke, looking deeply into Susana's eyes. "Eres de la tierra, y no te puedes escapar." Susana felt her heart jump. "Ven, walk with me," the woman said, "I am here every day. Todos los días."

Susana answered, "I would like that, Señora. What did you say your name was?"

The woman smiled and looked at the water Susana was carrying. "You know my name," she said, chuckling as she reached and took the oleander branch from Susana's hand, throwing it into the springs. "Do not drink that," she said, motioning to the water where she'd placed the other branches. "It can kill you."

Susana realized she was speaking to Clarita but said nothing. Instead, after a long pause, she said, "Me llamo Suspiro, and I think I need to learn from you." Please help me, she prayed under her breath. The woman nodded, turned, and walked on.

Susana did not follow her and instead returned to take a seat by the springs, taking a deep drink of water from her water bottle and smiling, realizing that she was not tense or frightened for the first time in a long time. "Yes, I think I am going to enjoy walking along here with you, Doña Clarita, and todas las madres." She sat there looking after the place the woman had walked long after she had disappeared, not noticing the sprig of oleander that was still floating in her bottle or the face of Doña Clarita looking at her from the depths of the springs.

"En el desierto, las semillas nunca mueren, siempre esperando la agua."

CHAPTER 14

my baby wanted an *el camino*; that's real

Diego Medina

mile marker 9

(you see, my love, we met in a sacred way—
some way of perfect alignment. how we got here
is a story that this holy land shares with us.
our migrations were determined long ago,
when the earth was in prayer,
when the mountains and valleys
made their pacts, and the rivers
sung themselves into being, carving through the land.
these landscapes we see are ancestors, my love,
they knew we were coming, intended us,
and they shaped themselves
so as to require our course.
our migration patterns were stories
that the rivers and mountain ranges
told to each other, and these formations shaped
connections, they spoke every love story,
and our unfolding futures are in credit to
the form of the land. she determined our movements
and settlements, our dances, our languages, our first kisses.
she would shape us, and in return
ask that we shape with our hands
that which God has asked of our imagining spirit
to bring upon the earth in a prayerful way.

she would ask that we hold our lovers tight
and kiss them goodnight. she would ask that we press ourselves
upon her with only loving intent. we must live as a dream
of our Holy Land's beauty. that is it.
and darling, though my hands are worn,
when I run my fingers
along your body, the land moves with you,
and in these moments of prayer
landscapes become.)

mile marker 191
baby, this isn't the oldest story of our love,
but that doesn't matter. A sharp blade
will still cut even after its maker is gone

we bought your used hyundai
santa fe in the bethlehem of new mexico, belen
and baby, all you wanted was an el camino.
a long way from galilee, from the stone in your belly,
from the buffalo hides we traded our salt for,
2000 cash for a santa fe you never wanted,
it didn't make it past

mile marker 79
truth or consequences before breaking down
and we stayed the night there,
where they built the dam, 1911,
and destroyed a river older
than our concept of time.

there was an el camino for ten grand,
real nice
up near alcalde

and you were afraid to stall out,
like all left feet in alcalde fear.

i saw you plead with the santa fe in t or c, mad
and entreating desperately its never-coming sentience.
the transmission was done,

dead there on el camino real,
and what was it about this highway that people
believed in. the real road is underneath the tar

where countless love stories are enslaved
to mythological bitumen.
before they called it el camino

she was real. there were lovers here,
loving though shackled,
and some were separated in 1680
crying across the halves of the state
and sending each other rain.

truth or consequences;
where the seen isn't, the unseen is.

before t or c, we were in hot water,
and now there is no water in the Holy Land,

it's all waiting behind the big dam.

creation leaves no mere coincidences,
only seeds of meaning for fertile minds to sprout.

today there is no water in the Holy Land
there are no turtles in Turtle River,

and the bends in the river
where fertility gushed,
where minerals made their beds for millions of years
are all gone and straightened
leaving only the plants with the deepest roots to survive.

this is where your santa fe will be forgotten,
and your tongue will be too dry to call it by its original name.

it will beg for water but only say juarez,
none until you get to

mile marker 0, wet and wild waterworld
The last place to get baptized
on this side of the border.

pilgrims come a long way, sniffing
for wet on the wind,

to find an oasis in the desert,
a heaven in the Holy Land,

and they churn their stomachs sick
when they get there,

going through the vortex
and chugging.

this is our last stop
before lupe de los mansos.

our mission, nuestra senora,
passed the old clay spot, now

the texas transportation stockyard,
to our rock in juarez

on the same line of latitude
as jerusalem, and with the same storyline.

the mission figs will bless our bellies,
and we, too, will bloom from within.

that is what the mission always failed to know,
what the figs already do:

the only way to know God
is within.

my love, there's holy string
between us too. there are fig

seeds i left in your body.
they will grow poems in your heart.

nothing sacred can be separated by a history,
even one dark enough

to see the same stars
from different missions.

Mile Marker 147

when we are brought to this earth
we are given a mission,
we are called by creation to offer up our
love to the holy fire,
to feed the eternal flame
with our passion and breath.

we are given a verse
borrowed from God
to return back to God
in another's heart

when we were brought to the missions
we were taken from our earth,
but we kept our verse;
we kept enough words
of our language to pray.

never call this language extinct,
for even in our exodus to the south
the first word of this language spoken upon this land
will forever remain.

in the prayers, in the music, the pueblo never ends.
in the footsteps and induction fields, the pueblo never ends.
we are still there if we are still here,
even after the centuries

there are still dances in Salinas,
where we were brought to this earth.

there is still salt in our blood,
so that we may sweat.

Mile Marker 165

we had a war for salt in this holy land
as i prayed for your sweat once more.

there's no water in the holy land
but there's salt,

the crystal memory of water,
the prayer behind the words.

we made our offerings to
the Holy Beings

when we arrived
and to our families left behind.

from one salty area to another
but a timeline warped and off-course.

somewhere a girl longed
to grab her beloved's hand,

somewhere salt woman
longed for my kiss again.

love has enslaved something in you
and like the ocean, love knows not its own vastness

until it's dried up
and only the sacred salt remains.

this is how i will remember our love,
how i have to.

that big ocean
now a desert

this holy road
now a highway

this mission
now our home.

i keep my heart open
to the thought of you appearing before me

i keep up this virtual pilgrimage to
something more than half-real.

our ancestral highway is a holy one
and it was mapped by the stars.

we've used it for thousands of years before this,
and there is more to that story than this one.

the way they use it now is wrong.
wrong for our hands

to be torn apart on
el camino real

Mile Marker 282
and that's all you wanted
at age 25.

all you wanted was something
to cruise slow in

and show me the desires
the sun never gets to see

slow enough, you and me,
to feel everything,

letting shadows fall soft
across the desert

briefly disappearing
a small sherd of history;

the steam leaving
clay and straw bricks drying in the sun.

drive it down to the border, then, little girl
where the world ends,

take your el camino
and fly!

they don't make them anymore
just a thing left

a small sherd
of history, there

like what the jirds did to bless
the flower children at shanidar

who could only dream
of jericho.

no AC, but it's worth
the vision you seek.

the false water on the highway,
the shadow of a saltbush swallowing.

there are no better shadows than shadows
in the desert.

only true pleasure
can be felt in the dark.

fear not, my
angel

i will love you in a million more
timelines than this.

This one is your
el camino.

Mile Marker 169, or thereabouts
even if just your tongue and mine
we'll hold every word

and what's next for our love?

will we love beyond the horizon of time,
where we know the sun by the silhouette first?
will we love in bodies like these

or bodies like the riverbed,
or the bed of an el camino?

my sun has danced across your sky
leaving your horizons glowing pink and flowering
every morning and every night

and now, on this day of parting

we are designated a candle to light
for the memory of it all, our monsoon
season of pleasure,
to keep a record of God's knowing,
so that it may be called upon in a future time.

and in that way
in the beating heart of creation
the love never goes.
hundreds of miles, and yet
we've loved for longer.

through all of the geological strata,
and yet we still take this salt.

i loved you, kissed you at the acomilla rest stop,
looking out over the rio salado,

and that was the last time for this life.
a historical marker on the el camino real,

and you'll go that way,
and, little one, i'll go this way.

Mile Marker 6, WSMR 20,000 BC

your body will always belong to my eternal love, baby.

the eagle above, golden,
circling, cleansing,

i knew you were with me,
the mammoth, camelop, the dire wolf,

i knew you were with me.
even after these months,

after thousands of years in the lifetime of a pilgrim,
there are further aparts we could be.

every migration that has been made
to reach salvation

to reach the proverbial salt,
is recorded in the heart.

The lives we live are portals to the memory of God
and we must always think bigger than us.

We were pulled from a place centuries ago
but we will always return home to each other's hearts somehow.

The eagle brings every dimension forward,
spins a triskele with its fractal feathers

and opens up the window to every timeline,
like a vision of spinning constellations

speaking, with light alone,
in tongues.

constellations are sacred sites,
made from an allegiance long ago

and you and i always return to these sacred sites together.
we were made there together and shall be there forevermore.

stepping through the same white sands
as the Holy Ones

we become landscapes.
the white sand

this beautiful body,
i'm here to give my gift of love.

relinquish the past,
set it free from your grip and let it run.

that which you truly love
will return again in time.

we left our footprints
but we took our shadows.

our footprints know what it means
to never leave home, but only

shadows know what it means
to be inside

another's heart.

CHAPTER 15

Cry Baby

Kathleen Alcalá

Oh, that moan was cold. It swept in under the door, crept across the floor, up the walls, crouched in the window corners, ready to come down on her at a moment's notice. She felt that chill, heard that baby blue hiccup that meant Baby was up.

What's up? she asked, as she lifted Baby from the crib, a safe crib, a guaranteedto keeplittlesnookumsoutofthewoodswhenthewolvesareout crib.

Cindi longed to climb into the crib herself, babe in arms, and sleep forever. Instead, she changed Baby, who didn't try to flip off the table for once, and plopped her into a highchair while she heated the bottle.

Who's to know what the cat knows? He had brought her a mouse again. Did this mean an extra-cold winter? Need to fill the larder with fat mice? Or just get fat? She patted her own belly, still loose and jellified from the pregnancy, the extra thirty pounds she gained down to maybe fifteen or twenty. Maybe a little more. As long as she was nursing, the clinic told her, she would lose weight. It didn't happen. Her hunger was not as raging as during the pregnancy, but it still turned noisily inside of her, like an internal combustion engine craving coal in order to burn, burn, burn.

She came to when Baby started her hic-uppy cry again, to find the water boiling around the bottle—now too hot.

Oh, baby oh . . . I love you so! So many songs to Baby, but they didn't mean Baby, did they? They meant the one who would end up with baby when it was all over—when the music stopped, when all the lovers went home, when no one would save the last dance for you.

My Mama done told me—but no, her mama did not tell her, told her nothing, not how it happened, only not to let it happen, which Beto guaranteed he would not let happen—murmuring in her ear, his hand creeping down her pants—until it did. Then he was gone—from town, to the Army, to work, to the Good Girl it turns out he was cheating on with you. But still. Cindi had never been happier, if only for those few weeks. The wind hummed a little louder.

Oh Baby, let's try the bottle again. Baby grabbed it like a bear cub and practically turned the bottle inside out she sucked so hard.

The birds twittered. The sun came up. There were playful gusts of wind, like the day straightening its sheets as it got up from bed. She changed Baby again and put her in the playpen. She was just starting to pull up, trying to stand, so she could not be left by herself for a minute. Cindi grabbed some clothes and threw herself in the shower. As soon as she had shampoo in her hair, Baby started screaming. Cindi jumped out and grabbed a towel. Baby had fallen backwards in the playpen, but stopped crying as soon as she was picked up. Cindi brought her in the bathroom and tried to hold the wriggling infant while rinsing her own head in the sink.

By 7:00, Cindi had Baby in the car seat and was on her way to Mama's.

That cold moan got in the car with her. It threatened to drown out the people on the radio who covered the news from overnight—floods, money, disasters, rich people getting richer. More floods. Cindi remembered she had not paid her credit card yet, and she would pay more if she did not pay that day. It started to sprinkle and she turned on the windshield wipers, the left one always sticking just a little before returning.

Cindi's mother was at the door to take Baby. All frowns for Cindi, all smiles for Baby. Told her she looked fat. That she'd never get a husband looking like that, and of course, already with a baby. Baby.

At work, Cindi parked, got out of the car and straightened her shirt. She would eat only an apple for lunch today, she promised herself. Mondays were hell. Everyone was frantic, hung over, bright-eyed, meaning to do better, be nicer, eat only an apple for lunch.

Cindi's desk was already stacked with forms to enter. Bruce must have brought more after she left work on Friday. At least the software was fixed. She put on her glasses and set to work. Every five forms she allowed herself to stop, initial them, and put them in a separate stack.

At 11:50, Natalie stopped by Cindi's desk, wondered if she wanted to go to lunch with her and some others for Gale's birthday. Cindi liked Natalie, and sort of liked Gale. But she said no, conscious of her tight top, her promised apple.

Oh, come on, Natalie said. Just once.

Cindi winced. That was exactly what he had said, just once, and nothing would happen. Nobody ever got pregnant the first time. That burn in her belly set in, that engine that wanted to be stoked, and she said yes.

The Daily Special was a Rueben sandwich, and Cindi ordered it. She had to lean forward to keep the juices, the dressing, the sour kraut, from dripping down her front. She told the whining apple part of her brain to shut up.

When she got back to the office, there were more forms. Bruce must not take lunch, she thought. Although about fifteen people processed, he was the only one who checked the forms before dividing them up among the processors. Only once did Cindi find an omission he should have caught.

Cindi called her mother to check on Baby. Baby's fine. Maybe Dad and I should take her more of the time. Why? Asked Cindi. Dad's not getting any younger. So you want to watch the baby more on top of watching Dad? Her mother was silent.

At 4:30 Cindi grabbed her purse and was pulling her hair back into a ponytail when she ran into Bruce in the hall. I was just coming to see you, he said. Oh yes? We are going to alter the form again, just one line, make it easier for the adjusters. If she left right then, she would beat the worst traffic on the Valley Highway. Can we talk about this tomorrow? She asked. Oh, sure. He continued on towards her cubicle with his load of forms. She knew he would drop some off along the way, the Johnny Appleseed of insurance claims. Cindi suddenly loathed the office, her job, her coworkers and their simple lives. She loathed the greasy spots on her blouse and the computer glasses she had forgotten to take off and leave on her desk. But she would not go back and risk running into Bruce again.

The wind was blowing fitfully, stronger, when she got outside. She shielded her face in the crook of her arm from the dust devils picking their way across the parking lot. Bits of rock and dirt pelted her head and arms.

At her mother's house, the wind tried to shut the car door on her leg. She limped to the door and struggled inside. Her Dad was asleep in the recliner in the living room, a game on television, the low roar of the crowd backwash through the dim room. She heard Baby call out, a rising note of a question.

Baby broke into a smile as Cindi picked her up out of the highchair. Those sharp little teeth in front, that dimple just like his. Baby broke Cindi's heart every day. She had a little bruise on her forehead.

What's this? asked Cindi, kissing it.

Oh, I'm so tired, said her mother, holding her back with both hands. Baby was into everything today.

She's pulling up. She wants to stand.

I had to put her in the highchair to get anything done. Baby wore a bib full of soggy Cheerios.

For how long? Oh, I don't know. She wouldn't nap today.

She always naps. Baby bounced her lips off Cindi's shoulder. She was hungry. She was also soaked.

We've got to go before the storm gets any worse. Cindi could hear the wind calling around the corner, whispering sour nothings in the ears of the house.

Leave her here. She'll be okay.

What's with you, mom? Thank you. I'll see you later.

It's just . . .

What?

I ran into my friend Sylvia at Safeway. She has a son.

Yeah . . . so?

I, I gave her your phone number. Maybe he'll call.

I told you mom, the last thing I want to do right now is date. End of story.

Cindi picked three empty bottles out of the sink and crammed them into Baby's diaper bag. I have zero time for pendejos.

Who else is going to date you? Cindi's mother could be mean. She wished she could afford real daycare.

I'll see you tomorrow. It's Tuesday, remember, so I have to be there a half hour earlier for our staff meeting.

I know. You think I don't remember anything.

I don't think that.

Outside, the sky had turned a swirling gray. Cindi tucked Baby's face against her shoulder. Opening the door to the back seat, it whipped back and hit them both. Baby screamed. She kept screaming, arching her back, as Cindi struggled to buckle her in. She might have hurt her a little, pinched her leg with the buckle, but there was nothing she could do about it. It's okay, it's okay, she kept murmuring.

Pain. Without pain there is no change.

The rain started up again. The farther they drove, the heavier it got. Cindi was worried about the underpass. It had flooded at least once recently, but it was the quickest way home. She could not think through Baby's screams. She wondered if something else was wrong with her. Maybe mom had put one of those old-fashioned diapers on her she liked to use. Sometimes the safety pins came open. Baby was braying like a donkey, unable to catch her breath. She smelled really bad. Traffic was at a crawl, and Cindi could barely see out through the windshield.

That low moan got louder and louder, a growl filling the car like a trapped animal. The rain drummed on the roof of the car. Pain is growth, she began to chant to herself.

Some space opened in front of Cindi's car, but she hesitated. She couldn't tell how deep it was. The car behind her honked sharply. Cindi gunned it, but the car lost traction, began to drift with a quick flow of water across the roadway. She felt her blood surge in fear, a metallic taste in her mouth when she bit her tongue. Pain is.... A truck driver in the oncoming lane blared his horn. Cindi's car began to rotate slowly to the left as Baby screamed. Cindi realized the moan was rising from her own throat as it turned to a scream. Oh Baby.

Cindi loosened her seat belt, and struggled onto her knees, reaching back to release Baby from her car seat. She could not open her door, the rising waters holding it shut. Finally, Cindi lay on her back and kicked a window out.

Cindi squirmed out through the window, only to find herself waist deep in water, the surrounding cars and trucks beginning to float and bump into each other. The rain was so hard, it hurt her skin. She could barely see. Baby was quiet now, as though she knew her mother needed to concentrate. It's okay, Baby. She held the little girl close, reassuring herself as much as Baby.

Cindi walked up the embankment and made her way to the overpass, heedless of the traffic that continued to pass her by inches. At the top, Cindi looked down to where she had left her car with everything still in it—Baby's car seat, Cindi's purse, her phone. She realized she was barefoot. She must have lost her shoes along the way. By now the water was beginning to close over the top of the car.

As she gazed down through the windshield, Cindi realized with a start that she could see a woman inside, lying inert in the driver's seat. It must be someone else's car. Where was hers?

Cindi looked at the child in her arms. All she held was Baby's coat. There was something hard inside of it, a knife. It looked ancient, stone. Is this what obsidian looks like? No wonder Baby was crying! But Baby was not there. Baby! Where's Baby? she called. By now it was dark. Cars continued to stream past Cindi as she tried to make her way back below the underpass, trying to find her car. Find Baby. Her wet clothes made clanking noises, buckles or something hitting each other. Her feet were oddly numb from the water, and she could not feel them as she walked.

Time passed, and the waters began to subside. The light was failing, and Cindi had trouble seeing. A dense fog had settled over everything. Cindi could hear a police radio down the street, where police cars and flashing lights surrounded a barrier keeping drivers away from the scene. She kept wiping her eyes, as though this would make Baby appear. A tow truck came and the driver hooked her car up to it. There was no one inside that she could see. She must have imagined the body. Cindi stood by the side of the road all night. She did not feel tired, and did not know where to go. I have to think, she said to herself. I have to go to the police. I have to find Baby. She kept trying to remember those final moments in the car. How she picked up Baby. How she got out. But she could not.

She couldn't go to the police if she had left Baby behind. She imagined being taken to her parents' home like this, without Baby. She imagined the things her mother would call her, would accuse her of. She would present the knife to the police and say, This is all I know.

She did not leave the intersection. I am Cihua, she thought. Pain is growth.

A day passed, and the underpass was swept out and reopened to traffic. Cihua crouched by one end of the underpass, her arms wrapped around herself, wet and dirty, barefoot, watching each car as it entered the tunnel, looking for Baby. No one seemed to notice her.

Night fell.

Cihua stood and realized she was rooted to this place, that she could not stop looking for her child. Her office clothes had turned to a white dress, stained with mud and blood, her hair an elaborate statement. The whine started in the pit of her stomach. Up through her chest, it rose to a growl in her throat. It burst out of her mouth and filled the street, echoed down the tunnel below the overpass, down the dank asphalt byways, the water still draining down the walls of stained stucco buildings, down the alleys and sidewalks and gutters of a city she did not recognize.

Pain is.

Baby! she called. I love you, Baby. Nimitztlazohtla Noyollotzin. She twisted her hair in grief. Oh, my child, your destruction has arrived! Where can I take you?

Cihuaconeti, amotepoloaya ohualahcic. Canin namechmamaz?*

*Thank you to David Bowles for this translation.

CHAPTER 16

Becoming Indigenous Again
Returning Home and Making the Ghosts Visible

Juan Pacheco Marcial

A decade and a half later:
I am going back home.
Death awaits.

Home is filled with
Memories of sunshine, thunder, lightning, rain, and rainbows
Memories of the beautiful smell of wet dirt after rain
Memories of playing out in the dirt until sundown.
Memories of having scraped knees and elbows.
Memories of walking down the mountain for school
Memories of having tortas de jamon for recreo.
Memories of having to wear a uniform to school.
Memories of birthday parties, fiestas, and jaripeos.
Memories of amazing food made by the elder hands.
Memories of putting dirt inside beer bottles after parties.
Memories of limpias para el susto.

A decade and a half later:
I am going back home.
Death awaits.

But home is filled
Memories of sadness after seeing my mami cry.
Memories of loneliness after being left alone for most of the day.
Memories of having to choose between my amá and apá.
Memories of yelling.
Memories of late-night crying.
Memories of being kicked in the head.
Memories of not being good enough.
Memories of drunk nights every payday.

A decade and a half later:
I am going back home.
Death awaits.

I fear that everything has changed.

The Ghost of Nostalgia and Loss

What does an undocumented indigenous Latinx immigrant living in the US respond when asked, "If you could go anywhere in the world, where would you go?"

One of my biggest pet peeves when it comes to icebreakers is being asked "If you could go anywhere in the world, where would you go?" My response to that question is always the same: a loving one, full of hope. I say that I want to go back home: my place of origin, my genesis. *Oaxaca*. However, I do not say the real response. Home has so many memories. *Too many memories.* Some are full of pain . . . and others are full of joy. The memories either implant a smile on my face or make a knot in my throat to the point where the ghosts start to speak themselves into existence. *I rush to catch and bury them before anyone notices.* But now, it is time for their release.

I miss home.

Even writing these words does not fully justify their existence or paint the true emotions behind them. It has been a decade and a half since I was there. At the time of my departure, I remember being excited because I was finally going to El Norte. There, I was going to eat all the burgers and make so many friends. At nine years old, my imagination quickly filled with endless possibilities of a new future, a new life. The news of crossing the border happened like lightning. In a matter of one week, my life changed before my eyes. *It all happened so quickly.* To prepare for El Norte, I invented my variant of the English language while playing with knockoff Hot Wheels on the techo of my old house. I was good with languages. My abuelita, Teresa, helped me practice Mixteco, her first language, my priceless heredity.

There were so many hopes for El Norte. *Freedom. Healing. Prosperity.* It was supposed to be a place where everyone was free. This place was promised with no more abuse, no more yelling, no more being scared. Yet, for some reason, as soon as I crawled under the border's barbed wire fence and into the unknown, home and everything I previously knew was all that I ever wanted again. It is painfully funny, damning almost, how life does this. But for now, I reside in OaxaCalifornia. Living in between, romanticizing my return home, and dreading the ghosts left behind.

I am proudly from Oaxaca—the state most populous of Indigenous people in the country of Mexico. I am a descendant of the people of the rain and people of the clouds, Mixteco and Zapoteco. Born from proud Oaxaqueño parents and wise Oaxaqueño grandparents. Till today, my family practices our indigeneity through our foods and traditions. We eat from the land through plants, seeds, fruit, animals, and insects. However, this was not considered normal in my semi-urban upbringing. My Indigenous identity was gradually being stripped away over time. *Peeling my body and soul until I was left with an exposed, fragile core.* The deterioration of my indigeneity created hate, despise, denial, and disgust toward everything that had to do with being Indigenous.

My mother was born in the beautiful pueblo of Santa Cruz Papalutla, just a forty-minute drive from Oaxaca de Juarez, the capital of the state of Oaxaca, Mexico. The pueblo is known for its work on artesanía de carrizo, the mayordomías, and jaripeos. Everything done in the pueblo is embedded in Indigeneity along with catholic practices. The people's prayers are done to their patron saints and La Virgencita, followed by limpias for el susto. Not so long ago, the pueblo was losing its fight to retain its Zapoteco language. In my family, we lost our ancestral language to conformity and survival. Everything had to be done in the Spanish language. Zapoteco, to us, became code language that only the elders would use to hide things from us. Recently, protectors of the language began fighting for the reconstruction of it through programs benefiting the public in learning basic words and sentences and institutionalized curricula placed in public schools for becoming proficient in the language. *Biciatao, nuestra raiz, our founder, with your strength, we carry forward our fight. In your protection, Papalotl continues.* The Zapoteco language is becoming stronger. The pueblo of Santa Cruz Papalutla is entering a new beginning.

My father was born in the beautiful mountain pueblo, El Gachupin. A two-hour drive up the mountains from Oaxaca de Juarez. The pueblo is surrounded by forestry, rivers, and wildlife. It is grounded in learning and living off the land. Their beautiful and complex Mixteco language is thriving along with the Spanish language used in their public schools. Unfortunately, because of its distant location to the capital of the state, hard terrain, and limited transportation to travel back and forth, poverty, and the lack of access to resources are predominant. El Gachupin has a devastating history of migration to northern Mexican states and the neighboring country north of the border, the United States. The people migrate to work in lands of greedy farmers and abusive governments. Stories of starvation, death, and violence haunt my father's kin. However, through sacrifice and the shredding of their bodies, they have become tenacious.

I was born and raised in the city of Oaxaca de Juarez, the capital of the state of Oaxaca. Ever since I was born, my family moved to live in the poverty-ridden colonias outside of the city. My neighborhood sits atop the hills on the Cerro del Fortin, with breathtaking views traversing throughout the capital of Oaxaca. We lived twenty minutes away from the beautiful architecture and blends of Oaxacan culture, food, and music that resided in the city. My parents' pueblos were far away, and we could only visit on special occasions. I went to a public kindergarten and elementary school where indigeneity did not exist. The goal of the public schools was to push a mestizo, white supremacist ideology. In school, I was taught nationalism by being forced to join the Banda de Guerra, a marching band where we would play military marching songs and violence through all the beatings my classmates and I endured at the hands of the instructors and staff. During and before the time of my journey to El Norte, the people of Oaxaca, led by teachers, educators, farmworkers, Indigenous people, working-class people, punks, and revolutionaries, organized against the corrupt state seeking better living wages, more funding for rural schools, and the resignation of a corrupt governor. Months passed where I did not attend school due to the strikes and protests, thus giving my father and mother a greater excuse to cross the border. Six months after El día en que Oaxaca se rebeló,[1] I immigrated to the United States at the age of nine, mojado.

The Ghost of Rejecting Indigeneity

"¡Como eres indio, igual de burro!"
    "Pero, yo soy un indio."

I spent most of my childhood in Greenfield, California, a small rural town in the heart of the Salinas Valley, the Salad Bowl of the World. This town has a vast amount of Oaxacan indigenous immigrants. They are mainly indigenous people from the Triqui pueblos of Oaxaca. The Triqui people in Greenfield carry on their pueblos with them through their traditions, clothing, language; however, it is detested by the non-Indigenous mestizo and white residents. Anti-indigeneity and antiblackness run deep within the town. As much as I love Greenfield, the place that saw me grow and where I hold the dearest memories of my teenage years, I have the same dislike towards it. Much of the Greenfield community projects so much hate and disgust directed at indigenous peoples. This disgust towards Indigenous communities of Oaxaca makes the racial slurs directed at us valid in their eyes. "Oaxacas, Oaxaquitas, Oaxacos" are just some of the many slurs we must face every day. The people of this community made claiming my indigeneity unbearable, and so, I, and many others, denounced, hated, despised, and became disgusted with being Oaxaqueños. "I'm not from Oaxaca, yo soy del estado en donde están los tornados," I would say. All for the sake of survival.

Throughout the years, there have been cases of towns and cities in the US with high populations of indigenous Oaxacan peoples experiencing unjust treatments from their new communities (Barillas-Chon, 2010; Johnston, 2004). Greenfield, CA is one of those towns. The gut feeling that I obtained immediately after crawling under the barbed wire was right. *I missed home.* My arrival in the United States was not an easy one. After settling in with my father in Greenfield—who had crossed the border before my mother, brother, and I—there was a small gap of time in which I tried to become adjusted to life in El Norte.

As a child, I was a sponge for knowledge; I would read and learn from everything I could get my hands on. However, my sponginess also absorbed prejudice linked to being an Oaxaqueño. Racism in the United States was visible. It was something I never observed while living in Oaxaca, although now I understand the many injustices indigenous peoples face there. In Greenfield, the blatant slurs spewed at Oaxaqueños, the immigration raids, and physical and mental abuse, all were visible. No one denied their racism and prejudices. *It was all a competition on who could be the more racist, and who could be the most heartless.* The change, from a place where I thought racism did not exist, to a place where racism was visible, changed my perspective on life. On being an indigenous person existing on someone else's stolen land. This change reflects the many injustices and the countless stories that, sadly, are not unique to me alone.

Having no family, no relatives of my same age or close to it—aside from my brother, who was also trying to survive. He just wanted to make it through the day, make it home safe—there was no one to empower me or my Oaxacan identity. Being immigrants, my family felt the outside pressures forcing us to assimilate into the ways of living in the United States. This left me with few choices regarding my identity: one of them was to reject it for the sake of survival, so I did. After experiencing the hate that Oaxaqueños received daily, after being bullied because I ate with my fingers, after being called Oaxaquita over and over, there was nothing appealing about being indigenous from Oaxaca. I began to deny everything that had to do with me being from Oaxaca and being Indigenous. I denied where I was born, where I came from. The craving to fit in and be safe from the trauma overwhelmed me. *I wanted to be seen as one of them. I wanted whiteness.* I tried so hard to become someone else. The ghost that lingers after rejecting my indigeneity still haunts me. As I join spaces of indigenous peoples, there is a lingering feeling that I cannot shake off. Am I Indigenous enough to belong in these spaces? Fortunately, as I reflect on my journey up until now, one can never completely shed their indigeneity.

I would work in the fields during high school, cleaning the lettuce fields and picking strawberries and green peas. There was a time when the cuadrilla, which I was working for, became a toxic environment for fieldworkers from Oaxaca. The foreman in charge, a white-passing mestizo, would create our workplace a living hell. The quotes at the beginning of this section are from insults I vividly remember. We were all a bunch of youngsters trying to make some money to pay for expenses for the next academic year. The insults from the foreman's tongue were yelled at us for not being able to understand, for being slow, for not getting the hang of things quickly, for being indigenous.

"¡Como eres indio . . . "—You are such an Indian. As this was being yelled at me, my mind traveled to my parents' pueblos. Their stories were filled with a tenacity that gave them strength in the toughest of times. Their indigenous culture, embedded in their Mixteco and Zapoteco languages, their traditional foods from insects to the plants by the side of the river, and traditions to their patron saints and La Virgencita empowered me. The response which resided in my head, after these rushing thoughts of my genesis, was, "Yes, I am an Indian."

" . . . igual de burro!" —just like a donkey! Many times, I have seen and heard people compare indigenous peoples to animals. We have been seen as a lesser race. As nothing else but savage humans, the uneducated, in need of salvation. *The conquered.* However, being compared to a donkey has a different, more painful meaning. The donkey is the mindless worker. This animal does all the dirty work and does everything as told. The dumb and abused animal, from its cries for help to the neglect and terrible treatment it receives. The donkey is of lesser rank and weaker than that of a majestic horse. The donkey, nonetheless, has endured. Indigenous peoples, my families, have endured.

"Pero . . . "—but. The first sign of resistance starts with questioning. In my case, I questioned the terrible phrase comparing me to a donkey which diluted the understanding of my indigeneity but at the same time reinforced it. The thought of whitening is instilled in my parents' generation. Their loss of language and violent assimilation to whiteness as they both left their pueblos to work, seeking a better wage to support their poverty-ridden families, drained them of their indigeneity. Nonetheless, as they fight to reconstruct and become closer to their indigeneity, they must endure and heal from the years of name-calling and diminishing acts of hate. Through this endurance, the resistance starts.

"Yo soy un indio"—I am indigenous. A powerful statement acknowledging my indigeneity then becomes the peak of the resistance towards whiteness along with its dangerous tactics for the erasure of indigenous peoples. By consciously admitting that I am indigenous, I begin to reverse my implanted de-Indianization. I start my journey to challenge mestizaje and white supremacy along with their racist, antiblack demeanors embedded in me. I begin to become indigenous again. Sin embargo, this conscious admittance towards my indigeneity did not come overnight, and it was long overdue. The acceptance of my indigeneity was a long process of reversal against the learned behaviors taught to me by these outside pressures that impeded me from rejoicing in it.

After my indigeneity had been stripped to its core. Two layers of internalized oppression had arisen. They had to be painfully peeled for me to rejoice once again in my indigeneity. The first is the battle towards whiteness in Oaxaca, the city in which I was raised. The subtle racism in the city made it almost impossible to critically assess the differences between indigenous and white individuals. The second layer revolved around departing the survival mode that was created to survive in someone else's land—Esselen/Salinan land—and not be discriminated against. Being raised in a town where hate and oppression towards indigenous Oaxacan individuals was almost a sport, I needed to do anything to survive. Once the two layers were peeled, true re-Indianization began.

I challenge myself to learn from the painful experiences I experienced growing up while denouncing my indigeneity. As a result, swarms of memories fill my mind about times when I claimed to be someone else. From a different place, a different ethnicity, a different cultural genesis. However, there is one incident that I remember clearly. I first once again began to rejoice in acceptance towards my indigeneity in the year 2017. After being involved with a student group that organized on immigrant rights and undocumented solidarity, I was invited to dinner with some of the members. After a couple of drinks and food, we began to have intimate conversations. "Where are you really from?" was the question of the night. As people began answering, giving the names of the places they were from and sharing the fond memories of their childhood, I was caught in a battle within myself. "What do I say? Who am I, really?" While I was being overwhelmed by the question, the temptation to deny my indigeneity once again did not seem too bad of a choice. One person answered, "I'm from Oaxaca." And then, another person added, "I'm also from Oaxaca!" That day, my life changed once again. I witnessed two amazing people acknowledge their indigeneity and proudly call themselves Oaxaqueñas. I instantly replied, "I'm from Oaxaca, too!"

I found the community I longed for.

The Ghost of Going Back Home

The guilt begins.

I am a displaced Mixteco and Zapoteco from Los Valles Centrales of Oaxaca. Because of educational and economic barriers, my family decided to immigrate to this hostile country. Unfortunately, my identity as an indigenous individual from Oaxaca deteriorated even further after I crossed the border. I had no sense of belonging, felt no love, and exhausted my will to live.

I was nine years old when I crossed the border. Back home in Oaxaca, my loving family was shocked at knowing that we were going to immigrate to the US. Throughout the years after crossing the border, my family would keep in touch through phone calls using ten-dollar calling cards, and now through unlimited calls and texts to Mexico. I did not call or talk to anyone back home in about a decade. Too much pain lingered, and hearing my family's voices would make the wounds deeper.

Not calling for such a long time left a pang of guilt inside of me. I knew that my grandparents were always asking for me. They would send homemade tla-yudas, cafe de olla, carne seca, and semillas through a paisana that delivers to the United States. My abuelitas are always thinking of me. What have I given in return? Nothing. Not a single call. I have forgotten my grandma's priceless heredity, her language.

Death awaits.

As I write this, my petition for advance parole to leave the country is in process. I am going back home. But at what cost?

My grandfather, the pillar of my brother's upbringing, the person who shares the same name as my beloved brother, the giver of life to my mother, has unfortunately passed away. Both of my abuelitos have now passed. The Ghost of immigration continues hunting my undocumented body—the one living in stolen land, forcing me to grieve from afar. The more I think about it, the more guilt I feel.

The Ghost lingers as I complete my application for advance parole. It calls my name as I ask for my grandfather's death certificate. *I am not worthy. No merezco esta oportunidad.* The Ghost shames me for the years that I have not reached out and asked the simplest question of "How are you?" It guilts me as I ask my uncle for my abuelito's death certificate.

My ghost, you who shames me for trying to go back home, will you haunt me forever? Will you stop tormenting me? I am only an illegal alien trying my best to find the broken pieces.

I close my eyes. I see the hill in which I lived, traversing the beautiful Zapotec land.

My ghost, will you let me go back? There are many broken pieces of myself that I hid by the flower bed in my old home. Let me watch the sunset once again.

From the techo of my old home, I will scream at the top of my lungs. The pain, anger. I will finally let go of it all.

My ghost, my protector, my border, let me go home. You can haunt me forever, then.

I am going home, and unfortunately, death awaits.

In my dream, it is all planned out. I close my eyes, it begins:

My visit home starts by once again crossing the physical manmade border, separating my citizenship from my alienship. The one that says I do not belong here. The racist fucking border that impedes me from going home. To be a person with dignity. To dream without fear. I will once again cross the inner borders that have harbored so many dilemmas within me. I will no longer ask who I am because I will know. A beautiful Indigenous boy, born from the tears and blood of my ancestors: the survivors, with tenacity, and un chingo de ganas. Arriving home, the person holding my passport will look at me, smile, punch it, and say, "Bienvenido a casa." I will say "gracias," that it is good to be back. I will pick up my belongings and head over to the exit, where my family will anxiously await me. We will look at each other, smile, and cry over the reminisce of our old familiar wrinkled faces. At last, I will hear the magical words, "Vamonos a casa!" As we get into the car and proceed to our lands, my thoughts will drift as I try to remember the streets, the buildings, the people, and my home. By then, home will be much closer now, at hands grasp. No more Google Maps to traverse; no more sitting in front of a computer reminiscing about my neighborhood by traveling through it using street view. No more "mobile media" to obsess with as I reminisce about the roads of my pueblito (Vasquez Ruiz, 2022). Once we arrive home, my precious family will be waiting for me. I will see my grandparents' firm stance, their rough, tired hands waving at me. I will see their wrinkled smiles and their fierce, sunken eyes. I will smell the wet dirt after a summer rain, the fire burning to keep the clay comal warm, the fresh blanditas ready to be turned into huge tacos de queso con sal, the cold tejate and agua de chilacayota ready to be sipped. I will hear laughter, birds chirping, children playing, and my name being called out. I will feel the moist air touch my skin, the hot sun pressed against my thick black hair, and an overwhelming sensation of love. I will taste the tears of joy that travel down to my lips and the glorious food made by my abuelita's hands. I will be home, and it only took a decade and a half to make it there.

My dream, a psychedelic utopic episode, does not tell the truth. I will come home to death. The only motivation this past decade and a half for me to want to go. Death will await me. Change will await me.

The Ghosts gnawing at my mind, bickering thoughts as I call them into existence, will forever be part of me. As this path of decolonization, towards re-Indianization, continues, the ghosts continue to roam around me. They remind me of the struggle for survival in this stolen land, of lingering displaced bodies. The experiences that have been created after crossing the border are deeply tied to my ancestral knowledge and to the lands of rain and the clouds. To this day, the memories with my abuelita maintain me on this path towards the decolonial of conocimiento (Anzaldúa, 2002). These memories aid in my acceptance of indigeneity, to shed the colonial thought that created layers upon layers of doubt and uncertainty. Most importantly, my reconciliation with Madre Tierra, the body, and the spirit become aspects of those teachings that, for so long, have been forgotten.

I am still afraid of what could happen when I call myself Indigenous in places where I grew up, such as Greenfield. I am afraid that one day my bravery will extinguish, and I will have to retract my body to the place where it used to feel safe. But for now, I return to these memories, to the ghosts, to the place where my life changed, evolved. As I delve into the universe residing inside my brain, I find peace, comfort, and distortion.

My ghosts, we are going home!

* * *

Para mi abulelito Beto y mi abuelito Alvaro,

Algún día regresaré a nuestra tierra natal.
Regresare al lugar en cual ustedes me criaron.
Iremos otra vez a caminar hacia el campo y el río.
Juntos venderemos frutas y verduras en el mercado.
Tomaremos mezcal y brindaremos a las cosechas.
Algún día llegaré con ustedes.

¿Saben? Los extraño mucho.
Extraño el bigote en sus caras. Sus manos duras y frías.
Extraño los días en cual me hicieron sentir seguro.
Extraño su saviduria.

Abuelitos,
A ustedes, los que nos dieron vida.
Gracias por mi vida y las vidas más que darán.
Gracias por su bendición.
Nos vemos pronto, en el otro mundo.

Note

1. The day Oaxaca rebelled. A phrase derived from the title of an online article commemorating the tenth anniversary of the intervention of the state of the peaceful strikes from protestors of Oaxaca, ending in people injured, dead, and scarred, since June 14, 2006. https://aristeguinoticias.com/1406/mexico/el-dia-en-que-oaxaca-se-rebelo/.

References

Anzaldúa, G. E. (2002). Now let us shift . . . the path of conocimiento . . . inner work, public acts. In G. E. Anzaldúa & A. L. Keating (Ed.), This bridge we call home: Radical visions for transformation (pp. 540–78). New York, NY: Routledge.

Barillas-Chón, D. W. (2010). Oaxaqueño/a students' (un)welcoming high school experiences. *Journal of Latinos and Education.* 9:4, 303–20.

Johnston, P. (2004). The blossoming of transnational citizenship: A California town defends indigenous immigrants. In J. Fox & G. Rivera-Salgado (Eds.), *Indigenous Mexican migrants in the United States.* (pp. 385–99). Center for US-Mexican Studies.

Vasquez Ruiz, M. (2022). Mobile postcards: Zapotec imagined mobility. *Mobilities.* 17:2, 285, 299.

CHAPTER 17

cortando las nubes, or, death came on horses

ire'ne lara silva

I. Maravillas

We cling to our mother, wanting only the touch of her breath. She holds us tight against her, but then she sighs, her arms fall to her sides, and she begins to scream. I want to say, Mami, please sit, rest. I'll pat your back. I'll wipe your tears. I'll bring you water. Drink. It will soothe your throat. Please, Mami, I'll take care of you. I'd say anything to keep her from screaming. Her screams echo along all the rivers and deep into the deserts.

When Iccauhtli cries, I pick him up and cradle him against me, humming so quietly it drowns out Mami's wailing. Tomás runs after her, whirling in the wind, howling and screaming till they are one voice. I run to keep up with them. Sometimes they're like that, building on each other's frenzy. Splintered trees and small animals scattering in their wake. They always leave me behind. Carrying Iccauhtli, I can never keep up. Before dark, I'll stop and make camp somewhere along the river. I carry Iccauhtli until he falls asleep. He's learned to sleep through anything. Even hunger. It's been days since Mami's been still long enough for Iccauhtli to nurse. I scoop up water from the river, tear tender corn from the fields, and when there is nothing else, give him my fingers to soothe his craving. His little gums hurt, leaving my fingers red and swollen.

We walk and walk. Mami and Tomás whirl, whooping and wailing. I sling Iccauhtli on my back, freeing my hands to work on shelling corn. Sometimes I leave Mami and Tomás to their running and sit by the river, telling Iccauhtli stories and playing with his toes. When he falls asleep, I rest, combing my hair and massaging my feet. Our sandals faded away a long time ago. My feet are bone and callous, callous and bone. We're always walking. Mami never says where we're going.

The land keeps changing. Before, we followed the puddles until they became creeks, the creeks until they became rivers. Always, the people lived along the waterways. But then the ground was parceled out and fences came up. The rivers were contained and leashed, run through the centers of towns and into irrigation ditches leading only to fi lds and fi lds of strange new crops. All our memories were lost to the changes and their newness. Circles and circles. For a while, at least, we found refuge with the people. But the people have changed. They don't listen for our steps at their door anymore. They've forgotten how to feed us and speak to us, how to lead us to our sleeping places on their floors.

It's rare now to find those who remember that we need them to hold our hands and lead us into their homes, speaking softly until we remember speaking, leading us to our beds and lighting candles to rest our heads by. Even fewer remember what to do when Mami suddenly cries out in the night and leaps up from her bed. Pulling at her hair. Breaking windows and tearing apart chairs. Rubbing wooden splinters and glass shards into her hands. They don't know to hold her, as hard as they can, singing quietly under their breaths. They don't know her name, the name they need to awaken her to comfort her to keep her from breaking things and harming people. They don't know to lead her to the door so she can run fast, run fast and away. They don't know she needs to feel the earth leaping up to her, the wind stinging at her eyes, strength and purpose growing within her as the cold lights of town fade away. They don't know us anymore. Only the land beneath our feet knows us.

The land knows who belongs to it, Mami says. Though Mami also says the land prefers enduring to fighting, and she always says it weeping. Those are the times she sits in trees, her strong legs wrapped around the branches, the machete cool against her hot face. She sings to that machete in the morning and at night, murmuring *mi vida mi amor mi vida* over and over again. Her eyes are always swollen, her lips bitten, her wideset face puffy and darkly pale. Sometimes she'll spend entire days sharpening the blade, holding it close and whispering against its edge, *mi vida mi amor mi vida*. We wait for her to rise. Sometimes whole days pass. Tomás attacks the trees with his machete, testing his strength and tiring himself. Iccauhtli sleeps, crawls around in circles. I'll hang a rebozo from low branches and set him inside, the wind causing him to sway slightly. And I take to singing low, oh so low, as low as my voice will sound, not disturbing anyone but making ripples in the river.

I'm learning how to make my voice weep as it sings. I imagine I am the river speaking and, on its own, my voice grows louder. Sometimes I think Mami hears me in the midst of her weeping. She checks her step and quiets for a second, body balanced delicately on the balls of her feet. But it's just for a second and then the silence I never disturb is gone. I wish she would sit beside me and tell me the story of where we came from. Where did we begin, I would ask her, why did our feet start this long walking? Where are we going?

Sometimes Tomás carries Iccauhtli on his back, ranging far and deep into the *monte,* teaching him all the names of things. Meanwhile, I help with Mami's work. It's going slowly, but I'm learning. I can't do everything she does, only the beginning of her work.

Mostly, I help with the dead. I'm careful, very careful. I cut the ropes away, pulling out the bullets or the knives or the sticks. I straighten the limbs or bring them together with the torsos. I pass my hands over their faces to close their eyelids, even when the vultures have already plucked the eyes away. I care for them with whatever I can find. Sometimes I gather enough wood to lay them on, covering body and wood lightly with palm leaves or bits of mesquite so the smoke will sink into the ground. When there is no wood, I bury them. When the ground is too hard, I drag them to nearby rivers or caves. The little ones I wrap in my rebozo and whisper, sleep little one, sleep. I lay all the dead to rest with my flowers, the little orange flowers I'm named for. I can always find them, even in the winter or in the dark of the desert.

I weep for them all. I remember their faces though sometimes all I can do is imagine what their faces might have looked like. Sometimes it's impossible to find all the parts, especially with the older ones who were cut apart, disemboweled, torn from the womb, beheaded, burned. For those I speak prayers with smoke or water to every part of the body. I hope my voice will reach them. I hope that what I've done is enough to give them peace.

I cut scars into my hands to remember them by. Little cuts that do not bleed but stay in the palm of my hand. Mami does it, too. She cuts bleeding scars into her legs to keep track of them all, to bring back their faces, dead and alive. It doesn't hurt her though she screams from the pain of the wounds inside her. Shaking her fists at skies and clouds, weeping for the lost, she runs, remembering and forgetting. Her face doesn't change. Her legs change. When she runs and her legs are bared, they look scaled in the moonlight.

She runs, clutching the machete to her side. She says she loves to run in storms and hear the thunder. She says she loves the lightning crashing around her and the water streaming down her face. But sometimes, when the clouds are still far away and dark shadows spread along the horizon, she'll sit in a tree and wrap her arms around her legs. Rocking herself slowly, back and forth, back and forth, she'll start muttering about horse prints in the sky. She says it rained the day before, it rained the day before It Broke. The sky was a strange color and the rain against her face tasted of metal and rotting things. It wasn't a good rain, she says, but they couldn't have known what would come. She remembers and growls. She leaps to the ground and races off along the river, machete in hand. She stays gone for days. When she returns, the machete is always bloody and there's at least one more scar carved onto her legs. She falls exhausted by the water, whispering, dark clouds such dark clouds.

It Broke, she says. The storm broke. The rain poured down, and the world broke. My life broke with the clouds and the storm. And what came in the rain killed everything. Why doesn't it ever stop? When will it end? Will the rain ever stop pouring? It never stops and nothing I do is ever enough . . .

And she beats the ground, weeping into her own arms.

from
the mouth of the river
de la desembocada to the creeks
a los arroyos por los ríos
along the rivers

Iccauhtli has stopped crying. He's too hungry to even cry now. He sleeps, but not well. I'm afraid to soothe him as he sleeps, afraid to wake him to hunger. Mami's gone. Tomás is spinning. Spinning the way only Tomás can spin, stamping his feet and throwing his eyes to the sky. Sometimes I don't know whether he's laughing or screaming. His voice switches back and forth unexpectedly, sometimes a boy, sometimes a man. I don't think I know him anymore, he's always screaming now. Long ago, we would play by the river, swimming and splashing water at each other until it grew dark. He had another name before, a name in a different language. But then we started walking and he put away the boy he'd been. "Cempasuchil," he said, "call me Tomás. I won't answer to anything else."

Tomás runs as if he wishes he could fly. His arms are raised in the air, the tips of his fingers bent, as if he were feeling for missing feathers. I know he'd love to have a horse or anything with wheels. But he knows that's impossible.

We've both heard Mami scream, in her fits, that in the beginning death came on horses and kept coming on horses and then afterward on things with wheels. She dreams of death coming on horses. She wakes to find herself already on her feet, already running away from death coming on horses. Death hasn't come on foot in years, she says. I'm going to run. Too fast for it to catch me. Too small for it to see me. Death will sometimes pass over one woman hiding in the river. Death hasn't come on foot in years.

from
the mouth of the river
to the creeks Medio Creek
Blanco Creek Coldwater Creek
Brady Creek Arroyo Guadalupe

Sometimes when she disappears for hours or days, she comes back with blood on her hands. Blood on her clothes. Blood on the machete. Blood on her skin. Blood sinking darkly into the notches running along her legs. Tomás goes with her then, and he returns silent and shaken, eyes almost completely white. He tells me very little.

Mostly, he tells me of Mami. That sometimes she seems to be Death. Grief. Fever. Ache and Struggle. He's seen her wield her machete like a sickle. And sometimes she is a shield. He's seen anger and love contort her face in terrifying ways. He says she hates it when it is too late and they surround her, the dead and the almost dead. There is no mercy, no grace, only the end of pain in what her machete does. Tomás hurries to his tasks, slitting throats or pressing guns to temples or rolling bodies into the waters.

Every time he comes back, Tomás has to learn how to speak softly again, though mostly his gentleness is reserved for Iccauhtli. And sometimes for Mami. It's hard for him to be gentle, as if he has to reach too far inside himself for it.

Slowly, though, he's learning how to hold the weeping ones to his chest, how to utter soft words, sing soft songs. All he could do at first was stand, close his eyes, and not hurt them anymore. Iccauhtli helps Tomás learn how to care for others. Iccauhtli is a pair of ears eager for Tomás's voice, a pair of eyes ready for his stories, his games, his face. Tomás leaves me alone with Iccauhtli less now. He says nothing, but I know he's afraid. Mami cries more now than she ever has.

I feel it too—the rage and the grief. Like a huge weight and like emptiness, like hunger but deeper and wider. It feels like fire flaming along my bones. It feels like rivers through my eyes, carving their course down my face. I want to be gentle and careful and to hum quietly but sometimes I want to spin and run and scream and wail. Sometimes I want to beat my fists against the sky and forget my name. But there's Iccauhtli and Tomás and Mami. There's hunger. And thirst. The land and the dead. There's the walking and the caring for the little we have left

There are flowers to pick and roads to find. Suns and moons to follow. And sometimes I think there is already too much rage. At the beginning at the ending and in the curving of it. So many deaths. So much evil spreading hate and grief and hardship.

Mami is the hero. Mami is the fighter. I am here to watch. Here to listen. Here to remember what happens and what has been forgotten.

The dead ones can never stop speaking, never stop telling their stories, never stop crying out for all the things they loved when they were alive. The dead know nothing about mercy. They only know they're dead. They know loops of pain that burrow into the ground and shoot up through the roots, shoot up through the earth.

In the beginning, I wept from sadness. I wept for the dead ones' pain, but now it's rage I feel boiling away inside me, in the core of me. Anger I feel swirling and hardening, sending out tendrils through my veins, making my heart pound with the sudden thickness of my blood. It reaches into my head with a clawed hand and pushes out against my skull. My eyes seem to run. My teeth forget they're human. But I make myself remember. I'm here with the dead ones. They need their last flowers, their remembering words, their sprinkling of water or scattering of leaves, and the weight of the earth or the lightness of air.

Only the dead ones and Iccauhtli keep me from spinning off into the air, screaming out my lungs against the wind and throwing my body against the rocks. The dead ones need something from me different from what Mami or Tomás could give them. I care for the dead.

por los ríos along the rivers
Calavera Colorado Nueces Frio San
Miguel Pecos Washita Tahoka riverwater
atoyac Yanaguana atl

Mami has run off past the outskirts of the next town. Tonight she's breaking lights along the river, deepening the shadows, distracting the men in white vans, with rustling sounds that seem to come from everywhere and nowhere. Afterwards, she'll take her sharp machete and gut train cars, leading the suffocated to a safe clearing. She'll run to lock doors and gates against the rioting Navy men with Mexican blood and skin and zootsuit under their nails. She'll lend her voice to the protests and the marches and whisper in the ears of poets. She'll save the children of the Adelitas who armed themselves and fell in battle. She'll swim along the rivers and pull the ones returning to the land of their ancestors away from the strong currents and the lights and the traps. She'll lead the Rangers' horses into falling over the cliff's edge rather than letting them carry death to the Indio villages. She'll fight with the campesinos to hold their land, their homes, their ties to the earth. She'll spend the night with the Yaquis fighting the pale ones. Running alone, she'll cover miles and miles, decades and centuries before dawn.

Tomás and Iccauhtli have gone deep into the *monte*, running with the coyotes and speaking to the sleeping snakes. They've left me alone. I haven't been free to wander by myself for a long, long time. I should be preparing food or making us shelter for the night. I should be finding flowers or searching for dead. But I feel restless, as if something in the clouds overhead is calling me.

I walk away from the river, following the path of irrigation ditches, stepping from all time to a single time. The sky looks different, brighter somehow. It hurts my eyes, and the colors of things are strange, as if they're trembling even when they're still. I haven't felt earth this solid beneath my feet in more time than I can remember. Streaming clouds overhead darken the earth and gentle the colors. I walk into the wide cotton fi lds and touch the swollen white buds with my fingers. I kneel on the ground to touch the plant stem and the place where it merges with the earth. I place a leaf in my mouth and taste nothing. I hear voices in the distance. I shouldn't risk their seeing me.

I don't look like them. Wrong clothes, no shoes. My braids so long they almost touch the ground. If I was one of them, I wouldn't be walking alone out here. I would have a family I belonged to, one that would come looking for me. They don't know what I am. They wouldn't believe anything I told them.

But then I see the woman. No, she's young. Barely a woman. The end of her long braid rests against the small of her back. She has only a kerchief wrapped around her head, but she's stiff with layers. Thick durable skirts over denim pants. Over the dress's waist, a man's shirt, buttoned and cuffed tightly around her wrists. The burlap bag with its rough-made yoke is slung across her back. She's deep into the cotton rows, far away from anyone else. Something metal glints in her hands—a knife, her fingers worrying the handle. Her darkness and her grace remind me of Mami. I come closer and see the very same frown on her face as she glances up at the rain-clouded sky.

II. Maravillas

The knife hurt in my hands. I knew it was wrong, but the clouds were leaving me no choice. I'd carried it all day. Had thought about raising the knife to the sky and slashing through the dark storm clouds. It couldn't rain. Not today. Not tonight. If I was still here in the morning, my life would be worth nothing.

Chuy and Lazaro were leaving tonight. They were ready to pretend there was no police, no *rinches*, no landowners to keep us from leaving Texas in the middle of the work season. Everywhere one looked, there were miles and miles of cotton to be picked. And even though Chuy and Lazaro had been born north of the river, if the *rinches* found them on the road, they would strip them of their papers and threaten to deport them— or worse, beat them and leave them for dead.

North, Lazaro had said, we could go up North and find better work. There were factories of all kinds. In the ten years since the second world war, Lazaro had said, there was work without end to be had at good pay. And from that moment, Chuy's eyes had been set on going North instead of being set on me.

Three months had passed since I'd realized I was with child. Sometimes I was afraid that Chuy had lied when he said he loved me and that he wanted to marry me. Time kept passing. It was harder and harder to hide my thickening waist. My mother knew, but she said nothing. Chuy still hadn't asked my father for my hand. Said my father would kill him for getting me with child. Chuy said it would be better for us to go away, up North. My child could grow up far from fields and mud and labor camps, he'd said.

But not if it rained. Lazaro hadn't wanted me to go with them at all. He said there was too much risk in taking a woman with them. They would have to move quickly through the fields and the *monte*, reaching the railroad tracks by dawn where friends of his would be waiting. I had begged to go with them, hating to have to cry to Chuy in front of Lazaro. Lazaro had finally agreed, on the condition that it not rain. The mud would make it easier to track them and I would be too great a burden. But I had to go. My father would throw me out of the house if I was still here when my belly grew large and rounded. And then what would I do, without Chuy, without my family? There would be nowhere for me to go. No choices for women like me—my father had said a thousand times—but to become prostitutes, at the mercy of all men. It would be better for me if I took the knife and slit my wrists and died in these fields.

It couldn't rain.

I looked away from the dark sky for a second and saw her. From far away, I thought she was an old lady. Made of earth and clay wrapped in dried leaves and dusted with a hundred roads. Her skirts and shawls dragged slightly on the ground, but she walked lightly. Her braids were so long they whipped in arcs around her body. She walked as if walking was like breathing, something done without thought. It was only as she came closer, stepping out of the shadows and lifting her face to me that I saw she was only a girl. Her face was wide and dark. Her eyes black and deep. She stared straight at me, stopping two rows away from me. Her bare toes dug into the loose earth filled with sharp sticks and dried stems but she didn't grimace. I gave her the knife when she held out her hand.

"Don't. It's bad luck." Her voice sounded rusty, her Spanish overrun and underrun with the rhythm and pull of another language. "Indian," my father would have spit out and then gone on to recite his claim to pure Spanish ancestry.

The knife looked heavy in her hands.

I fell to my knees in front of her, taking her hands in mine, "It can't rain today. My life is worth nothing if it rains. Please, only an innocent can cut the clouds," I pressed the knife into her hands.

Innocence was protection. That was what I had been taught. Only small children ever took the knives and cut upwards at the dark clouds to keep storms from breaking. Disaster resulted otherwise. My mother had told me the story of a priest who tried to cut the clouds. Instead, the earth had shifted, swallowing an entire village and all its inhabitants.

I thought the girl would help me. But she laughed and spun away from me, "I can't cut your clouds." She tilted her head to one side as if she was listening to a far-off sound, her eyes focused on the horizon. "My mother could, though. My mother could cut all the clouds in all the skies of the world." She whirled as she said this, dancing along the ditch. One second, she looked like a carefree child, and in the next, she was an old woman dragging one foot.

"My mother could cut them for you and chase the storm clouds away. Change the things that have happened, might have happened, are happening, will happen. She's innocent. If she's sad, she cries. When she falls, she hurts. When she runs, she flies. When she sleeps, she sings. She suffers and she fights." Her little-girl eyes were bitter, "But you and me, we just do what we need to survive. That's all I know how to do. I only know how to survive."

I thought she would cry, but she tightened her trembling lips and squinted her tear-glazed eyes. I didn't want to say anything. I didn't know what to say.

I'd heard the river in her voice, heard something that made me a little afraid. After too many long moments, she lifted her head heavily from her arms, her eyes shadowed, "I can't help you with the rain. I can't cut the clouds. You can't either. You can't keep the rain from falling."

The sound of my own sobs startled me. I had no strength. I fell, my face against the earth. My whole body shook. I didn't even realize I was weeping until I felt her fingers touching the tears on my cheek. The dark clouds were still overhead.

She touched my shoulder, "You'll feel better if you get up." She rose from the ground and held her hands out to me.

I don't think she saw the knife fall from her grasp, the dull edge gleaming as the blade opened and closed with the light, spinning in the air to land with its handle buried in the dirt.

The blade reflected sky and clouds, cutting long lines into their rounded shapes. I rose, twisting my body slightly, hiding the knife with my skirts, my foot laying the knife flat and into the soft ground. I prayed it would be enough.

I reached out to her slowly and touched her shoulder, "Thank you." I wiped my face, bit back the rest of my tears, told the part of my mind that was screaming to be silent. I couldn't think about the future now. "Can you help me with the cotton, please? If I don't finish this row, my family won't be paid for the work I've already done."

She nodded. I passed her the smaller bag, and watched her push the yoke over her head and one shoulder.

I helped her with the burlap bag, tugging on the yoke until it crossed her chest. I started talking, the words coming up from my insides, flowing out like bright blood, "My family came here to pick cotton. We follow the crops every year. A few months here, a few months there. We live in the *baracas* the owners built for the workers. One room per family. The only crop I hate worse than cotton is onion. It's so heavy and in the heat, it stinks."

She listened to me with her head tilted towards me, yet we advanced quickly. She didn't seem to need to straighten up from her bending. I offered her some of my water to drink, "I can't wait to leave all of this behind. Chuy, my *novio*, he's going to take me away. We're going up North. He's going to marry me. We're going to have a family."

We kept picking cotton. Stayed far ahead of everyone else. A slant-roofed metal shed came into view.

Hesitantly, she began to speak, her voice reedy, "My mother and my two brothers and me—we've been traveling for a long, long time. I barely remember what our home was like." She paused, as if trying to decide what she could tell me. "My mother won't ever answer me when I ask her where we're going."

The scent of the earth reaching towards rain grew stronger. I glanced up at the sky again. The clouds hadn't heard my prayers. They were churning violently. The sky thundered. It grew darker and darker. Far away I heard a harsh voice shouting in Spanish, "Hurry up, all of you, hurry!" and another man yelling, "Ramirez, 28 pounds. Noriega, 60 pounds. Garza, 43 pounds." They were emptying out all the burlap bags before the rain came. I grabbed the yoke of her bag and pulled it off her. I tossed it over my shoulder and started running towards the voices, "Wait here," I shouted back to the girl, "Wait here!"

But we were too far away from everyone else. In the next moment, the sky fell. The cotton fields were smashed down as if by a tremendous fist. The wind came howling from the north, blowing earth and leaves in furious waves. Blackness spilled out of the already dark sky. Deafening thunder overlapped the piercing flashes of lightning. The earth felt unsteady beneath our feet. We were suddenly alone. No lights. Impossible to hear anyone else's voice. I fell to the earth, the rain stinging and cold on my skin.

It should have worked. The knife spinning in the air, the blade reflecting the clouds—it should have been enough to stop the rain. One day. One night without rain was all I'd asked for. Chuy wouldn't take me now. My father would throw me out. I wouldn't have anywhere to go. I wrapped my arms around myself and felt the muddied earth against my cheek. I wanted to let the rain soften the earth around me until I sank into it, letting it swallow me, my love for Chuy, and the child in my womb.

Nothing mattered anymore. No reason to keep struggling. The girl kept calling my name—how did she know it when

I'd never told her? She pulled at my arm, calling my name, insisting I go with her. I pushed her hands away, "Leave me here. I don't care. Go away!"

She wrapped an arm around me and hauled me up against her side. A sudden gust of rain-laced wind blinded us. Nothing but the dark shadows beyond the fields. Nothing but mud all around us, no firm ground anywhere.

She shouted against my neck, "Don't give up—walk!"

It was almost more than I could do to keep lifting my feet. I took a step and sank until I felt the mud closing around my ankle. She pulled at me, but I couldn't help her with my weight. I felt so weak. I pulled against her shoulders and lifted my feet out. Forced myself to put one foot in front of the other.

The howling wind changed direction and, for a second, the rain stopped pouring into our eyes. The shed wasn't that far. Step after step through the mud, through the rain and the wind, we headed towards it. The mud gave away to soft grassy ground. We started running.

I was three feet behind her when I heard her make a sound. I reached for her as she started to fall. I held her tight against me, intent on reaching the shed. Her head was feverish against my shoulder, but her arms were wrapped tightly around my waist. Her fingers dug into my ribs. I could feel her heartbeat in my arms, against my chest, in my chin against her head. She was shivering, her body cold against me. I'd lost sight of the shed when I crashed into its walls. I pushed us through the rusted aluminum doors, falling hard against the musty ground.

The little girl clung to my neck, and I sobbed with relief. It was so dark inside I could hardly see anything. The wind howled through the thin wooden planks. The rain was a heavy, echoing pressure against the walls. We crawled on our hands and knees, huddling against the pile of burlap sacks in one corner of the shed. I held her close and rubbed her cold hands between mine. She was shivering, her hair streaming and wet over her face.

"Mari, Mari!" I heard a boy's voice yell from outside as he hammered at the walls of the shed. The little girl lifted her head at the sound of it. Bruises bloomed across her face, her eyes darkening and swelling, a bloody gash opening her upper lip. She quickly ducked her head against my shoulder, her body shaking though she said nothing and made no sounds.

The boy's voice came closer. He called and called for her, in English and in Spanish and in some other language, always calling the name of that little orange flower. Somewhere, a baby was crying and screaming. The doors shrieked when he threw them open. The rain and the wind fought against his closing the door. He started calling for her again, his voice breaking with sobs as he came closer. Three steps away from us, he slowed and stilled. He was tall but too thin, his clothes as ragged as the girl's.

He'd brought the scent of blood with him. Old and new. The scent of copper, the scent of fear, the scent of burning. He held a crying baby in his arms. The girl pushed herself out of my arms, stumbling towards the boy. He was gasping for air and coughing, as if he was choking on blood. As I watched, he shuddered as if someone had struck him a blow. His left arm fell off his body in a spray of blood. His knees folded, and he fell to the ground. With one arm the girl took the baby and cradled it against herself. With her other arm she gathered up the boy as he crumpled to the ground. He called to her weakly, "Cempasuchil."

Lightning flashed. I couldn't help gasping when I saw her face in the light, swollen and bleeding, one eye a massive burst of purple. The blanket fell away from the baby and I saw it, pale and bloody and naked. She stood, holding both brothers, unable to scream or cry or speak. In the light, the blood streaming from her was black. She endured, bleeding, without whimpering, holding herself together only because her brothers would collapse into flesh and pain without her.

I couldn't move. Couldn't speak. Didn't know what to do or say. How to help her. I didn't want to touch them. Didn't want to take them from her arms. Didn't want to see their faces any closer, any clearer. I turned my face away, not wanting to see the desperation in her eyes.

Thunder. Then more thunder, too much thunder. One of the walls tumbled down, and though the rain poured down and the trees outside were bent sideways with the wind, it was strangely quiet, strangely still inside the shed.

I cowered away from the woman who was suddenly standing there. Her terrible eyes were bright and clear, translucent as a child's. Her body was all corded muscle. Long scars divided the colonies of little scars up and down both legs. Her scaled legs seemed carved from wood or bone. A machete was slung across Her chest, blade naked against Her skin. Her eyes frantically searched the shed. Her eyes passed over me without seeing me. She held her arms straight out in front of her, her hands moving wildly through the air, as if she didn't trust her eyes. She crossed and recrossed the room, searching its walls and corners with anxious hands. I heard Her whispering, heard the words swelling and bleeding on her tongue.

Her voice was so low I could barely hear it, "*Hijos.*" Called and screamed and choked on it, "*Mis hijos, mis hijos.*" They answered Her. Boy and girl and baby. They touched Her, tried to cling to Her. She kept calling for them, beating at the air in frustration, whirling and calling. They fell away, still calling to Her. Her movements grew more frenzied, beating on the walls and tearing at her hair. Her arms kept closing around nothing. "Mami, Mami," they followed her around the shed, but she never stopped screaming for them, "*Mis hijos, mis hijos!*"

And all at once I understood. She didn't know they were there. Didn't know they'd answered Her. Didn't know She could touch them.

The baby was a cold dark bundle in the little girl's arms, and the boy was a mindless heap of limbs and flesh around her legs. She was shaking with the effort to stay on her feet. She let go of the boy and reached towards the Mother, "Mami." But her Mother kept screaming and I saw the shock on the girl's face as she realized her Mother couldn't see her, couldn't hear her, didn't even know they were there. She had never known they were there, behind Her, following Her, never leaving Her. Her Mother walking and running, searching for Her children and never finding them though they followed Her everywhere.

The girl swayed. Blood poured from her slight body. In that moment, she remembered everything and relived her own death. She wept without sobbing, her shoulders shaking soundlessly.

I stared at the Mother, at Her unclouded eyes. And though I was barely a mother, though I'd worried more about my future with Chuy than my child's future, in that moment I understood Her blindness. What would it do to Her to have to see—to remember—them as they'd died. Better to be blind. Better not to have it driven into Her Mother's Heart at every moment. Better to search for Her children, whole and unhurt, somewhere along the rivers. For as long as it took, the years becoming decades becoming centuries.

I don't know what the girl understood. I don't know what changed in her in that moment. She took a deep breath and straightened her limbs. Wiped away her own blood and smoothed away the bruises and swelling on her face. As her Mother whirled around and around, screaming with the wind, the girl rocked the baby against her. She sang low and soft against his cheek, and his body lost its terrible pallor, its terrible stillness. She loosened a long length of fabric from her clothing, wound it around her body, and secured him against her chest.

She knelt on the floor and gathered up her brother's broken body parts with both hands. She called his name and called his name and called his name as she fitted limbs to torso, as she smoothed the flesh into wholeness. When he lay, whole and breathing, she rose to her feet and then helped him up.

The three breathed and moved in the odd half-light half-dark of the shed. It was no longer raining, and the wind had died down. With sad eyes, the girl looked at her Mother, now quiet and still. After a moment, she took one of Her hands. The boy went to Her other side, took Her other hand. They led Her out of the shed.

I didn't see where they went. Didn't see if they went towards the road or towards the river. Didn't see if they faded away like smoke or if they walked, one step in front of the other, until they were too far to see in the darkness. I'd fallen to my knees in the shed, my hands moving over my baby. For the first time, I'd felt him or her move inside my womb. My child, I thought wonderingly. Not laughing, not crying, only filled with a sudden echoing silence. I imagined I could hear both our heartbeats. I'd never known such terror, feeling that endless, enduring love spiraling out of me.

I was a mother. I heard those words ring in my head, ringing through my body as if it was a bell. And I would hold my child in my arms the way She never would again. And in that moment I knew I would be a fierce mother. I would protect my child. I would find us a place in the world, with or without Chuy, with or without my family.

III. Cempasuchil

The beginning.

A hundred times, a hundred hundred times they came to the door. In metal armor, in stiff leather, in uniforms of a dozens colors. They came with swords and spears and bayonets and guns and cannons. Death came on horses. Death and disease and poverty. Acts of violence soaked the ground with blood again and again, hunting the people with dark skin and darker eyes and sky wide faces. Death came on horses. And with the rain. The pounding hooves echoed the rain the day It Broke. And each time it hurt. It hurt to die, to live, to suffer. Death came on horses the first time. And so she ran on foot, hardening her skin against rock and sand and earth. She wept and she wailed and she screamed into the wind but she ran.

They say she wept and wailed for her children and wandered all the rivers of the world, but they never say she ran. She ran like a deer. She ran like a bird flying or a fish swimming. They forgot that she needs to run, run fast and away, feeling the earth leap up to her feet and the wind stinging her eyes. They forgot that she's strong running, holding herself together through all the screaming and all the weeping and all the wailing. She clutches the machete to her side as she runs.

They forgot her name and gave her another. A name that barely contains the story. A name that says she only weeps, only knows how to weep. They gave her a name that always makes her remember the beginning. The name is a cage. A truth. A lie. But she answered to it, staying with her people and defending them. It wasn't just for her children that she ran searching but it was always her children. Death came on horses. She ran on foot. Protection and vengeance came naturally to her when Death came on horses. She ran on foot after it, hunting Death coming on horses.

It hurt each time to die. It hurt each time like the first time they had run her to the ground. They held her down and broke her limbs. The men spread her legs and violated her. They took a dagger, slit her belly, and pulled out the bloody baby. She had sung songs to him inside her, calling him *mi chiquito mi chiquito mi vida*. Iccauhtli had lived for a moment, gasping for air, his eyes flying open. His blue veins throbbed against his delicate and bloody skin.

Sometimes their rough hands dashed Iccauhtli's head against the rocks. Sometimes she lifted the dagger and slit the baby's neck before he could look at her with those white-less eyes. Sometimes she thrust the blade into her belly before they could pull him out. Sometimes she was able to escape, holding Iccauhtli in her arms and falling into the water, deep into the water.

Tomás was the first. They spotted the young Indian boy by the river, alone and unarmed, fishing with a stick. They were riding through, Death coming on horses, and they had dogs. Feverishly patient dogs who knew how to tear flesh without killing their victim. He screamed with the first bite and with the second and with the third as they laughed and watched him flail about. Four dogs swarmed over him, tearing out long ribbons and short chunks of flesh. And then they called the dogs away and left the boy with one eye to watch them go, to watch his blood slowly pour itself out, to hunt out the parts of himself spread over the riverbanks, all the blood leaking into the clear green river.

And then she came. His mother found him like that. Without knowing what she would see and then seeing all of it, not knowing she would never speak another word that was not wailing, she said his name. His single eye stared up at her with an odd calmness and pleaded, begged. There was nothing, her hands held nothing. She made herself go into the river and lift one of the heavy water-polished rocks. She made herself come out of the river and then she made herself dash it against his head. Once he was dead, she stained her face and her chest and her swollen belly with his blood.

She staggered towards the village, knowing what she would see. Smoke stained the entire sky. Her eyes strained against the hazy and oily heat. Women were still screaming on the other side of the village, and the whimpers in her own throat couldn't be heard over the screams of burning animals. Her daughter. Where was her daughter. She saw her home but heard no screaming. Saw fire eating its way across the roof. Horses had churned up the ground around the house, and newly dead animals had spilled their blood against its walls. She couldn't see. She went to the doorway and found her daughter. Boneless flesh. Unfurled, unraveled, unmade flesh. Her skin was bruised to blackness. Her limbs lay at odd angles, eyes set sightlessly on the ceiling.

Fire forced her away from the window, and she threw herself to the ground. But Death came on horses. She heard the shrill whinnying and the human shouting. They chased after her and she ran, holding her belly. She struggled to see through the smoke, but burning hands singed her flesh and made ashes of her name.

Woman and machete never parted, wandering all the rivers and all the creeks and all the places her people went, the people of dark skin and darker eyes and sky-wide faces, following all her children. She would search for her children, her children whole, unbloodied and unbroken. She never found them, though sometimes it seemed she could hear her daughter's voice singing, her son's shouting, feel Iccauhtli nudging against her breast. She would wander all the rivers and all the creeks and all the places her people went, finding and losing her children in all their faces. She saw her son in the dark bodies hung from gnarled trees, the men with hollow eyes who died running from guns, the ones who lost their footing in the river's rushing. She saw her daughter in the suffocated women she found in sealed boxcars, the women she found curled around their babies in the desert, the women attacked walking home at night from the maquiladoras. The people who remembered her, remembered her by the wrong name. But the ones who saw her, the ones she saved, the ones whose pain she ended, the ones for whom she was death's face, the ones her own hands put to rest, they recognized the rage and tenderness in her eyes and called her Mother. She watched over everyone, listening for their cries. The ones who'd forgotten heard only the echoes of her wailing and thought it was the wind.

CHAPTER 18

Thru the Veil and 32.2480° N, 112.9161° W (Sonoran Desert)

Roxanna Ivonne Sanchez-Avila

Artist Statement

In my self-portrait photography, I search for a sense of self and how I navigate the world as a Honduran-American. I explore how children of Honduran immigrants, like myself, create identity, especially when their parents began anew and left many of their traditional knowledges and kinships behind. Often putting the responsibility on their children to create or inhabit fragmented identities. The selected images *Thru the Veil* and *32.2480° N, 112.9161° W (Sonoran Desert)* capture the interconnected relationships between fragmented multilayered identities and haunting testimonios of displacement and migration.

In *Thru the Veil*, I used multiple exposure on black and white film to orchestrate a liminal state of mind that visualizes shapeshifting. Presented as a diptych, a visual storytelling format that pairs two images that are connected by contrast or theme, it shows my multidimensional Honduran-Americanness. As Graciela Iturbide, a famous black and white photographer, said about the language of photography, "What the eye sees is a synthesis of who you are and all you have learned" (as quoted in Richardson, p. 56). In this portrait, I *shapeshift* within the multiple layers representing being displaced within various planes yet, blending together through the dance between light and shadow. It highlights how a multitude of life experiences overlap to make

ure 18.1. *Thru the Veil*, photo by Roxanna Ivonne Sanchez-Avila.

Figure 18.2. *32.2480° N, 112.9161° W (Sonoran Desert)*, photo by Roxanna Ivonne Sanchez-Avila.

you who you are and gives you the opportunity to synthesize and create identities out of fragments.

In *32.2480° N, 112.9161° W (Sonoran Desert)*, I expanded film, a technique to increase contrast and the film grain, to highlight nighttime migration and the (e)motion migrants conjure traveling through the Sonoran Desert in Arizona. A common trope in migration narratives, the moon has served as the light that guides in the darkness. In the image, the full moon is visible in the sky where white specks that look like stars surround it, but it is dust on film, visualizing residue that ghostly matters leave behind. At the center, a shack made of aluminum sheets reminded me of my Honduran mother's migration testimonio and nostalgia for home. In the foreground is a moving shadow figure facing the shack and the moon. I used long exposure, a photography technique that allows more time to capture movement, to emote ghosts as energy entities.

My cultural identities are decontextualized inheritances that only exist by words. I live in a liminal status. Even when there is limited accessibility to concrete archives of my family lineage or history, my embodiment is not always legible to me and/or others. Central America is an important landscape of the Americas that, through forced trauma to the land and people, connects two bodies of water, the Pacific and Atlantic Oceans, yet the people and region are often misconceived in discourse. I feel my identity is much like the perceptions people have of Central America, a phantom figure. I turn to photography to unravel these absent, limited, or misrepresentations of Central Americans.

References

Bradu, Fabienne. (2005). "Graciela Iturbide speaks with Fabienne Abdu." *Conversations with contemporary photographers*. Umbrage Editions.

Iturbide, Graciela. *PhotoQuotations.com.* "Graciela Iturbide." http://www.photoquotations.com /a/343/Graciela+Iturbide. (accessed June 29, 2020).

Roberts, Elisabeth. (2012). "Geography and the Visual Image: A Hauntological Approach." *Progress in Human Geography* 37, no. 3: pp. 386–402.

PART III

Bringing the Borderlands Home: Public Discourses and Theories of the Flesh

CHAPTER 19

Hauntology of the Oppressed
The MeXicana Gothic and Spectral Geographies in Sandra Cisneros's "Woman Hollering Creek"

Cathryn J. Merla-Watson

"Monsters and the phantasmagoric have long been central to the Chican@ experience as reminders of our unresolved haunted histories of violence and oppression."
(W. A. CALVO-QUIRÓS, 2017, p. 39)

"Because ultimately haunting is about how to transform a shadow of a life into an undiminished life whose shadows touch softly in the spirit of a peaceful reconciliation."
(GORDON, 1997, p. 208)

It was New Years Eve in San Antonio, Texas, in the mid-1980s, when I first heard of La Llorona. I was six years old. Monica, my older cousin, was baby-sitting us younger cousins. Shutting off the living room light, she sat us in a circle, and began telling us a story in a hushed tone of a dark-skinned woman who is abandoned by her Spanish gentleman lover, returning to his fiance in Mexico. In a fit of desperation and rage, the impoverished woman drowns her children in a nearby river and then herself. She is condemned to wander the river banks for eternity calling and crying for her children in inconsolable grief. According to my prima, that New Year's evening La Llorona haunted the drainage creek that ran behind my parents' working class apartment—perhaps looking for us. The older cousins smirked appreciably.

Monica's purpose in telling this tale was apparent: to scare us into sitting still and not making trouble until our parents came home. Like many Chicanas and Mexicanas, I have remained haunted long after my initial hearing of this folklore in childhood. The claustrophobic aspects of La Llorona's afterlife have always given me goosebumps as I think about how her specter must remain forever at the river. As a young mixed-race Chicana who was always on the move and loved to play sports and was often called a "tomboy," my elders frequently reprimanded me to sit still (*stop playing soccer with the boys in that dress!*) and to stay small (*close your legs and stop sitting like a frog m'ija!*). As a woman now approaching middle age, a tenured college professor, and once a semi-professional bicycle racer, my life has been defined by mobility in multiple senses.

The claustrophobic and ghostly matter of La Llorona disinters and reanimates historical trauma in relation to the Indigenous and contemporary Chicana subjectivity in the US-Mexico borderlands. Bound up within a "historical triangulation" (González, p. 10) of demonized Mexican indigenous women, mythic and actual, such as, for example, La Llorona is interlocked with Cihuacoatl and Malinche (Malintzin or Malinalli), that is, respectively, the Aztec fertility and motherhood goddess as well as Hernán Cortés's lover and translator, also known as "La Chingada" or "The Fucked One" (see also R. Perez, 2008). Sonia Saldívar-Hull expounds: "When we trace the legend of La Llorona, we find that this tale actually chronicles the historical moment of violence against the indigenous female subject in the Americas" (p. 157). These cognate Indigenous figures together suture a gendered and sexualized collective colonial imaginary, a "memory / of some ancient / betrayal" (Moraga, 2000, p.38) that inheres in and colors representations of Mexicanas and Chicanas–as well as stifle our material realities and desires, entrap and contain us. As such, La Llorona transmits gendered and sexualized spatial knowledge in relation to the "LatIndigenous," a neologistic identification signaling the complex ways that Chicana and Latinx identities are informed by and entwined with Indigeneity. Further, structuring La Llorona's folklore qua colonial imaginary (Pérez, 1999) are constrictive binaries—virgin/whore and passive victim/aggressive agent—that suffocate and immobilize Mexicana and Chicana subjectivity. "The whore figure, the damned mother, overly sexual," Bernadette Marie Calafell (2015) affirms, "is always put in her place" (p. 20). However, just as importantly, her figure is an im/material site for potential decolonial intervention, transformation, and liberation.

It is the horrific gendered, racialized, and sexualized elements of spatial constraint that are contoured by these pernicious gendered and sexualized binaries within the folklore of La Llorona that Sandra Cisneros's 1992 short story "Woman Hollering Creek" (WHC) explores. The titular short story of *Woman Hollering Creek and Other Stories* (1992) centers on Cleófilas, a young woman from a small town in Mexico, who, after marrying, immigrates with her new husband Juan Pedro to "Seguín, Tejas," a remote Texas town west of San Antonio. Romanticized fantasies of marital bliss quickly morph into a dystopian nightmare: while pregnant and caring for an infant, Cleófilas becomes entrapped in not only a foreign place where she does not speak English but also in the vice grip of domestic violence. La Llorona, whose figure is evoked by the story's title, invisibly though palpably animates the story's geography, delimiting where Cleófilas can go and whom she can become, her very horizons of possibility. To be sure, Chicana feminist literary scholarship has incisively analyzed the ways in which WHC foregrounds how working class Mexican immigrant women become ensnared by patriarchal social structures, limning out the story's claustrophobic features. While Mary Pat Brady (2002) underscores the story's "urgency of space," Dalia Kandiyoti (2009) teases out themes of enclosure and confinement permeating this diasporic immigrant short story. Saldívar-Hull (2000) further illuminates how transnational popular forms of representation and discourses function to constrict Chicana and Mexican immigrant women's gender roles.

Yet, curiously, given the salient presence of the spectral and the central motif of entrapment in this short story, WHC has yet to be approached through the related lenses of the gothic or theories of the spectral. To further flesh out the urgency of space in WHC, I reinterpret the story through the prism of what I call the "meXicana gothic," borrowing from Rosa Linda Fregoso (2003), to make visible, however partially, how the ambivalent colonial imaginary and ghostly matter of La Llorona animates Cleófilas's affective experience of space in WHC, both the feeling of terror and a decolonizing sense of hope and the utopian. The meXicana gothic, I submit, reroutes the specterly within the US-Mexico borderlands, a complex and intersectional terrain of the LatIndigenous, engendering a culturally specific interpretive practice to recognize and analyze the ghostly within Latinx literary and cultural productions. As I explore in the conclusion, the meXicana gothic deploys a "hauntology of the oppressed" that helps us to collectively conjure and exorcise our ghosts.

The MeXicana Gothic

Although the gothic genre emerged in Britain in the eighteenth century, it is notoriously mutable and portable, appearing throughout history and within diverse cultures across the world. Its subgenres continue to proliferate across hemispheres, as evident in the recent appearance of the tropical, Latin American, and global gothic genres, which remap and reconceptualize the gothic beyond the white British and US pale. In this vein, scholars of the US gothic have begun to rethink the gothic genre to recognize diverse BIPOC contributions to or reengagements with this fraught genre. After all, gothic literature's beginnings in both the US and Britain uncovers how the abject and terror have historically been figured by xenophobia and racial anxieties, that is, the "darker side of modernity" (Mignolo xix, 2011). Observing how the gothic displays "generic instability" (p. 5), Teresa Goddu (1997) offers a model to begin reconceiving the genre by approaching the American gothic as a discourse that must be contextualized within its "network of historical representation" (p. 2). Acknowledging how "history invents the gothic and in turn the gothic reinvents history" (p. 132) brings into relief the heretofore occluded horrors of history to which BIPOC communities have been subjected to and subjectivized by. This taut relationship among history, subjectivity, and the gothic permits a more pluralistic view of the gothic that encompasses texts authored by US ethnic writers whose work is not normally recognized as gothic, such as the autobiographies of Harriet Jacobs and Richard Wright. Maisha Wester in the *African American Gothic: Screams from Shadowed Places* (2012) builds on Goddu's repurposing of the gothic by exploring how black writers do not just "mimic traditional gothic conventions," but instead "appropriate and revise the genre's tropes in unique ways to both speak back to the tradition's originiators and to make it a capable and useful vehicle for expressing the terrors and complexities of black existence in America" (p. 2). Through appropriation, Wester maintains, "black writers introduce profound variations that make the gothic something new" (p. 28).

Indeed, as Tanya González (2007) observes, analyzing Latinx literature through the gothic or American gothic "is not a common practice" (p. 46). Although relatively scant attention has been dedicated to theorizing an emerging Latinx gothic genre, there is a growing body of scholarship that builds on the work of Goddu, Wester, and others that has begun to enunciate the gothic and horror in relation to the Latinx epistemology, lived experience, and sense of place. This scholarship focalizes how the Latinx gothic makes visible what has become naturalized and ordinary: the "violentologies" (Olguín, 2021) animating LatIndigenous subjectivity and social life—or death. What is more, these scholars underline how the gothic is not simply a genre but also "a mode of reading" (Merla-Watson & Olguín, 2017), and I would add, *rereading*, Latinx or LatIndigenous texts. The Latinx gothic is thus a project of reclamation, as evinced in how Cordelia Barrera (2022), Tanya González (2007), Tace Hedrick (2017), and Paul Wickelson (2013) have reclaimed texts like Mary Castillo's Lost in the Light (2012), Sandra Cisneros's *Caramelo* (2002), and Cherríe Moraga's *The Hungry Woman: A Mexican Medea* (1995) as gothic. These scholars recontextualize the gothic within the borderlands and the "haunted Southwest" (Barrera, 2022). They excavate how the violences of US imperialism and settler colonialism, as perhaps most obvious through the Mexican American War and the signing of the Treaty of Guadalupe Hidalgo, have carved out and continue to invisibly contour Latinx or LatIndigenous lived experience. Analyzing *Caramelo*, Wickelson (2013) states how the US West "emerges less as an uncomplicated beacon of youth and possibility" but more as, drawing on José E. Limón's work, "a 'bedeviled' colonial space, not separate from Mexico but haunted by a history of low-grade war between ethnic groups, genders, and classes" (p. 93). Similarly, reapproaching the complex site of the borderlands as a gothic frontier, Barrera writes, "Border places, however, encompass liminal sites of memory with histories all their own. The spatial poetics of the desert configure a palimpsest, a space worked upon, etched over in terms of history and modernist practices that occluded or erased earlier practices, belief systems, and ways of being" (p. 71). Resituating and remapping the gothic within the LatIndingenous space US-Mexico borderlands, Wickelson and Barrera aver, exhumes other histories, epistemologies, and even ontologies, calling for a critical reassessment and rereading of one of the gothic's central figures–the specter.

In the groundbreaking 1997 monograph *Ghostly Matters: Haunting and the Sociological Imagination*, Avery Gordon performs a sociological analysis of contemporary ethnic literature that reframes the ghost as an affective mode of knowledge production that testifies to collective traumas and demands collective reckoning. Gordon contends that haunting is "neither premodern superstition nor individual psychosis; it is a generalizable social phenomenon of great import. To study social life one must confront the ghostly aspects of it" (p. 7). Reframing the specterly as a structure of feeling and a social figure that accrues particular significations in minority writing that is qualitatively different than white western conceptions of the ghostly opens up space for understanding how the specterly is culturally constituted. Doing so, begs further questions about the relationship between the ghostly and the epistemological and ontological. Though María DeGuzmán (2012) theorizes the ghostly within a queer tropics of night in Anglographic queer Latinx

Caribbean poetry, DeGuzmán's discussion of the specter is relevant to interpreting ghosts in LatIndigenous letters more broadly. DeGuzmán argues that
the specter "transports readers into a different space-time and horizon of values, not only into deconstructed categories of race, ethnicity, nationality, sexuality, class . . . but into a project that reconstructs these variables by refracting
them through dislocation, diaspora, exile, and transculturation" (p. 79). This
reconstructive and refractive function of the specterly, moreover, dovetails
with Barrera's (2022) hermeneutic for interpreting the haunted southwest that
requires a "shifting of the lens between a discursive mixture of registers from
American literary forms . . . alongside conceptions that speak to Indigeneity,
Aztec and Mayan mythologies, and preconquest ways of living in the world"
(p. xvi). LatIndigenous specters indeed "materialize a unique borderland
standpoint" (Calvo-Quirós, 2017, p. 41)—one inflected by mestizaje and diaspora, serving as a "valuable source of epistemic information about those histories of subjugation" (p. 39).

I have previously noted with B. V. Olguín (2017), Chicana feminist
scholarship has produced the most developed scholarship on Latinx or
LatIndigenous ghostly matters within the context of the US-Mexico borderlands through focused attention on La Llorona, collectively loosening her
from the clutches of coloniality and overlapping heteropatriarchal structures
(p. 16). Domino Rene Perez writes that La Llorona "haunts the cultural landscape of our imaginations, reminding us of the necessity and consequences of
acting out against oppression" (2008, p. 73). La Llorona inheres within transnational imaginaries that in turn haunt and constrict Mexicana and Chicana
desire, sexuality, and material worlds. As Norma Alarcón (1999) argues, La
Llorona and related figures including Aztec goddesses and Malinche, who
together span the US-Mexico borderlands, cement, borrowing from Gayatri
Spivak, "regulative psychobiographies" (p. 68) that continue to consolidate
and exert heteropatriarchal control of Chicanas and Mexicanas, restricting
Chicanas both in terms of imaginative horizons and actual mobility.

I propose interpreting La Llorona and cognate figures through what I call
the meXicana gothic, borrowing Rosa Linda Fregoso's term (2003), in Chicana
and Latina literary and cultural productions to more fully understand how
these fraught figures as colonial imaginaries mark, shape, and even extinguish
Chicana and Mexicana subjectivity. The meXicana gothic permits an inter-
pretation of these figures on their own grounds: the US-Mexico borderlands.
While he "X" draws visibility to the intersection between and "complicated
imbrication of 'Chicanas' and 'Mexicanas' in the formation of the nation" (xiv),
Fregoso also adds:

As the interface between Mexicana and Chicana, "meXicana" draws attention to the historical, material, and discursive effects of contact zones and exchanges among various communities on the Mexico-US border, living in the shadows of more than 150 years of conflict, interactions, and tensions. "meXicana" references processes of transculturation, hybridity, and cultural exchanges . . . (p. xiv)

In this manner, the meXicana gothic captures the hybrid and shifting nature of LatIndigenous identity and specters. This genre adumbrates how "[h]istorical meaning and ethnic identity are established through the process of haunting" (Brogan, 198, p. 18).

In addition to Fregoso's original use of the X, which indexes the intersectional and hybrid identities and spaces of the borderlands, the X accrues other spatial and bodily significations within the context of the meXicana gothic. The "x" multiply marks. It demarcates geographic sites more generally ("x marks the spot") and sites of crime and violence, that is, not only crime scenes but also the crosshairs of a scope used to sight a firearm (Seltzer, 2016). Thus the MeXicana gothic is attuned to how gendered, sexualized, and racialized bodies are marked and targeted for specific forms of overlapping violence, social and real death, as well as as how those bodies are situated and ensnared within discursive and material structures and gridlocks of oppression. However, the "x" is also semantically slippery, polysemous, mysterious, and even subversive (Seltzer, 2016). In other words, like the spectral, the x is not totalizing and nor is it completely transparent, but rather the x is mutable and open to other future possibilities and decolonial imaginaries.

Before proceeding to the analysis of WHC in the following subsection, a quick note on my perhaps unorthodox engagement with genre. Conceptualizing the Latinx gothic more broadly (as well as non-white or non-western forms of the gothic) calls for the dissolution of sclerotic binaries and distinct formal features that have historically informed this genre. Traditionally, distinctions have been made between the gothic and gothic horror as well as between gothic horror and the contemporary popular horror genre. The contemporary horror genre also encompasses myriad discrete subgenres, including body and domestic horror. As well, there are ongoing and lively debates surrounding definitions of the female and feminist gothic. For the purpose of this essay, though, I do not engage in these debates as I am less interested in the stability and discreteness of genres and subgenres, and I am more interested in how Latinx cultural producers such as Sandra Cisneros intentionally draw from multiple genres *a lo rasquache* (Ybarra-Frausto, 1990) to reconfigure and authorize new genres that speak to the lived experiences of LatIndigenous peoples. This blending not only echoes the cultural mestizaje of Latinx ethnicity but also the speculative more broadly, an umbrella term that includes the gothic and horror genres, and "draws genre boundaries expansively to encompass heterogenous forms and genres of writing" (Streeby, 2017, p. 74). What is more, this maneuvering between and among confuses generic boundaries, opening up interstitial sites wherein our ghosts emerge.

La Llorona and LatIndigenous Spectral Cartographies in WHC

When I teach WHC in the undergraduate classroom, I have students break into groups and use markers to map out the story on butcher block paper. Students are encouraged to depict the multiple spatial scales described in the story, ranging from the location of Cleófilas's home to the locale of her neighborhood and the town Seguín to the larger region of the Texas-Mexico borderlands as well as Mexico. This exercise brings into sharp relief the multiple and overlapping scales in which Cleófilas—and other working class immigrant women—are trapped and unable to escape the horrors of domestic abuse. As in much of Chicana fiction and cultural production, domestic space is not limited to the "private sphere." In a similar vein, WHC "underscores the domestic as connected to the many political and recurring debates about domestic place, race, gender, and immigration affecting the lives of Mexicanas and Chicanas" (McMahon 2013, p. 4). Indeed, this mapping of WHC powerfully demonstrates how "violence is closing in on" Cleófilas (Brady, 2002, p. 134), and how, more broadly, how "for women of color, home and homeland have not been safe place—our bodies are constantly targeted, trespassed, and violated" (Anzaldúa, 2015, pp. 14-15).

To that end, the mexicana gothic is an incisive vehicle for critique, drawing from the feminist gothic and domestic horror, whose prominent formal convention is the isolation of the female protagonist in the ostensibly most sacred and safe space of the home. While WHC has traditionally been approached through realism or the bildungsroman, Cisneros's oeuvre is known for breaching generic borders (Karafilis, 1998). Interpreting WHC through the meXicana gothic unearths how Seguín and the borderlands is haunted in particular ways, and how haunting itself is experienced differently or "differentially" (Sandoval, 2000) according to intersecting and relational forms of difference. Approaching WHC through the meXicana gothic, moreover, reveals how La Llorona inspirits the LatIndigenous terrains of the borderlands and both delimits and potentially liberates Chicana and Mexicana lived experiences and futures.

The very first paragraph of WHC is quintessentially gothic, laced with fore-boding as it portends a failed marriage and a return home:

The Day Don Serafín gave Juan Pedro Martínez permission to take Cleófilas Enriqueta DeLeón Hernández as his bride, across her father's threshold, over several miles of dirt road and several miles of paved, over one border and beyond to a town en el otro lado—on the other side—already did he divine the morning his daughter would raise her hand over her eyes, look south, and dream of returning to the chores that never ended, six good-for-nothing brothers, and one old man's complaints. (p. 43)

This passage conveys, too, another trope of gothic—entrapment—as it charts a closed circuit of patriarchal control that spans the borderlands; before Cleófilas even departs from her childhood home her father foresees his daughter returning. Absent is a mother or other female figures who might provide guidance, helping to navigate a way out. This patriarchal enclosure, which is further developed throughout WHC, moreover, is animated by the specter of La Llorona. Conspicuously, though, the title of the story and the name of the arroyo is not "woman weeping" or "weeping woman" ("la llo-rona") but rather "woman hollering." Saldívar-Hull explicates that

. . . La llorona functions as an unspoken, perhaps unspeakable presence for Cleófilas. Trusting that her audience will know the plot of the leg-end, Cisneros need only have her character be drawn to a creek whose name only hints at the Spanish name Llorona; it has become Woman Hollering. (p. 119)

To slightly rephrase and reframe Saldívar-Hull's assessment of La Llorona's role in WHC, this fraught figure operates as an invisible though tangible structure of feeling and colonial imaginary contouring the affective and inter-sectional experience of space in this story: to wit, a ghostly matter. It is also significant that La Llorona, who is not named but remains a spectral pres-ence in WHC, is articulated as a form of Indigenous knowledge that escapes the white gaze and distribution of the sensible: "The natives only know the *arroyo* . . . was called Woman Hollering, a name no one from these parts questioned, little less understood. *Pues allá de los indios, quién sabe*—who knows the townspeople shrugged . . . " (p. 46). WHC refuses to endow La Llorona with full legibility, whereby the story participates in a larger project

of decoloniality: not only does WHC resist the all-consuming optics of coloniality, but also, in doing so, makes imaginative space to reenvision La Llorona
into a more agentic figure or decolonial imaginary who maps her own path
within and against or even outside of patriarchal gridlocks.

Elaborating how La Llorona saturates, haunts and shapes WHC's spectral
geography of the borderlands, the exposition employs terrifying imagery,
sonic formal devices, as well as intertextuality to map out Cleófilas's affective
state. Gloria Anzaldúa (1999) conceptualizes "intimate terrorism" as a feeling
as though the "world is not a safe place to live in" (p. 42):

> We shiver in separate cells in enclosed cities, shoulder hunched barely
> keeping the panic below the surface of the skin, daily drinking shock
> along with our morning coffee, fearing torches being set to our build
> ings, the attacks in the streets. Shutting down. Woman does not feel safe
> when her own culture, and white culture, are critical of her; when the
> males of all races hunt her as prey. (p. 42)

Intimate terrorism refunctions the traditional notion of gothic terror, which
is more concerned with suspense and dread, by giving notice to the daily and
persistent forms of heteronormative and patriarchal forms of constraint and
necro-subjection (Rosas, 2019) that are naturalized and rendered invisible.
Now married to Juan Pedro, Cleófilas lives in Seguin, trapped at home in her
bedroom where "she lay on her side of the bed listening to the hollow roar of
the interstate, a distant dog barking, the pecan trees rustling like ladies in stiff
petticoats—*shh-shh-shh, shh-shh-shh*—soothing her to sleep" (p. 44). Evoking
Charlotte Perkins Gilman's 1892 female gothic story "The Yellow Wallpaper,"
the domestic is refigured as a site of terror, constriction, and disquiet. Even
within the bedroom Cleófilas is immobilized, stationed to her side of the
bed. Background noise becomes menacing: the highway takes on a terrifying
and animate quality as it "roar(s)" (p. 44). While highways have the capacity
to connect, they also have the ability to sever individuals and communities
from other social bodies and vital resources (Villa, 2000), such as those in San
Antonio where Cleófilas attempts to flee in the story's conclusion. Cleófilas
also hears "distant dogs barking" (p. 220), sounding alarm, which is further
amplified through alliteration. It is relevant, too, that dogs were used as tools
of conquest throughout the Américas to torture, control, and contain indigenous peoples, further heightening Cleófilas's experience of intimate terrorism.

The incorporation of popular Mexican and borderlands cultural productions of telenovelas and fotonovelas in WHC allude to dichotomies informing La Llorona's figure, which in turn constrain Cleófilas and Chicana and Mexicana subjectivity more broadly. While telenovelas portray an overly romanticized version of married life and reality, prompting Cleófilas to leave her Mexican hometown for an idealized vision of "el otro lado" and marriage and family life, fotonovelas such as ¡Alarma! Magazine . . . sensationalize and normalize violence against women" (Saldívar-Hull, 2000, p. 109). Saldívar-Hull further explains, "These often sexually explicit fotonovelas gush their class and sex-role contradictions" (p. 109) in which women are demonized—deemed a whore—for men's adultery while men are exonerated. WHC highlights how this contradiction prompts violence against women. For instance, Maximiliano, one of the men in the bar Juan Pedro frequents "was said to have killed his wife in an ice-house brawl when she came at him with a mop" (p. 51). When this vulgar "foul-smelling fool" (p. 51) then jokes that he "had to shoot . . . she was armed," eliciting disgust from Cleófilas and laughter from the other men at the bar. This normalizing of violence against women and women being cast singularly as a whore or hapless victim is also echoed through news stories reporting the murder of women. Cleófilas recalls:

This woman found on the side of the interstate. This one pushed from a moving car. This one's cadaver, this one unconscious, this one beaten blue. Her ex-husband, her husband, her lover, her father, her brother, her uncle, her friend and coworker. Always. The same grisly news in the pages of the dailies. She dunked a glass under the soapy water for a moment—shivered. (p. 52)

This passage unveils how patriarchal violence is inscribed into the social geography of Seguín, how geography is haunted, and how this spectral matter is felt differentially, for it describes a woman who has been shoved out of a car onto the interstate—a conduit promising escape. Concluding with Cleófilas washing dishes, this passage also underscores her own confinement to the domestic sphere with femicide as her horizon of possibility. Cleófilas's predicament mirrors that of La Llorona, whose figure is conjured by "soapy water" that elicits a shiver: in the same way that La Llorona is stationed to a body of water for the rest of eternity, Cleófilas also lacks agency and cannot see or imagine a way out of her domestic situation.

La Llorona also haunts and circumscribes Cleófilas's actual domestic sphere. Cleófilas's home is flanked by and surrounded by female figures comprising an unholy trinity of toxic femininity—Dolores (Pain), Soledad ("Loneliness"), and Woman Hollering/La Llorona. The short story emphasizes, too, that Cleófilas's name also references "[o]ne of those Mexican saints . . . A martyr or something" (p. 54). While the arroyo Woman Hollering runs in the back of Cleófilas's house, Dolores and Soledad live to the right and left of Cleófilas, respectively. Dolores and Soledad allegorize key features of La Llorona. Like La Llorona they embody vexed binaries of the virgen/whore or active aggressor/passive victim or martyrdom, and are fully defined through their relationships to men, as their names betray. While La Llorona's name is based on the tragic consequences that transpired due to her reaction to an erstwhile lover and father of her children, the names Dolores and Soledad index how these women are defined through their relationships to their husbands and sons as they "were too busy remembering the men who had left either through choice or circumstance and would never come back" (p. 47). Soledad is figured by her reaction to a husband who abandoned her: "Her husband had either died, or run away with an ice-house floozie, or simply gone out for cigarettes one afternoon and never came back" (p. 46). Similarly Dolores lives a life of pain and mourning since her two sons who died in war and her husband died of grief for them; her house "smelled *too much* of incense and candles from the altars that burned *continuously*" (p. 47; emphasis mine). Whereas Mexican altars serve as a vital, sacred place of remembrance through which we honor and celebrate our dead(Pérez, 2007), Dolores's altar is portrayed as excessive, verging on grotesque—incense that smells "too much" and velas that "continuously" burn. Dolores also organizes

> her time around the memory of these men and her garden famous for its sunflowers—so tall they had to be supported with broom handles and old boards; red red cockscombs, fringed and bleeding a thick menstrual color; and, especially, roses whose sad scent reminded Cleófilas of the dead. Each Sunday la señora Dolores clipped the most beautiful of these flowers and arranged them on three modest headstones at the Seguin cemetery. (p. 47)

Within gothic literature more generally the garden functions as an ambiguous space of both entrapment and freedom; Dolores's garden operates more as the former. Cisneros again employs a language of excess and the grotesque: sunflowers "so tall" that require support from a broomstick, tellingly, a domestic tool, and cockscombs that are "red red" and resemble menstrual fluid. Her roses are associated with death and decay; they have a "sad scent" that reminds Cleófilas of death, and are grown for the purpose of decorating her sons' and husband's headstones. Dolores's flowers symbolically underscore how her selfhood is wholly figured through an all-consuming relationship to men, a patriarchal vampirism, as it were. Dolores's martyrdom recalls La Virgen de Guadalupe, the archetypal good/passive woman who is tethered to vexed related female colonial and cultural nationalist imaginaries, including La Llorona. Dolores's garden and flowers, particularly when interpreted alongside mention of murdered women in WHC, thus suggest not only entrapment but also how Chicanas and Mexicanas become trapped in the crosshairs of patriarchal violence.

WHC represents and maps out a multiscalar nexus haunted by intimate terrorism as embodied by La Llorona and cognate figures. La Llorona qua femicide also looms large in the narrative, giving shape and form to the story's sense of space. *Woman Hollering Creek and Other Stories* was published 1991, shortly before the North American Free Trade Agreement (NAFTA) went into effect in 1994. Saldívar-Hull explains: "In addition to posing crucial questions about female sexuality and gender inequities within Mexican and Chicano culture, Cisneros exhibits her feminism on the border with her equally incisive critique of US economic policies" (p.107). NAFTA, in particular, "has served as one more legally sanctioned economic mode to exploit female labor" (p. 107) in the US-Mexico borderlands. Since 1993 maquiladoras or border factories have been linked to several hundred victims of femicide, which have involved rape, sexual assault, and other unspeakable and heinous forms of terrorism. Many of these women are poor, darker-skinned women from rural areas who have immigrated north to find employment due to, ironically, the economic devastation wreaked by globalization on Mexico's rural sector. While the reasons for the femicides are multicausal, feminist scholars have exposed the gendered and sexualized dimensions of discourses of disposability wielded by the Mexican state to justify and dismiss these murders. This patriarchal cultural logics follow that these women have transgressed normative patriarchal spatial boundaries by stepping out from the private or domestic sphere of home into the public sphere or labor market, thereby becoming public women or whores in the eyes of the dominant public and state (Wright, 2011, p. 713). As such, Fregoso contends that the femicides attest to how globalization in Mexico and the borderlands has worked to "intensify earlier and more traditional forms of patriarchy in the nation-state" (p. 18); that is, these femicides are enmeshed in a "nexus of violence that spans from the state to the home" (p. 20). This nexus of gendered violence, though in its incipient stages in the early 90s, inflects the spectral geography of WHC, its traces energizing La Llorona's figure.

However, and unlike traditional gothic heroines, Cleófilas's fate is not forever cemented or tethered to La Llorona, as insinuated by the name of the arroyo, Woman Hollering. La Llorona may be reckoned with and reimagined through "a collective exorcism" (Gordon, 1997, p. 183). Mobility and a route (literal and figurative) toward realizing agency becomes a shimmering horizon of possibility in the conclusion of WHC when Cleófilas encounters Felice ("happiness") and Graciela ("grace"). Juxtaposing Dolores and Soledad, Felice and Graciela are self-realized and do not depend on men to define them. In contrast, these allegorical figures offer connection and direction rather than isolation and stasis. Cleófilas meets Graciela, a physician, when she is administered a sonogram whereupon Graciela recognizes signs of domestic abuse. Graciela subsequently calls her friend Felice to drive Cleófilas to a bus station in San Antonio on her way home. To Cleófilas's dismay, Felice picks her up in a truck. And when Cleófilas asks Felice if the pickup belongs to her husband, Felice retorts that she does not have a husband and that she paid for the truck herself. When they drive across the arroyo Woman Hollering, Felice "let out a yell as loud as any mariachi" (p. 55). Felice then explains to Cleófilas:

Every time I cross that bridge I do that. Because of that name, you know. Woman Hollering. Pues, I holler. She said in a Spanish pocked with English and laughed. Did you ever notice, Felice continued, how nothing around here is named after a woman? Really. Unless she's the Virgin. I guess you're only famous if you're a virgin. Felice was laughing again. That's why I like the name of the arroyo. Makes you want to holler like Tarzan, *right*? (p. 55)

Cleófilas is initially shocked that Felice "started yelling like a crazy" (p. 56), and contemplates "Pain or rage, perhaps, but not a hoot like the one Felice had just let go" (p.56). But then Felice begins to laugh again and Cleófilas realizes in the last lines of the story that it is actually her laughter as she feels a "gurgling out of her own throat, a long ribbon of laughter, like water" (p. 56). Cleófilas's and Felice's laughter register a "transformative recognition" (Gordon, 1997, p. 8) that senses La Llorona and the vexed colonial imaginaries and binaries she carries and transmits, but also detects other decolonial ways of being or haunting, for the specter of La Llorona, like other clamoring ghosts in US ethnic fiction, such as the specter in Toni Morrison's *Beloved* (1987), are "pregnant with unfulfilled possibility, with the something to be done that the wavering present is demanding" (p. 183).

The collective exorcism in WHC and other ethnic fictions, as Gordon reminds us, is not about banishing the ghost but learning to live with her, collectively inspiring her with new life through rewriting, reimagining, and redistributing the sensible or seeming common sense. Gordon insists that, returning to my epigraph, "ultimately haunting is about how to transform a shadow of a life into an undiminished life," which is "necessarily a collective undertaking" (p. 208). Exorcising La Llorona, then, holds her in abeyance, and opens up new potential routes for Cleófilas, enables her to locate a way out of patriarchal gridlocks and constrictive colonial imaginaries, even if momentarily. This time Cleófilas, and by symbolic extension, La Llorona, do not murder her/their children, but rather choose to try to leave and save herself/ themselves and her/their children, to chart other possible endings, or rather, beginnings. It is also significant that Cleófilas, her son Juan Pedrito, and Felice cross a bridge, which Anzaldúa (2002) conceives as "thresholds to other realities, archetypal, primal symbols of shifting consciousness. They are passageways, conduits, and connectors that connote transitioning, crossing borders, and changing perspectives . . . transformations occur in this in-between space, an unstable, unpredictable, precarious, always-in-transition space lacking clear boundaries" (p. 1). This bridge, this geography-in-flux wherein La Llorona is collectively reimagined, stands in contradistinction to the oppressive and static geography of Seguín. Nonetheless, Cleófilas is not guaranteed a happy ending; after all, even though she is leaving Seguin and escaping domestic abuse, it is also implicit that she is returning to her father's household where "her future safety and happiness" is not ensured (Brady, 2002, p. 134). Yet, this momentary third or liminal space at the conclusion of WHC exposes the utopian impulse of the ghostly–to imagine and potentially become otherwise. The meXicana gothic thus begets a rereading of WHC that focalizes the LatIndigenous figure of the ghost, La Llorona, that accounts for not only how she structures space in WCH as a colonial and transnational patriarchal imaginary, but also brings into sensibility how her figure may be collectively exorcised and transformed into a decolonial imaginary that moves within and against or even beyond seemingly concretized patriarchal structures.

Speculative Rasquachismo: La Llorona attends UTRGV, Or, a Hauntology of the Oppressed

The work of analyzing and theorizing LatIndigneous ghostly matters falls squarely within the purview of Latinx speculative studies, which examines how LatIndigenous or Latinx cultural producers dare to ask, "what if?" and imagine otherwise, despite how totalizing neoliberalism or extractive and racial capitalism might feel or how intersectional structures of oppression seem to be closing in. Latinx speculative aesthetics remembers and makes vital imaginative space even as it reckons with the ostensibly dead. To that end, Anzaldúa's 2003 speculative meXicana gothic poem "The Postmodern La Llorona" conjures and reconstructs La Llorona—"La Llorona attends UCSC, goes on picnics / and to the movies" (p. 280) prompts me to wonder: *What if Cleófilas as La Llorona/La Gritona were to have caught the Greyhound in San Antonio, but didn't go home and instead came to the Río Grande Valley, Anzaldúa's birthplace, and attended the University of Texas Río Grande Valley, where she could go on picnics and to the movies?* Conjuring LatIndigenous specters is indeed a collective project of reconstruction wherein we gather and creatively recycle traces of the past in the present and project other possible future routes.

This essay has engaged two new neologistic concepts—the meXicana gothic and LatIndigenous, and now, by way of closing (and opening), briefly highlight two more related neologistic concepts central to studying our LatIndigenous ghosts, which I hope inspires future studies: speculative rasquachismo and hauntology of the oppressed. In a 1990 essay, Tomás Ybarra-Frausto conceptualized the Chicanx sensibility of rasquachismo, namely, a creative recycling of what dominant society has cast aside as detritus to engender something beautiful and aesthetically pleasing, something more than the sum of its parts. Building on this foundational concept, I (2017) have explored how what I reframe as a "speculative rasquachismo" (p. 355) disorders dominant imaginings of the future and the utopian—where LatIndigenous and BIPOC communities are often elided. These neologisms themselves perform rasquachismo, gesturing toward a necessary and practical endeavor for those of us who study minority and subaltern modes of knowledge production—to create new vocabularies for new (or at least heretofore occluded and devalued) subjects/objects of study, including our collective ghosts, and by extension, our collective futures.

In yet another speculative rasquache act, I merge Jacques Derrida's (1994) "hauntology" and Chela Sandoval's (2000) "methodology of the oppressed," a *hauntology of the oppressed* foregrounds a methodology and an understanding how ontology is always haunted: "Ontology is a conjuration" (Derrida, 1994, 161). This methodology and interpretive hermeneutic is deconstructive, and functions as "a deregulating system" (Sandoval, 2000, p. 10) that ferrets out the interstices or third spaces where our specters linger, and it disturbs ossified narratives and colonial imaginaries. But at the same time, a hauntology of the oppressed is uncertain and open, a "methodology of renewal, of social reconstruction, of emancipation" (Sandoval 2000, p. 10). Importantly, this "hauntology of the oppressed" demands ontological specificity (regardless of how slippery) that apprehends the idiosyncrasies of our LatIndigenous ghostly matters and is central to my articulation of the meXicana gothic. Doing so makes room for not only rereading now established texts such as those by Cisneros, but also new, emerging work by Myrium Gurba and ire'ne lara silva, among many others. Hauntologies of the oppressed eschews passive modes of reading, and instead insists upon collective reckoning and decolonial imaginings of the future.

References

Anzaldúa, G. (1999). *Borderlands/La Frontera: The New Mestiza*. (2nd ed.). Aunt Lute Books.

Anzaldúa, G. (2002). Preface: (Un)natural bridges, (Un)safe spaces. In A. Anzaldúa, & A. Keating (Eds.), *This Bridge We Call Home: Radical Visions for Transformation*. (pp. 1–5). Routledge.

Anzaldúa, G. (2009). The Postmodern Llorona. In A. Keating (Ed.), *The Gloria Anzaldúa Reader* (pp. 280–81). Duke University Press.

Anzaldúa, G. (2015). Let us be the healing of the wound: The Coyolxauhqui imperative–La sombra y el sueño. In A. Keating (Ed.), *Light In The Dark, Luz en lo Oscuro: Rewriting Identity, Spirituality, Reality*. (pp. 9–22). Duke University Press.

Barrera, C. The Haunted Southwest: Towards an Ethics of Place in Borderlands Literature (2022). Texas Tech University Press.

Brady, M. P. (2002). *Extinct Lands, Temporal Geographies: Chicana Literature and the Urgency of Space*. Duke University Press.

Brogan, K. (1998). *Cultural Haunting: Ghosts and Ethnicity in Recent American Literature*. University of Virginia Press.

Calafell, B. M. (2015). *Monstrosity, Performance, and Race in Contemporary Culture*. Peter Lang Inc.

Calvo-Quirós, W. A. (2017). The Emancipatory Power of the Imaginary: Defining Chican@ Speculative Productions. In C. J. Merla-Watson & B. V. Olguín (Eds.), *Altermundos: Latin@ Speculative Literature, Film, and Popular Culture* (pp. 39–54). University of Washington Press.

Cisneros, S. (1991). Woman Hollering Creek. In *Woman Hollering Creek and Other Stories*. (pp. 43–56). Random House.

DeGuzmán, M. (2012). Buenas Noches: American Culture, Latina/o Aesthetics of Night. Indiana University Press.

Derrida, J. (1994). *Specters of Marx: The State of Debt, the Work of Mourning, & the New International*. (P. Kamuf, Trans.). Routledge.

Fregoso, L. 2003. *Mexicana Encounters: The Making of Social Identities on the Borderlands*. University of California Press.

Goddu, T. A. (1997). *Gothic American: Narrative, History, and Nation*. Columbia University Press.

González, D. J. Malinche Triangulated, Historically Speaking. In R. Romero, & A. N. Harris (Eds.), *Feminism, Nation, and Myth: La Malinche*. (pp. 6–12). Arte Público Press.

González, T. (2007). The Gothic Gift of Death in Cherríe Moraga's *The Hungry Woman: A Mexican Medea* (2001). *Chicana/Latina Studies*, 7(1), 44–77.

Gordon, A. (1997). *Ghostly Matters: Haunting and the Sociological Imagination*. University of Minnesota Press.

Hedrick, T. (2017). "The Spirits Talk to Us": Regionalism, Poverty, and Romance in Mexican American Gothic Fiction. *Studies in the Novel*, 49(3), 322–40.

Kandiyoti, D. (2009). *Migrant Sites: American, Place, Diaspora Literatures*. Dartmouth College Press.

McMahon, M. R. (2013). *Domestic Negotiations: Gender, Nation, and Self-Fashioning in US Mexicana and Chicana Literature and Art*. Rutgers University Press.

Merla-Watson, C. J. (2017). (Trans)Mission Possible: The Coloniality of Gender, Speculative Rasquachismo, and Altermundos in Luis Valderas's Chican@futurist Visual Art. In C. J. Merla-Watson & B. V. Olguín (Eds.), *Altermundos: Latin@ Speculative Literature, Film, and Popular Culture*. (pp. 352–70). University of Washington Press.

Merla-Watson, C. J., & B. V. Olguín. (2017). Altermundos: Reassessing the Past, Present, and Future of the Chican@ and Latin@ Speculative Arts. In C. J. Merla-Watson & B. V. Olguín (Eds.), *Altermundos: Latin@ Speculative Literature, Film, and Popular Culture* (pp. 1–36). University of Washington Press.

Mignolo, W. D. (2011). *The Darker Side of Western Modernity: Global Futures, Decolonial Options*. Duke University Press.

Moraga, P. (2000). *Loving in the War Years*: lo que nunca pasó por sus labios. South End Press.

Olguín, B. V. (2021). *Violentologies: Violence, Identity, and Ideology in Latina/o Literature*. Oxford University Press.

Pérez, E. (1999). *The Decolonial Imaginary: Writing Chicanas into History*. Indiana University Press.

Perez, D. R. (2008). *There Was a Woman: La Llorona from Folklore to Popular Culture*. University of Texas Press.

Rosas, G. (2019). Necro-subjection: On Borders, Asylum, and Making Dead to Let Live. *Theory and Event*, 22(2), 303–24.

Saldívar-Hull, S. *Feminism on the Border: Chicana Gender Politics and Literature*. (2000). University of California Press.

Sandoval, C. (2000). *Methodology of the Oppressed*. University of Minnesota Press.

Seltzer, L. F. (2016, March 3). What's So Fascinating About the Letter X? *Psychology Today*. https://www.psychologytoday.com/us/blog/evolution-the-self/201603/whats-so-fascinating-about-the-letter-x.

Streeby, S. (2017). Reading Jamie Hernandez's Comics as Speculative Fiction. In C. J. Merla-Watson, & B. V. Olguín (Eds.), *Altermundos: Latin@ Speculative Literature, Film, and Popular Culture* (pp. 72–92). University of Washington Press.

Villa, R. H. (2000). *Barrio-Logos: Space and Urban Place in Chicano Literature and Culture*. University of Texas Press.

Wester, M. L. (2012). *African American Gothic: Screams from Shadowed Places*. Palgrave Macmillan.

Wickelson, P. (2013). Shaking Awake the Memory: Gothic Quest for Place in Sandra Cisneros's *Caramelo*. *Western American Literature*, 48(1 & 2), 90–114.

Wright, M. (2011). Necropolitics, Narcopolitics, and Femicide: Gendered Violence on the Mexico-US Border. *Signs*, 36(3), 707–31.

Ybarra-Frausto, T. (1990). Rasquachismo: A Chicano Sensibility. In R. Griswold del Castillo, T. McKenna, & Y. Yarbro-Bejarano (Eds.) *Chicano Art: Resistance and Affirmation, 1965–1985*. (pp. 155–16). Wight Art Gallery.

CHAPTER 20

Haunted by Settler Nostalgia

(Lat)Indigenous Specters, White Vampires, and the Historical Amnesia of *Twilight*

Susana Loza

To raise the Indigenous undead is to unsettle and to resettle, to reenter and reclaim old home places.
—Eric Anderson, "Raising the Indigenous Undead" (2016)

In "Settler Colonialism as Structure: A Framework for Comparative Studies of US Race and Gender Formation," Evelyn Nakano Glenn argues that the specificities of racisms and sexisms affecting different US racialized groups can only be comprehended through a settler colonial framework (2015, p. 52). In addition to facilitating comparability within and across regions and time, such a framework reveals the "underlying systems of beliefs, practices, and institutional systems that undergird and link the racialization and management" of Natives, Latinxs, Blacks, and Asians (Glenn, 2015, p. 67). However, as Shantel Martinez and Kelly Medina-López remind us in their introduction to this volume, the line between Native and Latinx has always been blurred in the US, a settler nation built on indigenous land and peopled by natives from North, South, and Central America. Their term, LatIndigenous, speaks to the collective histories, colonial traumas, and intergenerational experiences that bind indigenous people from the Southern hemisphere to their native kin in the North. To mark this cross-continental kinship but honor the cultural specificities of distinct indigenous groupings, I will utilize a variation of their term, (Lat)indigenous, when referring to natives from across the Americas.

This chapter unmasks the inextricable connections between gender construction, national formation, and (Lat)indigenous monsterization in the US settler colonial state through a close analysis of the *Twilight Saga* (the film series based on Stephenie Meyer's book series). Since its publication in 2005, the *Twilight* book series has sold over one hundred million copies, while the five films that comprise the saga have amassed $1,363,537,109 at the box office (Abbott, 2018, p.3). It has also spawned a prolific and profitable fandom. *Twilight's* fans have mounted conventions, manufactured merchandise, curated museum exhibits, launched online roleplay communities, crafted digital games and YouTube videos, produced websites and blogs, and, of course, written countless fanfics (Siegel, 2011, p. 82). Clearly, *Twilight* seized the public's imagination, which is why it is necessary to consider how the fantasy "saga upholds dominant ideas about race that associate whiteness with civility, beauty, and intellect on the one hand, and indigenous people with animality and primitivism on the other" (Wilson, 2010, p. 55).

In addition to contemplating how the *Twilight Saga* uses conflicts and territorial disputes between white settler vampires and (Lat)indigenous monsters to express and manage white anxieties about invasion, contamination, segregation, miscegenation, conquest, and demographic change, this chapter documents how the series obscures settler violence through its (mis)remembrance of the US past. The importance of developing modes of critical pedagogy attentive to the task of recollection cannot be denied, especially when confronted with the fact that histories of racial and sexual violence not only inform present contexts and conditions but also shape the future (Pollard, 2014, p. 144). In her potent contribution to this collection, Brenda Lara introduces the concept of "epistemic haunting," a dualistic form of knowledge that reveals the histories that the heteropatriarchal colonial nation suppresses, a knowledge that lives on even if its creator is absent or dead. This is a vital tool that allows us to engage in what cultural studies theorist Tyler Pollard calls a "pedagogy of conjuration" (2014). A pedagogy of conjuration teaches us how to "live with, hear, and speak to, those specters of racial injustice that emerge in popular culture and which are in danger of being conjured away, or exorcised, by their 'domestication' or 'naturalization' within these very popular texts" (Pollard, 2014, p. 154). Consorting with ghosts, grappling with the settler colonial past reminds us that the past is never really past in a haunted nation. But before we engage with the (Lat)indigenous specters of *Twilight*, let us detour through a short synopsis of the saga.

The *Twilight Saga* tells the story of Bella Swan (Kristen Stewart), a socially awkward white teenager who relocates to the small town of Forks,

Washington, to live with her single father. Soon after her arrival in the rainy Northwest, our human heroine falls in love with Edward Cullen (Robert Pattinson), a moody seventeen-year-old that is actually a ninety-year-old white vampire. Their tortured romance is the central conflict of the saga. But other conflicts also shape the vampire series. Edward is part of a US family of "vegetarian" vampires that feed on animals instead of humans. Their vegetarianism distinguishes the Cullens from other vampires: the nomads in *Twilight*, Victoria's Newborn Army in *Eclipse*, and the European Volturi, the ancient ruling clan of the vampire world that appear throughout the saga. Last but not least, the Cullen vampires have an uneasy truce with a pack of indigenous werewolves that are based on a living human tribe (the Quileute). This truce is frequently threatened by Bella's (more than) friendship with Jacob Black (Taylor Lautner), a dark-skinned Native teen that lives nearby at La Push, the Quileute reservation. Now, with this narrative sketch in mind, let us turn our attention to the haunted settlers of the *Twilight Saga*.

Native Monsters, White Vampires, and the Fragility of Settler Memory

Indians, the original possessors of the land, seem to haunt the collective unconscious of the white man and to the degree that one can identify the conflicting images of the Indian which stalk the white man's waking perception of the world one can outline the deeper problems of identity and alienation that trouble him . . . Underneath all the conflicting images of the Indian one fundamental truth emerges—the white man knows that North America is Indian—and he will never let go of the Indian image because he thinks that by some clever manipulation he can achieve an authenticity that cannot ever be his.
—Vine Deloria Jr., "American Fantasy," Foreword to *The Pretend Indians* (1980)

In *Recovering the Sacred: The Power of Naming and Claiming*, Winona LaDuke suggests that the "descendants of settlers are, in a sense, haunted by nostalgia for the lost cultures and fabled pride their forbears worked so hard to annihilate. The sociopathology of the United States rests on its colonialist history and, in particular, on the awesome weight of genocide" (2005, p. 76). The *Twilight Saga* alleviates this genocidal guilt in a variety of ways. It disseminates falsified native legends that ignore the lasting effects of colonization

(Wilson, 2010, p. 69). It recreates the clash of colonizer and colonized with white vampires and native werewolves but has the battle end in a truce instead of brutal subjugation and forced assimilation (Leggatt and Burnett, 2010, p. 29). It masks the settler status of the Cullen family by juxtaposing it against their imperialist European counterparts: the Volturi. *Twilight*'s canny juxtaposition of the all-American vegetarian vampires against the vicious Volturi also allows the white vampire text to perform a range of functions: "constructing symbolic depictions of White crimes against humanity and wallowing in the guilt thereof; vicariously enjoying images of White aristocratic decadence and debauchery; flirting with constructions of racial superiority inherent in older constructions of racial Whiteness as superhumanity; offering audiences ambivalent images of White perfection and White corruption" (Kirkland, 2013, p. 110). Finally, the saga erases slavery and romanticizes The Lost Cause via Jasper Whitlock (Jackson Rathbone). Before being adopted into the undead Cullen clan, Jasper was a noble Confederate soldier. The young Texan was turned into a cruel and callous bloodsucker by a lustful and predatory LatIndigenous woman seeking to form a vampire army on the US-Mexican border. By depicting Jasper as an innocent white victim of Brown aggression, the series replicates the deliberate reconfiguration and reimagining of places, spaces, and lives, which is characteristic of settler colonialism (Wisker, 2016, p. 119). It is worth emphasizing before we go further that the indigenous peoples of Mexico and the indigenous peoples of the Southwest have largely the same ancestry because the Spanish mainly colonized Mexico with soldiers instead of white settler families (Gordon, 2020, p. 534). In other words, the US-Mexico border may divide these populations, but they are kin. And like the Quileute, North America is their home.

Twilight's (mis)remembrance of the US settler past can be seen as a cinematic remix of what scholar Renée Bergland dubbed the "discourse of Indian spectrality" (2000), a form of literary annihilation which saw its heyday in the nineteenth century (Schoch-Davidson, 2020, p. 144). In *The National Uncanny: Indian Ghosts and American Subjects*, Bergland asserts that "the interior logic of the modern nation requires that citizens be haunted and that American nationalism is sustained by writings that conjure forth spectral Native Americans" (2000, p. 4). In the white settler imagination, "Native American ghosts function both as representations of national guilt and as triumphant agents of Americanization" (Bergland, 2000, p. 4). For US settlers like the Cullens to claim an authentic indigenous identity in North America, they must symbolically subjugate the natives they have displaced. Indigenous peoples, and the long history of settler colonial violence against them, serve as "the fundamental raw material out of which American Gothic narrative is manufactured" (Burnham, 2014, p. 227). *Twilight*'s problematic reimagination of the Quileute past and Mexican history in the Southwest testify to the persistence of this extractive relationship, how native cultures continue to serve as a resource that settlers like Meyer mine to craft tales of terror that simultaneously spark and assuage genocidal guilt.

The *Twilight Saga* attests to the longing of settlers to return to a past that never existed and to places that they irrevocably changed (Adams, 2012, p. 5). Its white settler vampires suffer from what Renato Rosaldo once diagnosed as "imperialist nostalgia," a colonial disease that uses the pose of "innocent yearning" to capture the white Western imagination and "conceal its complicity with often brutal domination" (1989, p. 108). *Twilight*'s construction of whiteness is thus "dependent upon and secured through a process of forgetting—both strategic and collective—akin to amnesia" (Bebout, 2016, p. 84). In *The Racial Contract*, political philosopher Charles Mills argues that misunderstanding, misrepresentation, evasion, and self-deception on matters related to race are central to whiteness. They are the foundations of the "cognitive and moral economy psychically required for conquest, colonization, and enslavement" (1999, p. 19).

Twilight reveals the fragility of white settler memory, its obsessive reiteration of false national narratives, its symbolic (re)colonization of the Americas as the home of European explorers and migrants. The fantasy saga illuminates how white goodness is preserved by projecting evil onto Brown colonized bodies. Eve Tuck and K. Wayne Yang have designated such maneuvers: "settler moves to innocence" (2012). Settler moves to innocence are strategies, positioning, or evasions that "attempt to relieve the settler of feelings of guilt or responsibility without giving up land or power or privilege" (Tuck & Yang, 2012, p. 10). These settler moves rely upon historical amnesia to forge what James Baldwin christened the "willed innocence" of whiteness (Ioanide, 2014). The remainder of this chapter will track four "settler moves to innocence" in the *Twilight Saga*: 1) its promulgation of the Noble Savage trope, 2) its problematic revisioning of colonial contact, 3) its suspiciously sympathetic view of settler vampires, and 4) its monsterization of Mexicans in order to justify Manifest Destiny and the Civil War. In each case, stereotypical representations of (Lat)indigeneity are "deployed to fashion a robust benevolent whiteness that reinforces dominant narratives of American exceptionalism" (Bebout, 2016, p. 31). And, in all of these moves to innocence, the (in)humanity of white settlers is rationalized.

The Noble Savagery of Native Werewolves

The Noble Savage provides a fantasy for Euro-Americans wishing to escape dilemmas of their own culture.
—Lisa Aldred, "Plastic Shamans and Astroturf Sundances: New Age Commercialization of Native American Spirituality" (2000)

Midway through *New Moon* (Weitz, 2009), the second installment in the *Twilight Saga*, Bella Swan discovers that her friend and romantic admirer, Jacob Black, is descended from an ancient line of Quileute "shapeshifters" that assume wolf form when provoked. This revelation occurs when Bella goes to Jacob's house to confront him for not returning her calls; he has recently withdrawn from their friendship because he is afraid of "hurting her." When she arrives, Bella finds Jacob asleep in bed. When she lifts her gaze from his prone form, she spies four shirtless Native youths standing at the edge of the forest. Unbeknownst to Bella, the Quileute teens are part of the same shapeshifting wolf pack. As the half-naked posse stride menacingly towards the house, Bella rushes out and angrily blames them for Jacob's bad behavior. The pack scowl and laugh at her ridiculous charges but seethe with barely suppressed rage, rage which erupts when Bella punches one of them. The jab causes the Native youth to phase or change from human to wolf. As Bella dashes towards the house to warn Jacob to run for his life, he leaps over her head and phases in midair. Horror washes over her face as she beholds the fierce fight that ensues between the two indigenous shapeshifters.

In the *Twilight Saga*, new vampires are depicted as "slaves to their instincts" for a year or two, but the Quileute shapeshifters are portrayed as perpetually controlled by their bestial nature. The native wolves suffer from outbreaks of uncontrollable emotion long after they mature. These outbreaks cause them to "phase" from human to wolf, "suggesting that their instincts, rather than their rational thoughts and conscious emotions, control them" (Borgia, 2014, p. 168). Jacob is particularly temperamental, and his unrequited feelings for Bella often cause him to phase and threaten her romance with Edward. Though Jacob's character has a major role in the storyline, his character is severely underdeveloped. Jacob's role in *Twilight* testifies to the enduring appeal of the Noble or Romantic Savage trope for Euro-Americans like Bella. Jacob's ability to turn into a wolf also contributes to the romantic savage stereotype by reinforcing "the ideology that Indians live in harmony with nature and have a 'natural' existence . . . In fact, Jacob and his Indian brethren are so close to nature that they can transform into it. As (were)wolves, they become part of nature itself, conforming to the laws of wolf behavior and pack mentality" (Burke, 2011, p. 210).

In *Gothic Images of Race*, H. L. Malchow discusses how both gothic texts and "racist discourse manipulate deeply buried anxieties, both dwell on the chaos beyond natural and rational boundaries and massage a deep, often unconscious and sexual, fear of contamination, both present the threatened destruction of the simple and pure by the poisonously exotic, by anarchic forces of passion and appetite, carnal lust and blood lust" (1996, p. 5). The scene above speaks directly and viscerally to such anxieties. It also reminds us that white women have a double relation to difference. On the one hand, Bella occupies the role of object, much like the indigenous werewolves. On the other hand, she is also the colonizer who objectifies native bodies and consumes them. Remember how the encounter begins with her observing their half-naked Brown bodies on the horizon.

By encouraging viewers to take pleasure in the spectacle of savage were-wolves fighting over the fate of a white damsel in distress, *Twilight* simulta-neously exoticizes natives and constructs them as uncivilized and in need of subjugation by the white settler. The saga reinforces white settler desire by allowing Jacob's half-naked body (and the bodies of the other wolves) to be fully objectified, thus following "a long tradition in American culture that began with Columbus's study of the bodies of the half-clothed Indians on Hispaniola" (Burke, 2011, p. 211). The focus on the pack's perpetual state of undress is also in "keeping with a history of white representations of native men as more bodily, more brute, and more animalistic than white men" (Wilson, 2010, p. 65). As Curtis Marez points out, "these forms of ritual imperial spectatorship indirectly help to reproduce conditions of domination by constituting Indian cultures as property and by encouraging a proprietary relationship to images of Indians" (2004, p. 340). This simultaneous love and hate for the Indian, the yearning to venerate and exterminate "the indigenous peoples of the Americas—have been the preconditions for the formation of North American identities separate from European roots" (Schwarz, 2005, p. 298).

The noble savage stereotype in the *Twilight Saga* is far more than a plot device. White settler audiences "cannot help but leave the cinema or the library seeing the Native characters as less than human" (Antoine, 2011, p. 244). The ethical implications are particularly damning considering *Twilight*'s global popularity and the continued dearth of Native American images (Antoine, 2011, p. 244). But, perhaps, the most dangerous part of Meyer's depiction of Native peoples is that she renders them mythical creatures. By imagining her cosmic epic battle between good and evil, between civilized white vampires and savage Indian werewolves, Meyer "creates a binary that implies that Native peoples are as equally fantastic, as equally fictional, as vampires" (Burke, 2011, p.216). This is a bold and disturbing settler move of innocence.

When the Howling Quileute Met the Colonizing Cold Ones . . .

Although they threaten the American national project, [Indians] also nationalize the imagination. Guilt over the dispossession of Indians and fear of their departed spirits sometimes function as perverse sources of pleasure and pride for white Americans because they signify a successful appropriation of the American spirit. In Europe, people were haunted by their own ancestors. In America, they have the opportunity to be haunted by the ghosts of Indians.
—RENÉE BERGLAND, *The National Uncanny: Indian Ghosts and American Subjects* (2000)

In *Eclipse* (Slade, 2010), Bella hears ancestral stories of the Quileute, who transform into wolves to frighten settlers invading their lands. As the fire crackles around a beach campfire on the La Push reservation, a Quileute elder begins to describe the arrival of the first Cold One (Peter Murphy). In this imagining, we see semi-naked Quileute ancestors peacefully seated by the seashore, happily occupied in domestic tasks, and surrounded by their boisterous Brown children, when a painfully pallid white man, dressed in damp European clothing, emerges from the sea (the implication being that he has just arrived from far away). The scene then cuts abruptly to the unmoving and likely dead bodies of Quileute children lying at the feet of the male European vampire. The Quileute warriors stumble upon this awful tableau and immediately begin growling and quickly transform into snarling wolves. They quickly surround and slay the murderous interloper. But, a few days later, the Cold Woman (Monique Ganderton), distraught at the loss of her vampire lover, arrives to avenge his death. She nearly kills the Quileute chief spirit warrior, Taha Aki (Byron Chief-Moon), but his Third Wife (Mariel Belanger) distracts the Cold Woman by stabbing herself. As the Cold Woman rushes to the Third Wife to drink her blood, Taha Aki phases into a wolf and kills the vampire.

The scholarship on American Gothic has long argued that the figure of the Indian is central to the US imagination, symbolizing unresolved settler horror, guilt, and trauma from Poe to Meyer. More recently, Renée Bergland (2000) has contended that the "long history of colonial violence" against indigenous populations is the "fundamental raw material out of which American Gothic narrative is manufactured" (Burnham, 2014, p. 227). While Teresa Goddu has theorized that "the gothic tells of the historical horrors that make national identity possible yet must be repressed in order to sustain it" (1997, p. 10). The implications of these literary insights are rendered starkly in the previous scene: the peaceful natives are fulfilled and content until brutally ambushed by a genocidal white invader that is intent on taking their land and lives. Vampires in the *Twilight* series do not so much represent the anxiety of "reverse colonization" but rather a ruthless reimagining of colonization itself (Priest, 2013, p. 229)

While the European Cold Ones are represented as barbaric and cruel in *Eclipse*, the invasion and destruction of the indigenous community is ultimately not caused by settler colonial greed and white supremacist arrogance, but rather it is depicted as an expression of the demented grief of the vampire's bereft white lover. There are also other troubling settler moves to innocence in *Eclipse's* first contact scenario. First, although we see the lifeless bodies of Quileute children lying at the feet of the male European vampire, it is the wolves that are shown attacking first and are thus the instigators of violence. Second, the fact that the tribal warriors are shapeshifters implicitly renders them as monsters. As beings that kill. Wild beings to be feared. Beings that need to be tamed.

In "Raising the Indigenous Dead," Eric Gary Anderson suggests that the problem with gothic texts like the *Twilight Saga* is that they remain complicit with "settler colonial operations" (2016, p. 326). In *Eclipse*, the Quileute are literally howling savages who live in the wilderness and violently attack white people. Settler gothic is not just another story form. It is a way of seeing the world that serves the socioeconomic interests of white settlers. Whatever we might wish to say about its connections to other forms and archetypes, and whatever its transmutations and ironic recastings, settler gothic continues to depend in a remarkably straightforward way on the continued abjection of the native (Curry, 2008).

Defanging Vampires, Rehabbing Mormons: The Cullen Clan as Sympathetic Settlers

This story—of exceptionalism, democracy, and good intentions—is the story that Americans, and many around the world, wish to tell and be told about themselves. In its retelling of American history, the Twilight

saga retains the nation's most favorable characteristics while discarding its most unfortunate moments—the slave trade, Indian removal, and imperial interventions around the world.
—MICHELLE MALONEY-MANGOLD, "Manifest Destiny Forever: The Twilight Saga, History, and a Vampire's American Dream" (2013)

In *The Settler Colonial Present*, Lorenzo Veracini makes a compelling case for seeing the Cullen Clan as Euro-American settlers: "[T]heir abode is an isolated homestead surrounded by wilderness and wolves. These wolves are actual indigenous peoples . . . Carlisle, the Cullens' patriarch who moved to the 'New World' out of a deep dissatisfaction with the old one and its 'old' ways, rejected its hierarchies and its inescapable violence" (2015, p. 72). From the start, the Cullens are simultaneously pitted against the Old World Volturi and the indigenous pack (tribe). As Veracini avers, the *Twilight Saga's* "triangulation is typical of the settler colonial situation" (2015, p. 72). Meyer represents the Quileute as irrational, impulsive, and savage (if noble), while the settlers are rational, strategic, and colonially answerable to the Old World (a status that they seek to emancipate themselves from by rooting themselves in the 'New World') (Veracini, 2015, p. 72). *Twilight* rehabilitates its white settler protagonists by opposing their superhuman goodness with the elitist Euro-supremacism of the Volturi, who want to rule the world and have no qualms about destroying or enslaving inferior races in the process (Kirkland, 2013, p. 96). Moreover, as several scholars suggest, Meyer anchors the Cullens in the Americas and renders them sympathetic settlers through her creative incorporation of her Mormon religious beliefs (Ledvinka, 2012; Leggatt & Burnett, 2010; Maloney-Mangold, 2013; Wilson, 2014).

In "It's a Wolf Thing: The Quileute Werewolf/ Shape-Shifter Hybrid as Noble Savage," Natalie Wilson illuminates how the Mormon author interweaves Latter-day Saint (LDS) settler colonial ideologies into her vampire saga:

[T]he Book of Mormon contains the history of two warring races, not vampire and werewolf as in Twilight, but white and nonwhite: one a "fair and delightsome people," the other a "wild and ferocious, and a bloodthirsty people; full of idolatry and filthiness . . . wandering about in the wilderness" (Book of Mormon, Enos 20). Smith named these two races the Nephites, who were "peace-loving and domestic," and the Lamanites, who were "bloodthirsty and idolatrous" (Brodie 43–44). These two races supposedly fought for 1,000 years, with the evil, dark-skinned Lamanites eventually killing off the white Nephite race. In a reversal of genocide, the darker-skinned Lamanites were said to have slaughtered the Nephites, leaving only Moroni, son of the heroic Nephite leader Mormon, who would eventually lead [Joseph] Smith to the gold plates that contained the Book of Mormon. (2014, p. 201)

Returning to the *Twilight Saga*, it is easy to interpret the Cullen vampire clan as Nephites and the Quileute werewolves as Lamanites. The Cullens are depicted as exceedingly "fair and delightsome." They are highly educated, wealthy, and have an appreciation for art and classical music. The sparkly white vampires are constructed as representing the pinnacle of European civilization (Ledvinka, 2012, p. 207). In contrast, the dark-skinned werewolves are depicted as impoverished residents of a small reservation. We might also read the Native American wolves as "cursed" because of their ancestral history of shapeshifting and subsequent lack of free choice (and indeed, Jacob describes his fate as a curse in *New Moon*) (Wilson, 2014, p. 202). By associating LDS scripture with attractive, clean-cut twenty-first-century vampires, Meyer simultaneously defangs vampirism and rehabilitates Mormonism (Ledvinka, 2012, p. 210). Her amalgamation of Mormon settler mythologies with indigenous shapeshifting lore also creates a wolf/Other that is racially, spiritually, and socioeconomically inferior (Wilson, 2014, p. 202). The symbolic linkage of the Quileute with a dark genocidal race and the Cullens with a nearly eliminated white race also wholly reverses US colonial history and can thus be seen as a classic settler move to innocence. But, it is certainly not the only settler colonial move that the *Twilight Saga* makes.

In "Manifest Destiny Forever: *The Twilight Saga*, History, and a Vampire's American Dream," Michelle Maloney-Mangold underscores the centrality of two key settler colonial ideologies, American exceptionalism and Manifest Destiny, to Meyer's narrative (2013). As Maloney-Mangold notes, the Cullens' victories over the Volturi rehearse America's mythology "wherein a liberty-loving underdog overthrows the tyrannical oppressor and embarks upon a journey across the frontier" (2013, p. 34). The town of Forks, where most of the saga unfolds, thus "becomes a kind of vampire 'city upon a hill' to which the rest of the vampire world can turn for inspiration, leadership, and freedom" (Maloney-Mangold, 2013, p. 34). Sadly, much like US history books, the series retelling American history conveniently excises all the "unfortunate genocide, xenophobia, and imperialism of actual events" (Maloney-Mangold 2013, p. 34). I would like to conclude this section by considering one final settler colonial move to innocence that the Cullens make, and that is their treaty with the Quileute.

Law and territory are pivotal issues in the saga from the beginning. In a sepia-filtered flashback in *Twilight* (Hardwicke, 2008, 34:00), we witness two Quileute ancestors (William Joseph Elk II and Rick Mora), wearing ceremonial wolf-eared headdresses, discover the colonizer Cullens hunting on their lands. The native werewolves and the settler vampires negotiate a treaty that divides the territory along a stream, thus peacefully "reworking historical land disputes between indigenous nations and Mormons" (Hudson, 2017, p. 186). Both groups are barred from acting on the other's territory. The tribe can void the treaty if the Cullens create more vampires. In "Biting Bella: Treaty Negotiation, Quileute History, and Why 'Team Jacob' Is Doomed to Lose," Judith Leggatt and Kristin Burnett discuss the treaty that the actual Quileute people signed with the US government (2010). In the Treaty of Olympia, the Quileute agreed to "cede, relinquish, and convey to the United States all their right, title, and interest in and to the lands and country occupied by them" (Leggatt & Burnett, 2010, p. 30). In exchange, they were granted a reservation made up of their traditional settlements and retained the right to gather, hunt, and fish in their "usual and accustomed grounds and stations" (Leggatt & Burnett, 2010, p. 30). As Leggatt and Burnett observe, neither the Cullens nor the US government gave up anything in the treaty process; "the Cullens were already 'vegetarian,' so their lives were not altered to accommodate the Quileute, and the settler government acquired vast tracts of Native land without resorting to costly military solutions" (2010, p. 29). Like many other Native American tribes, real-life Quileute have struggled to protect their land from settler encroachment and resource development and continue to fight in the courts to guarantee their rights (Leggatt & Burnett, 2010, p. 30). By whitewashing the violence of the treaty process, downplaying the (continued) dispossession of natives, and portraying the Cullens as benevolent colonizers, *Twilight* once again demonstrates its settler colonial amnesia.

Undead White Supremacy: On *Twilight*'s Monsterization of Mexicans and Romanticization of the Confederacy

White supremacy has never been able to sustain itself on fear and hatred alone. Articulations of white goodness and heroism have structured and reinforced claims of innocence and victimhood. This has been the case since the creation of racial difference as a system of meaning, and it is even more critical within the post-break era when white supremacy has worked hard to smooth its rough edges of explicit domination and

degradation, making these "positive" aspects of whiteness more crucial for racial hegemony.
—LEE BEBOUT, *Whiteness on the Border: Mapping the US Racial Imagination in Brown and White* (2016)

While the previous sections concentrated on the saga's exploitation of the Quileute werewolves to absolve white settler guilt, I will conclude by pondering *Twilight*'s monsterization of LatIndigeneity and romanticization of the Confederacy via the backstory of Jasper Whitlock. In *Eclipse* (Slade, 2010, 102:00), Bella notices that Jasper's flesh is marred by vampire bites. He responds: "Battle scars. All the training the Confederate Army gave me was useless against the newborns." Jasper then tells Bella that he was "the youngest major on the Texas Cavalry. All without having seen a real battle." That is until he met an immortal named Maria (Catalina Sandino Moreno). At this point, the scene becomes a flashback to Civil War–era Texas. He recalls: "I was riding back to Galveston after evacuating a colony of women and children when I saw them. I immediately offered them my aid." Jasper dismounts and courteously doffs his confederate cap as he briskly strides towards three beautiful young women that he assumes are damsels in distress. Maria is flanked by white blonde Lucy (Kirsten Prout) and Brown-skinned brunette Nettie (Leah Gibson). As Jasper approaches, Lucy admiringly whispers: "Lovely and an officer." Nettie looks lasciviously at the major and murmurs to Maria: "You better do it. I can never stop once I've started." Maria nods. After Jasper introduces himself and offers his aid, she tells him: "I hope you survive. You may be of great use to me." She proceeds to turn him into a vampire. Jasper then tells Bella about Maria's plan to create an undead army on the US-Mexico border:

> They were very common in the south. Constant brutal battles for territory. Maria won'em all. She was smart, careful and she had me. I was her second in command, my ability to control emotions served her well. I trained her newborns, but in this occupation, since she never let them live beyond the first year, is my job to dispose of them. I could feel everything they felt. I thought what Maria and I had was love. But I was her puppet, she pulled the strings. (Slade, 2010)

In *African American Gothic*, Maisha Wester argues that the "Othered body—the "Not-Free, Not-Me" of American culture—is made to enact all of the deviance and failures the white rational body denies, and so becomes monstrous and unfathomable, necessitating the whips dealt it daily" (2012,

p. 5). In *Eclipse* (Slade, 2010), Maria, the sexy Mexican Vamp, the monstrous mother amassing an army of baby bloodsuckers on the US Southern Border, is that Othered body. She is the uncanny monster (m)Other enslaving whites and viciously murdering them when they have lost their utility for her. Jasper, the confederate soldier fighting to preserve actual chattel slavery, is just an old-fashioned Southern gentleman caught in her duplicitous schemes. While he comes to regret his killing of the newborn vampires, Jasper appears utterly untroubled by his confederate past. Jasper is thus a "metonym not only for the South's troubled history but also for the contemporary disavowal of that history" (Pollard, 2014, p. 151). This scene is a truly astonishing example of a settler move to innocence, given the South's violent and traumatic history of lynching Blacks and Latinxs that dare to contest white supremacy (Martinez, 2018). *Twilight*'s monsterization of Maria is particularly reprehensible in light of the dehumanization of Mexican women by Euro-American settlers in this era, specifically how they were labeled as witches and whores often as a prelude to sexual assault (González, 2003). As Chicana Historian Deena J. González points out, "Euro-Americans moving into this area of the country, which belonged to Mexico and was inhabited by Native and Mexican people, practiced terror and rage against the inhabitants of the land" (González, 2003, p. 255).

Like the Hollywood Westerns of yore, *Twilight* rationalizes and sanitizes the history of the US's North American imperialism and transforms it into a guiltfree narrative (Ramirez-Berg, 2007, p. 3). Charles Ramirez-Berg calls this settler cinematic process: "Manifest mythmaking" (2007). Manifest mythmaking justifies the extermination and deportation of (Lat)indigenous peoples. By representing Maria as a degenerate and deadly Mexican savage, *Twilight* rhetorically and ideologically vindicates Anglo expansion into Mexican/Indian lands. The erasure of Jasper's complicity with white supremacist settler colonialism and his projection of those historical horrors onto a LatIndigenous body reminds us that the fantasy series is not an embarrassing pop cultural aberration but is "part of a continuum of American colonialist and imperialist violence" (Trefzer, 2015, p. 200). In this brief flashback, *Twilight* demonstrates how US whiteness is constructed against a Mexican Other. And like previous figurations of the Mexican Other throughout the nineteenth, twentieth, and early twenty-first centuries, this one is also a hallucination, "a spectacular and spectral projection that met the needs of whiteness and Americanness, or whiteness as Americanness" (Bebout, 2016, p. 71).

Finally, let us consider the ideological work that the Mexican Vamp does in this romantic scenario. As Amanda Hobson establishes in "Dark

Seductress: The Hypersexualization of the Female Vampire," the archetype of the female bloodsucker as sexual temptress has been part of vampire narratives since Sheridan Le Fanu's *Carmilla* (1872) and the Brides in Bram Stoker's *Dracula* (1897) (2016, p. 9). This hypersexualized figure "blends violence and seduction with fears of the destructive beauty and charm of womanhood" (Hobson, 2016, p.12). *Twilight's* Maria certainly fits this description, but she fuses it with the "Erotic, Exotic Mexicana" trope (Bebout, 2016). According to Lee Bebout, the "Erotic, Exotic Mexicana" is a discursive formation, a racial script, overlaid and inscribed upon material bodies (2016, p. 156). Its "tropic embodiments are not simply objects of desire but critical fulcrums in the construction and imagination of white masculinity" (Bebout, 2016, p. 156). Maria's racialized embodiment of the vamp and her monstrous creation of a newborn army on the US-Mexico border taps into white settler fears of a Mexican reconquista. It also (accidentally) activates post-9/11 fears about foreign brown (m)Others coming to the US to birth so-called "anchor babies" and/or "terror babies." Maria and her violent progeny are thus "not only conceptualized as a threat, they are also articulated as a terrorist(ic) threat, which is to say, a threat with the potential to violently undermine the security of the nation" (Bloodsworth-Lugo & Lugo-Lugo, 2017, p. 71). But, perhaps, the true horror of the Mexican Vamp is not her inherent lawlessness and savagery but her ability to inspire such depravity in an innocent settler just fighting for his white supremacist way of life.

Reckoning with the Settler Past

The nation's narratives—its foundational fictions and self-mythologizations—are created through a process of displacement: their coherence depends on exclusion. By resurrecting what these narratives repress, the gothic disrupts the dream world of national myth with the nightmares of history. Moreover, in its narrative incoherence, the gothic discloses the instability of America's self-representations; its highly wrought form exposes the artificial foundations of national identity. However, while the gothic reveals what haunts the nation's narratives, it can also coalesce those narratives. Like the abject, the gothic serves as the ghost that both helps to run the machine of national identity and disrupts it. The gothic can strengthen as well as critique an idealized national identity.

—TERESA GODDU, *Gothic America: Narrative, History, and Nation* (1997)

On January 6, 2021, there was a white supremacist siege on the US Capitol instigated by then-President Trump. One of the most striking images to emerge from that day was of a white settler named Jake Angeli, better known as the QAnon shaman. In a widely circulated photograph, a shirtless Angeli stands on the dais of the US Senate. He is in a horned helmet holding a spear upon which he has hung the US flag. Angeli's face is painted red, white, and blue; a pair of eagle feathers decorate his fur-lined headdress (Pierce, 2021). His mouth is open in a scream of victory as if he had just conquered a new territory. As Joseph M. Pierce noted in his *ArtNews* Op-Ed, "White supremacists like Angeli pose as Indians in order to create an image of themselves as inseparable from the land itself. They imitate Indigenous people and they justify their actions by imagining themselves as the natural heirs to a land retroactively emptied of Native Americans" (2021).

Storming the US Capitol was an expression of the inability of white settlers to imagine a world in which they do not "automatically and inevitably wield the power over life and death in this country built on genocide and slavery" (Pierce, 2021). But this imaginary is unthinkable without first positioning (Lat)indigenous people as inherently closer to nature, only to erase and supplant their histories with the fantasies of white settlers as the *Twilight Saga* does. This is the history of US settler colonialism. Angeli and *Twilight* are both symptomatic of the white supremacist amnesia that makes "America" possible. Angeli's theatrics and *Twilight*'s settler moves are dangerous because they position natives as relics of the past that "must be erased, must be made into ghosts" (Tuck & Yang, 2012, p. 6). US whiteness is not and has never been natural nor innocent. Rather, it is a settler structure, a way of seeing the world, a sincere fiction that maintains itself by consciously misrecognizing the brutal reality of US race relations (Vera & Gordon, 2001, p. 265). *Twilight*'s settler moves to innocence attempt to absolve white guilt, but instead, they reawaken the (Lat)indigenous specters that haunt this settler state and force us to confront their suppressed histories yet again. If the US wants to move beyond its white supremacist past and present, there must be a "collective repudiation of the very idea of an American historical memory that omits ugly truths to instead create a fable of white lies and white American redemption" (Holloway, 2021).

References

Abbott, S. (2018). *Undead Apocalypse: Vampires and Zombies in the 21st Century*. Edinburgh University Press.

Adams, J. (2012). *Wounds of Returning: Race, Memory, and Property on the Postslavery Plantation*. University of North Carolina Press.

Aldred, L. (2000). Plastic Shamans and Astroturf Sundances: New Age Commercialization of Native American Spirituality. *American Indian Quarterly, 24*(3), 329–52.

Anderson, E. G. (2016). Raising the Indigenous Undead. In S. Castillo Street & C. L. Crow (Eds.), *The Palgrave Handbook of the Southern Gothic* (pp. 323–35). Palgrave MacMillan.

Antoine, D. M. (2011). Unethical Acts: Treating Native Men as Lurking Threat, Leaving Native Women Without Voice. *Journal of Mass Media Ethics, 26*(3), 243–45.

Bebout, L. (2016). *Whiteness on the Border: Mapping the US Racial Imagination in Brown and White*. NYU Press.

Bergland, R. L. (2000). *The National Uncanny: Indian Ghosts and American Subjects*. University Press of New England.

Bloodsworth-Lugo, M. K., & Lugo-Lugo, C. R. (2017). Race, Gender, Sexuality, and the Threat of "Anchor Terror/Babies." In *Feminism after 9/11* (pp. 69–90). Palgrave MacMillan.

Borgia, D. N. (2014). *Twilight:* The Glamorization of Abuse, Codependency, and White Privilege. *The Journal of Popular Culture, 47*(1), 153–73.

Burke, B. (2011). The Great American Love Affair: Indians in the *Twilight Saga*. In G. L. Anatol (Ed.), *Bringing Light to Twilight: Perspectives on a Pop Culture Phenomenon* (pp. 207–19). Palgrave MacMillan.

Burnham, M. (2014). Is There an Indigenous Gothic? In C. L. Crow (Ed.), *A Companion to American Gothic* (pp. 225–37). Wiley-Blackwell.

Curry, A. B. (2008). We Don't Say "Indian": On the Paradoxical Construction of the Reavers. *Slayage: The Online International Journal Buffy Studies, 7*(1). https://web.archive.org/web/20111128024707/http:/slayageonline.com/PDF/Curry2.pdf.

De Genova, N. (2006). *Racial Transformations: Latinos and Asians Remaking the United States*. Duke University Press.

Deloria, P. J. (1998). *Playing Indian*. Yale University Press.

Deloria Jr., V. (1980). Foreword: American Fantasy. In G. M. Bataille & C.L. P. Silet (Eds.), *The Pretend Indians: Images of Native Americans in the Movies* (pp. ix–xvi). The Iowa State University Press.

Glenn, E. N. (2015). Settler Colonialism as Structure: A Framework for Comparative Studies of US Race and Gender Formation. *Sociology of Race and Ethnicity, 1*(1), 52–72.

Goddu, T. A. (1997). *Gothic America: Narrative, History, and Nation*. Columbia University Press.

González, D. J. (2003). Lupe's Song: On the Origins of Mexican/Woman-Hating in the United States. In A. Gaspar de Alba (Ed.), *Velvet Barrios: Popular Culture & Chicana/o Sexualities* (pp. 251–64). Palgrave MacMillan.

Gordon, H. (2020). Cowboys and Indians: Settler Colonialism and the Dog Whistle in US Immigration Policy. *University of Miami Law Review, 74*(2). https://repository.law.miami.edu/umlr/vol74/iss2/6.

Hardwicke, C. (2008). *Twilight*. Summit Entertainment.

Hobson, A. (2016). Dark Seductress: The Hypersexualization of the Female Vampire. In A. Hobson & U. M. Anyiwo (Eds.), *Gender in the Vampire Narrative* (pp. 9–27). Sense Publishers.

Holloway, K. (2021). *Are We Witnessing the Emergence of a New 'Lost Cause'? The Nation*. https://www.thenation.com/article/society/capitol-riot-reconstruction-history/.

Hudson, D. (2017). *Vampires, Race, and Transnational Hollywoods*. Edinburgh University Press.

Huhndorf, S. M. (2001). *Going Native: Indians in the American Cultural Imagination*. Cornell University Press.

Ioanide, P. (2014). The Alchemy of Race and Affect: "White Innocence" and Public Secrets in the Post–Civil Rights Era. *Kalfou, 1*(1), 151–68.

Kirkland, E. (2013). Whiteness, Vampires and Humanity in Contemporary Film and Television. In D. Mutch (Ed.), *The Modern Vampire and Human Identity* (pp. 93–110). Palgrave MacMillan.

LaDuke, W. (2005). *Recovering the Sacred: The Power of Naming and Claiming*. South End Press.

Ledvinka, G. (2012). Vampires and Werewolves: Rewriting Religious and Racial Stereotyping in Stephenie Meyer's *Twilight* Series. *International Research in Children's Literature, 5*(2), 195–211.

Leggatt, J., & Burnett, K. (2010). Biting Bella: Treaty Negotiation, Quileute History, and Why "Team Jacob" Is Doomed to Lose. In N. Reagin (Ed.), *Twilight and History* (pp. 26–46). Wiley-Blackwell.

Malchow, H. L. (1996). *Gothic Images of Race in Nineteenth-Century Britain*. Stanford University Press.

Maloney-Mangold, M. (2013). Manifest Destiny Forever: *The Twilight Saga*, History, and a Vampire's American Dream. In C. Buccifero (Ed.), *The Twilight Saga Exploring the Global Phenomenon* (pp. 33–45). Scarecrow Press.

Marez, C. (2004). Aliens and Indians: Science Fiction, Prophetic Photography and Near-Future Visions. *Journal of Visual Culture, 3* (3), 336–52.

Martinez, M. M. (2018). *The Injustice Never Leaves You: Anti-Mexican Violence in Texas*. Harvard University Press.

Mills, C. (1999). *The Racial Contract*. Cornell University Press.

Pierce, J. (2021). *The Capitol Rioter Dressed Up as a Native American Is Part of a Long Cultural History of "Playing Indian." We Ignore It at Our Peril*. Artnet News. https://news.artnet.com/opinion/native-capitol-rioter-1937684.

Pollard, T. J. (2014). *True Blood*, a Critical Pedagogy of Conjuration, and Mediating Racial Histories in the Classroom. *Review of Education, Pedagogy, and Cultural Studies, 36*(2), 144–55.

Priest, H. (2013). Pack versus Coven: Guardianship of Tribal Memory in Vampire versus Werewolf Narratives. In S. Bacon & K. Bronk (Eds.), *Undead Memory: Vampires and Human Memory in Popular Culture* (pp. 213–38). Peter Lang.

Ramirez-Berg, C. (2007). Manifest Myth-Making: Texas History in the Movies. In D. Bernardi (Ed.), *The Persistence of Whiteness* (pp. 29–53). Routledge.

Rosaldo, R. (1989). Imperialist Nostalgia. *Representations, 26*, 107–22.

Schoch/Davidson, A. E. (2020). Indigenous Alterations. In C. Bloom (Ed.), *The Palgrave Handbook of Contemporary Gothic* (pp. 143–62). Palgrave MacMillan.

Schwarz, M. T. (2005). Native American Barbie: The Marketing of Euro-American Desires. *American Studies, 46* (3/4), 295–326.

Siegel, J. L. (2011). Vampires, Werewolves, and Other Humans: Learning from Participatory Responses to the Representation of Native Americans in *Twilight*. *Working Papers in Educational Linguistics (WPEL), 26* (1), 79–103.

Slade, D. (2010). *The Twilight Saga: Eclipse*. Summit Entertainment.

Trefzer, A. (2015). The Indigenous Uncanny: Spectral Genealogies in LeAnne Howe's Fiction. In E. G. Andersen, T. Hagood, & D. C. Turner (Eds.), *Undead Souths: The Gothic and Beyond in Southern Literature and Culture* (pp. 199–210). LSU Press.

Tuck, E., & Yang, K. W. (2012). Decolonization Is Not a Metaphor. *Decolonization: Indigeneity, Education & Society*, *1* (1), 1–40.

Vera, H., & Gordon, A. (2001). Sincere Fictions of the White Self in the American Cinema: The Divided White Self in Civil War Films. In D. Bernardi (Ed.), *Classic Hollywood, Classic Whiteness* (pp. 263–80). University of Minnesota Press.

Veracini, L. (2015). *The Settler Colonial Present*. Palgrave MacMillan.

Weitz, C. (2009). *The Twilight Saga: New Moon*. Summit Entertainment.

Wester, M. L. (2012). *African American Gothic: Screams from Shadowed Places*. Palgrave MacMillan.

Wilson, N. (2010). Civilized Vampires Versus Savage Werewolves: Race and Ethnicity in the *Twilight* Series. In M. A. Click, J. S. Aubrey, & E. Behm-Morawitz (Eds.), *Bitten by Twilight: Youth Culture, Media, & the Vampire Franchise* (pp. 55–70). Peter Lang.

Wilson, N. (2014). It's a Wolf Thing: The Quileute Werewolf/Shape-Shifter Hybrid as Noble Savage. In M. Parke & N. Wilson (Eds.), *Theorizing Twilight: Critical Essays on What's at Stake in a Post-Vampire World* (pp. 194–208). McFarland.

Wilson, N. (2011). *Seduced by Twilight: The Allure and Contradictory Messages of the Popular Saga*. McFarland.

Wisker, G. (2016). *Contemporary Women's Gothic Fiction: Carnival, Hauntings, and Vampire Kisses*. Palgrave MacMillan.

ABOUT THE EDITORS

Shantel Martinez (she/her) obtained her PhD in communications and media with an emphasis on Latinx communication and gender studies from the University of Illinois, Urbana-Champaign. As a practitioner-scholar, she centers storytelling and narrative practices to examine cycles of intergenerational trauma/survival in both familial and educational spaces.

Kelly Medina-López (she/her) has a PhD in rhetoric and professional communication from New Mexico State University. As a Piro-Manso-Tiwa Border-Indigenous scholar, her work focuses on histories, rhetorics, and storytelling practices of the US Southwest, New Mexico, and specifically Paso del Norte.

ABOUT THE CONTRIBUTORS

Kathleen Alcalá is the author of six books exploring migrations, identity, and our relationships with the land. A graduate of Stanford University (BA), the University of Washington (MA), and the University of New Orleans (MFA), Kathleen makes her home on Suquamish territory. She has recent work in *El Porvenir Ya!*, *Zócalo*, *New Suns*, and *The Madrona Project*, and her work was added to PALABRA, an audio archive of the Library of Congress. Kathleen and Norma Cantú are coeditors of *Weeping Women: La Llorona's Presence in Modern Latinx and Chicanx Lore*, Trinity University Press. Raven Chronicles Press is republishing her novels.

Sarah Amira de la Garza received her PhD from the University of Texas at Austin and is a Southwest Borderlands Scholar and associate professor at Arizona State University. A native sixth generation Tejana, she has received awards for her teaching, research, mentoring, work in spirituality, and the legacy of her original work in ethnography. She is a performance ethnographer whose critical cultural and creative work crosses disciplinary boundaries and specializes in decolonial and indigenously grounded methodologies, creative writing, and forms of performance praxis. Her most recent work is in the areas of Mindful Heresy and the recognition of the tradition of what she has coined as Chican@graphy, which predates the contemporary trend in auto-ethnography, as a collectively driven decolonialist form of creative resistance grounded in the real experiences of those who refuse to surrender their voices and dignity to those who oppress them.

Sarah De Los Santos Upton (PhD, University of New Mexico) is an associate professor in the Department of Communication at the University of Texas at El Paso. Her research and teaching explore nepantla identity, borderland pedagogy, and reproductive justice. She is the coauthor of

Challenging Reproductive Control and Gendered Violence in the Américas: Intersectionality, Power, and Struggles for Rights, winner of the NCA Feminist and Women's Studies Division's 2018 Bonnie Ritter Book Award. She is also the coeditor of *Latino/a Communication Studies: Theories, Methods, and Practice.* Her research has been published in the journals *Departures in Critical Qualitative Research, Women's Studies in Communication, Development in Practice, Action Research, and Frontiers in Communication,* as well as various edited volumes.

Moises Gonzales is an associate professor of urban design in the Community and Regional Planning Program at the School of Architecture and Planning at the University of New Mexico. Moises is coeditor with Enrique R. LaMadrid of the recent book, *Nación Genízara, Ethnogenesis, Place, and Identity in New Mexico* by University of New Mexico Press (2019). Moises Gonzales is also coauthor, along with Robert William Piatt, Jr., of the book, *Slavery in the Southwest Genizaro Identity, Dignity and the Law* by Carolina Academic Press (2019). He is a genízaro of both the Cañón de Carnué Land Grant and the San Antonio de Las Huertas land grant. He is a danzante of the Matachin and Comanche traditions of the Sandia mountain communities.

Luisa Fernanda Grijalva-Maza holds a PhD in cultural studies from Universidad de las Américas, Puebla, Mexico (UDLAP). She is a professor at the Department of International Relations, Universidad Popular Autónoma del Estado de Puebla, Mexico (UPAEP), and managing editor of Latin America of *Tapuya: Latin American Science, Technology and Society* (Taylor and Francis/Routledge). In her research, Grijalva-Maza seeks to identify the political potentiality of repetition and liminality from a post-humanist and decolonial perspective, particularly in Gothic productions. Her latest publications are "Melancholic Repetition and the Suspension of Identity: From Madness to Immanence in Wuthering Heights," to be published in *Studies on Gothic Fiction,* and "Giving Satanic and Divine Patriarchy a Run for Their Money: Hybridity, Liminality, and Female Empowerment in Chilling Adventures of Sabrina," to be published in *Chilling Adventures of Sabrina Collection* in 2023 (Lexington).

Leandra Hinojosa Hernández (PhD, Texas A&M University) is an assistant professor in the Department of Communication at the University of Utah. She enjoys teaching health communication, journalism, gender studies, and media studies courses. She utilizes Chicana feminist and qualitative approaches to explore Latina/o/x cultural health experiences, Latina/o/x journalism and media representations, and reproductive justice and gendered violence contexts. She is the Immediate Past Chair of the NCA Feminist and Gender Studies Division and the Chair of the NCA Health Communication Division. She has published the monograph *Challenging Reproductive Control and Gendered Violence in the Américas: Intersectionality, Power, and Struggles for Rights* (with Dr. Sarah De Los Santos Upton) and coedited *Latina/o/x Communication Studies: Theories, Methods, and Practice* and *This Bridge We Call Communication: Anzaldúan Approaches to Theory, Method, and Praxis.* Her research appears in *Health Communication, Women's Studies in Communication, QED: A Journal in GLBTQ Worldmaking, Frontiers in Communication,* and *Communication Research.*

Spencer R. Herrera is a professor of Spanish and Chicana/o/x Studies in the Department of Languages and Linguistics at New Mexico State University. His most recent coedited book is *Querencia: Reflections on the New Mexico Homeland* (UNM Press, 2020). He is also coauthor of *Sagrado: A Photopoetics across the Chicano Homeland* (UNM Press, 2013). He has published and guest edited/curated in leading journals such as *Aztlán* and *Casa de las Américas.* He was born and raised in Houston, Texas, but has enjoyed living in Nuevo México for over twenty years.

Brenda Selena Lara is a doctoral candidate at UCLA's César E. Chávez Department of Chicana/o and Central American Studies. Born and raised in Huntington Park, CA, Brenda is a first-generation student raised by a strong, hardworking Mexican mother who taught her feminist values. Her upbringing influences her historical and theoretical research analyzing LGBTQ+ Latinxs' lives, knowledge, deaths, and cultural depictions. Through archival methods, in her dissertation "Epistemic Haunting: Queer Latinx Ghosts in Academia," she coins epistemic haunting as a framework for understanding queer Latinx scholars' knowledge and the social violence they face in life and death. Brenda Lara has been awarded the Eugene V. Cota-Robles Fellowship, the Center for Black, Brown, and Queer Studies Fellowship, UCLA's Dissertation Year Fellowship, and the IUPLR/UIC Mellon Dissertation Fellowship. Alongside her graduate work, she is a UCLA First-Generation Graduate Student Councilmember and the editor for *Queer Cats: A Journal of LGBTQ Studies.*

Susana Loza is an associate professor of critical race, gender, and media studies at Hampshire College. She holds a PhD in comparative ethnic studies from the University of California at Berkeley. Her publications include "White Witches, Black Bitches: Race, Sex, and Settlerism in *American Horror Story: Coven*" (Forthcoming 2024), "Postracial Amnesia: *Doctor Who* in the Brexit Era" (2021), "Remixing the Imperial Past: *Doctor Who*, British Slavery, and the White Savior's Burden" (2017), "Hashtag Feminism, #SolidarityIsForWhiteWomen, and the Other #FemFuture" (2014), "Playing Alien in Postracial Times" (2013), and "Vampires, Queers, and Other Monsters: Against the Homonormativity of *True Blood*" (2011). Professor Loza's previous book, *Speculative Imperialisms: Monstrosity and Masquerade in Postracial Times* (2017), explores the resurgence of ethnic simulation in science fiction, horror, and fantasy in a putatively postcolonial era. Her current project, *Settler Gothic*, excavates the colonial ideologies and gothic elements of contemporary US horror television and film.

Juan Pacheco Marcial (he, him) is a proud Oaxaqueño, Mixteco, Zapoteco, and undocumented activist raised in the Salinas Valley of California and in his hometowns of Santa Cruz Papalutla and El Gachupin (Santiago Tlayozaltepec) in Oaxaca, Mexico. He earned his AA in Psychology from Hartnell College and his BA in Psychology from California State University, Monterey Bay. Currently, Juan is a PhD student of Chicanx studies at the land-grabbing University of California, Santa Barbara situated in Chumash territory.

Amanda R. Martinez, PhD is an associate professor and chair of the Department of Communication Studies at Davidson College. She studies media effects, gender, and intercultural communication with a focus on underrepresented populations, identity, intersectionality, race-based media stereotyping, humorous communication in entertainment contexts, health communication, and intergroup communication dynamics. Her publications appear in several peer-reviewed journals, including *Mass Communication and Society*, the *Howard Journal of Communications, Southern Communication Journal, Health Communication*, and *Women's Studies in Communication*, and several edited books. She is a coeditor of the *Latina/o/x Communication Studies: Theories, Methods, and Practice* (2019) book and Cultural Media Studies book series coeditor (Peter Lang Publishing). A Chicana feminist from New Mexico and Texas, her Latina/o/x communication studies research agenda angle aims to elevate the complexities of Chicana/o/x cultural roots and contemporary experiences by shattering the monoliths prevalent across important societal realms of representation, including health, education, and mass media.

Diana Isabel Martínez, PhD is an associate professor of communication in the Communication Division and Assistant Director for the Center for Teaching Excellence at Seaver College at Pepperdine University. Her research explores Gloria Anzaldúa's physical and psychological borderlands and her theories surrounding nepantla identity. Broadly speaking, Dr. Martínez is interested in issues surrounding social movements, public memory, and visual rhetoric. She has published the monograph *Rhetorics of Nepantla, Memory, and the Gloria Evangelina Anzaldúa Papers: Archival Impulses* and coedited *Latina/o/x Communication Studies: Theories, Methods, and Practice*. Her publications have appeared in journals such as the *Western Journal of Communication, Communication Quarterly*, the *Journal of Multimodal Rhetorics*, and edited books. Dr. Martínez currently serves on the editorial board of the *Quarterly Journal of Speech*. She teaches courses in rhetoric and leadership, communication studies, and culture.

Diego Medina is an artist and writer from Las Cruces, New Mexico and is a member of the Piro-Manso-Tiwa tribe. In addition to creating art and poetry, Diego has a passion for borderlands Indigenous history and currently serves as the Tribal Historic Preservation Officer for his tribe.

Cathryn J. Merla-Watson is an associate professor of Mexican American studies and the Director of Gender and Women's Studies at the University of Texas-Río Grande Valley. She has published articles in *Aztlán* and *MELUS* and has published chapters in *The Un/Making of Latina/o Citizenship: Culture, Politics, and Aesthetics* (2014); *Research Justice: Methodologies for Social Change* (2015); and *Latina Outsiders: Remaking Latina Identity* (2019); and *Uneven Futures: Strategies for Community Survival* (2022). Merla-Watson coedited *Altermundos: Latin@ Speculative Literature, Film, and Popular Culture* (2017), which won The Before Columbus Foundation's American Book Award (2018). She is currently coediting *Latinx Visions: Speculative Worlds in Latinx Literature, Art, Performance, and Protest* (forthcoming 2024).

Arturo "Velaz" Muñoz is an aspiring poet, activist, and public speaker. Just like a candle, Velaz hopes to bring light and warmth to the world through community organizing, presenting his work at community events and universities throughout the region, and with his podcast, *Varrio Voices*. His poetry has been published before in *The Lutrinae* and the *Mission Village Voice*.

Eric Murillo was born in El Paso, TX, and has lived in his ancestors' home-lands for most of his life. He is the proud father of Elio and Ollin Murillo and is a first-year Borderlands PhD student at the University of Texas at El Paso. He is a reconnecting Piro-Manso-Tiwa descendant and a member of the Piro-Manso-Tiwa Indian Tribe of the Pueblo of San Juan de Guadalupe community.

Saul Ramirez is a multidisciplinary artist who works in a diverse range of materials—painting, sculpture, video, photography, writing, and installation. Ramírez was born in El Paso, Texas, in 1995 to Morayma Paulina Ortiz, sec-ond of three children, and grew up in Juarez near their tightly knit family for six years before moving to the United States, spending another six years in Albuquerque, New Mexico until the family would move to El Paso where Saul would finish high school and would spend much of their time engaging the school and becoming close with their teachers who instilled a deep love and comfort in academic and educational spaces. In 2013, they would move to Las Cruces, New Mexico, to attend college at New Mexico State University, at first as a Physics and Astronomy student, but would then go on to receive a BFA in studio art and BA in art history in 2019. Having always been close to the Rio Grande, their life has been deeply guided and anchored by its shape through-out the constant migrations between homes, cities, schools, and friends, and it is within the diverse influences of history, family, landscape, and knowledge that their work takes shape as an intersection of ethics and economy which reveals the subtle intentions of behind work, especially when the artist takes on the intimate and politicized role of community educator.

Roxanna Ivonne Sanchez-Avila is a Honduran-American photographer based in South Central Los Angeles, California. She earned her bachelor's degree in studio art and women's and gender studies at Beloit College in Wisconsin. She is currently attending East Los Angeles Community College, earning skill certificates in portraiture photography, and black and white film processing and printing. By her mid-twenties, Roxanna became interested in further exploring the possibilities with black and white film over digital pho-tography. In the past seven years, her main focus has been to explore double/multiple exposures with black and white film, self-portraiture, and a combi-nation of both. She believes that multiple exposures grants her the opportu-nity to delve into the obscured multilayers of her own identities and solidify them. Her future goals include obtaining a Master's in fine art and becoming an educator for high school or college students.

ire'ne lara silva is author of four poetry collections, *furia*, *Blood Sugar Canto*, *CUICACALLI/House of Song*, and *FirstPoems*, two chapbooks, *Enduring Azucares and Hibiscus Tacos*, and a short story collection, *flesh to bone*, which won the Premio Aztlán. She and poet Dan Vera are also the coeditors of *Imaniman: Poets Writing in the Anzaldúan Borderlands*, a collection of poetry and essays. ire'ne is the recipient of a 2021 Tasajillo Writers Grant, a 2017 NALAC Fund for the Arts Grant, the final Alfredo Cisneros del Moral Award, and was the Fiction Finalist for AROHO's 2013 Gift of Freedom Award. Most recently, ire'ne was awarded the 2021 Texas Institute of Letters Shrake Award for Best Short Nonfiction. ire'ne is currently a Writer at Large for Texas Highways Magazine and is working on a second collection of short stories titled, *the light of your body*. Website: irenelarasilva.wordpress.com

Lizzeth Tecuatl Cuaxiloa grew up in Santa Maria Tonantzintla. From the age of fifteen, she approached local potters and learned how to work with ceramics. Her self-driven training has allowed her to experiment freely without prejudice. However, she has taken workshops in Antigua Academia de San Carlos and SOMA (CDMX) to supplement her knowledge. Lizz works with a diverse set of techniques, such as ceramics, textile, sculpture, stencils, artistic weaving, and poetry, to explore themes of colonialism and dispossession. She is also highly involved in the defense of land and territory in her local community to protect water sources against transnational corporations. Her work deals with the intersections of indigeneity, antiracism, and feminism. She currently lives and works in Santa Maria Tonantzintla, Cholula, Mexico.

Bianca Tonantzin Zamora (she/her) is associate director for Stanford University's School of Humanities and Sciences. In her role, she serves as the lead strategist for DEI initiatives for H&S staff. Bianca utilizes intersectional and arts-based approaches to lead national diversity, equity, and inclusion workshops. As a proud queer Latina poet and organizer for grassroots coalitions, she was recognized as an Honor 41 Latinx recipient. She received a Bachelor of Arts with distinction from Sonoma State University in women's and gender studies and a Master of Science from Miami University in student affairs with diversity and equity.

INDEX

Page numbers in **bold** refer to illustrations.

Printed in the USA
CPSIA information can be obtained
at www.ICGtesting.com
CBHW040731301223
2913CB00001B/2